Society's Final Solution

*A History and Discussion
of the Death Penalty*

Edited by

Laura E. Randa

University Press of America, Inc.
Lanham • New York • Oxford

Copyright © 1997 by
University Press of America,® Inc.
4720 Boston Way
Lanham, Maryland 20706

12 Hid's Copse Rd.
Cummor Hill, Oxford OX2 9JJ

Library of Congress Cataloging-in-Publication Data

Society's final solution : a history and discussion of the death penalty /
edited by Laura E. Randa.
p. cm.
Includes index.
1. Capital punishment--United States. 2. Capital punishment--
Delaware. I. Randa, Laura E.
KF9227.C2S67   1997   364.66'0973--dc21   97-1663 CIP

ISBN 0-7618-0713-6 (cloth: alk. ppr.)

⊖™ The paper used in this publication meets the minimum
requirements of American National Standard for information
Sciences—Permanence of Paper for Printed Library Materials,
ANSI Z39.48—1984

To Michael Reggio, my mentor and friend
who always strives to make a difference.

To Don King, my soul mate

Contents

Foreword

Much public debate and policy development have resulted from public reactions to and legislative debates focused upon the issue of the death penalty. Currently public opinion polls indicate overwhelmingly that a tougher legislative stance is needed with regard to the death penalty. Whether members of society are fully informed on this issue is the motivation behind *Society's Final Solution: A History and Discussion of the Death Penalty.*

This is the first publication to explore the historical basis for the death penalty utilizing multiple perspectives of legal thinkers, legal practitioners, public officials, family members of victims and convicted death row inmates to explore the ambiguities and complexities inherent in this issue. Current thinking on the topic is perhaps nowhere more specifically represented than through the "Violent Crime Control and Law Enforcement Act" of 1994.

Tougher death penalty provisions are part of the "Violent Crime Control and Law Enforcement Act" of 1994. But the federal death penalty is just one part of an aggressive, crime-fighting strategy. For example, we have had a federal *drug* death penalty on the books now for five years.

The "Violent Crime Control and Law Enforcement Act" of 1994 is the most bold, balanced, comprehensive attack on crime ever enacted. It includes the death penalty for federal prisoners who murder, the death penalty for drive-by shootings, the death penalty for terrorists, the death penalty for torture, the death penalty for fatal kidnappings, rapes and hostage takings, the death penalty for gun murderers during federal crimes.

The new legislation also includes a whole long list of aggravating factors—these are the factors that a jury weighs in *favor* of imposing the death penalty. On the list of aggravating factors are an offender's use of a firearm during the crime, or a history of firearms violence. Other aggravating factors that were included: when the crime is carried out in an especially cruel and depraved manner; if it involved dealing drugs to kids; or if the victim was especially vulnerable. Another request by many was the right for victim's family to tell about their pain and their sorrow, and for the government to induce a victim impact statement at the sentencing phase of the case.

However, a number of critical questions arise from such legislation. For example:

- Does the Death Penalty deter crime, especially murder?
- Does the state have the right to sanction murder?
- If execution is unacceptable, what is the alternative?
- Is the death penalty necessary, or is it merely retribution for victims' families?
- Have strict procedures eliminated discrimination in death sentencing?
- Does the law permit execution of juveniles and people who are mentally retarded or mentally ill?
- Are executions "cruel and unusual punishment?"

These and many other questions arise from exploration of this topic.

Society's Final Solution: A History & Discussion of the Death Penalty is the first book which focuses specifically on addressing multiple issues dealing with capital punishment. Major thinkers across the United States and individuals personally and tragically involved in this issue initiate a timely and necessary dialog with regard to the creation of public policy surrounding the death penalty. This book is a very thoughtful and thorough approach to the capital punishment and should be read by all practitioners and students interested in exploring all facets of capital punishment.

Joseph R. Biden, Jr.
United States Senator
Senate Judiciary Committee
July, 1996

Preface

In editing *Society's Final Solution: A History of the Death Penalty*, I wanted to represent a balanced look at the death penalty from multiple perspectives. I wanted this, not for myself, but for the many students who were the real inspiration behind this publication. The natural curiosity of those young minds led to this exhaustive study of the death penalty. In completing this labor of love, I wanted to include voices from all sides of the issue.

These voices had to include the families of victims, those who have committed murder, legal scholars of national reputation, prosecutors, defense attorneys, pardons board members and state attorney generals. Because my students deserved an honest response, I amassed a variety of spokespersons to address an issue which is rarely approached from multiple points of view.

I desired to create a work which has no ax to grind regarding the death penalty. I intentionally solicited articles for balance in exploring what is a very complicated legal, economic and social issue. I stood, face to face, with two separate mass murderers in order to gain their perspective. Both of these individuals who I had come to know over a three year period, have now been executed.

I networked to collect, over a period of more than five years, articles on the best thinking regarding this issue. It is my opinion that this work reflects the time, energy and effort of countless individuals to look at the issue of capital punishment in a way that no previous work has done.

Acknowledgments

Like any other major project, this book would not have been a reality without the aid and support of many people. I wish to acknowledge the assistance of Senator Joseph R. Biden, Jr. and his staff, Mr. Tom Wagner, a member of the Delaware Board of Pardons, Colonel Thomas P. Gordon, Police Chief of New Castle County, and all who contributed articles to this publication. On a personal note, I wish to acknowledge those who inspired me to complete this work: Annette Pratola for her undaunted faith in students and in my abilities; Captain Mike DeLoy, Lieutenant Michael Brittingham and the Delaware Department of Corrections for assistance in gaining valuable personal information from those facing the death penalty; and to Don E. King, Jr. for his constant patience, understanding and support.

Finally, I wish to thank Michael Reggio, not only for his contribution to the work, but for his perpetual belief in me. He was with me every chapter of the way, letting me know when to move forward, although it seemed at times I was standing still. He provided the feedback I could understand and use, so that the manuscript became continually better. Thanks for your tenacity in sticking with me — and for your belief that this book was possible.

Laura E. Randa

Introduction

Initially, I remained professionally detached from this project as I had so many research projects before. However, after coming face to face with two convicted death row inmates, following the subsequent execution of each of these individuals, and conducting interviews with families of murdered victims, I remain forever changed.

This collection began six years ago when I was writing an interdisciplinary public policy unit for *Newsweek* magazine. A sample group of students from the Phoenix Academy in Delaware conducted interviews and surveys in order to determine in which public policy high school students were most interested in our state. Concurrently, Delaware was about to execute the first man since the 1940's. Over 80% of students chose the death penalty as the number one public policy about which they wanted to learn more.

We began to develop and write this powerful 12-week unit. As part of this unit, students interviewed people with various viewpoints on the death penalty. One of the most compelling educational experiences for the students was a visit to Sussex County Correctional Institute to interview two inmates facing the death penalty. This was the first time in Delaware's history that students were allowed to come face-to-face with death row inmates.

This public policy study has now impacted over 3,100 students. The intent of this book is to share and inform the reader about the death penalty utilizing many different perspectives. I encourage you to read the material and formulate your own opinion on this compelling public policy. There are various perspectives in these pages.

It is my belief that the real strength of this publication is the lack of an ax to grind. Neither I nor this group of students wanted to do other than present all sides of this extremely complicated issue. Although I speak mainly for myself, I believe I also speak for all of those students when I say that our lives will remain forever altered.

Chapter 1

History of the Death Penalty

Michael H. Reggio

As far back as the Ancient Laws of China, the death penalty has been established as a punishment for crimes. In the 18th Century BC, the Code of King Hammurabi of Babylon codified the death penalty for twenty five different crimes, although murder was not one of them. The first death sentence historically recorded occurred in 16th Century BC Egypt where the wrongdoer, a member of nobility, was accused of magic, and ordered to take his own life. During this period non-nobility was usually killed with the ax.

In the 14th Century BC, the Hittite Code also prescribed the death penalty. The 7th Century BC Draconian Code of Athens made death the penalty for every crime committed. In the 5th Century BC, the Roman Law of the Twelve Tablets codified the death penalty. Again, the death penalty was different for nobility, freemen and slaves and was punishment for crimes such as the publication of libels and insulting songs, the cutting or grazing of crops planted by a farmer, the burning a house or a stack of corn near a house, cheating by a patron of his client, perjury, making disturbances at night in the city, willful murder of a freeman or a parent, or theft by a slave. Death was often cruel and included crucifixion, drowning at sea, burial alive, beating to death, and impalement (often used by Nero). The Romans had a curious punishment for parricides (murder of a parent): the condemned was submersed in water in a sack, which also contained a dog, a rooster, a viper and an ape.[1] The most notorious death execution in BC was about 399 BC when the Greek philosopher Socrates was required to drink poison for heresy and corruption of youth.[2]

Mosaic Law codified many capital crimes. In fact, there is evidence that Jews used many different techniques including stoning, hanging, beheading, crucifixion (copied from the Romans), throwing a criminal from a rock, and sawing asunder. The most infamous execution of history occurred approximately 29 AD with the crucifixion of Jesus Christ outside Jerusalem. About 300 years later, the Emperor Constantine, after converting to Christianity, abolished crucifixion and other cruel death penalties in the Roman Empire. In 438, the Code of Theodosius made more than 80 crimes punishable by death.[3]

Britain influenced the colonies more than any other country and has a long history of punishment by death. About 450 BC, the death penalty was often enforced by throwing the condemned into a quagmire. By the 10th Century, hanging from gallows was the most frequent execution method. William the Conqueror opposed taking life except in war, and ordered no person to be hanged or executed for any offense. However, he allowed criminals to be mutilated for their crimes. During the middle ages, capital punishment was accompanied by torture. Most barons had a drowning pit as well as gallows and they were used for major as well as minor crimes. For example, in 1279, two hundred and eighty nine Jews were hanged for clipping coin. Under Edward I, two gatekeepers were killed because the city gate had not been closed in time to prevent the escape of an accused murderer. Burning was the punishment for women's high treason and men were hanged, drawn and quartered. Beheading was generally accepted for the upper classes. One could be burned for marrying a Jew. Pressing became the penalty for those who would not confess to their crimes. The executioner placed heavy weights on the victim's chest. On the first day he gave the victim a small quantity of bread, on the second a small drink of bad water, and so on until he confessed or died. Under the reign of Henry VIII, the numbers of those put to death are estimated as high as 72,000. Boiling to death was another penalty approved in 1531, and there are records that show some people boiled for up to two hours before death took them. When a woman was burned, the executioner tied a rope around her neck when she was tied to the stake. When the flames reached her she could be strangled from outside the ring of fire. However, this often failed and many were literally burnt alive.[4]

In Britain, the number of capital offenses continually increased until the 1700's when two hundred and twenty-two crimes were punishable by death. These included stealing from a house in the amount of forty shillings, stealing from a shop the value of five shillings, robbing a rabbit warren, cutting down a tree, and counterfeiting tax stamps. However, juries tended not to convict when the penalty was great and the crime was not. Reforms began to take place. In 1823, five laws passed, exempting about a hundred crimes from the death. Between 1832 and 1837, many capital offenses were swept away. In 1840, there was a failed attempt to abolish all capital punishment. Through the nineteenth and twentieth centuries, more and more capital punishments were abolished, not only in Britain, but also all across Europe, until today only a few European countries retain the death penalty.[5]

The first recorded execution in the English American colonies was in 1608 when officials executed George Kendall of Virginia for supposedly plotting to betray the British to the Spanish. In 1612, Virginia's governor, Sir Thomas Dale, implemented the Divine, Moral, and Martial Laws that made death the penalty for even minor offenses such as stealing grapes, killing chickens, killing dogs or horses without permission, or trading with Indians. Seven years later these laws were softened because Virginia feared that no one would settle there.[6]

In 1622, the first legal execution of a criminal, Daniel Frank, occurred in Virginia for the crime of theft.[7] Some colonies were very strict in their use of the death penalty, while others were less so. In Massachusetts Bay Colony the first execution was in 1630, but the earliest capital statutes do not occur until later. Under the Capital Laws of New-England that went into effect between 1636-1647 the death penalty was meted out for pre-meditated murder, sodomy, witchcraft, adultery, idolatry, blasphemy, assault in anger, rape, statutory rape, manstealing, perjury in a capital trial, rebellion, man-slaughter, poisoning and bestiality. Early laws were accompanied by a scripture from the Old Testament. By 1780, the Commonwealth of Massachusetts only recognized seven capital crimes: murder, sodomy, burglary, buggery, arson, rape, and treason.[8]

The New York colony instituted the so-called Duke's Laws of 1665. This directed the death penalty for denial of the true God, pre-meditated murder, killing someone who had no weapon of defense, killing by lying in wait or by poisoning, sodomy, buggery, kidnapping, perjury in a capital trial, traitorous denial of the king's rights or raising arms to resist his authority, conspiracy to invade towns or forts in the colony and striking one's mother or father (upon complaint of both). The two colonies that were more lenient concerning capital punishment were South Jersey and Pennsylvania. In South Jersey there was no death penalty for any crime and there were only two crimes, murder and treason, punishable by death.[9]

However under the direction of the Crown, harsher penal codes were execution there until 1691. In Pennsylvania, William Penn's Great Act (1682) made passed in the colonies. By 1776, most of the colonies had roughly comparable death statutes which covered arson, piracy, treason, murder, sodomy, burglary, robbery, rape, horse-stealing, slave rebellion, and often counterfeiting. Hanging was the usual sentence. Rhode Island was probably the only colony which decreased the number of capital crimes in the late 1700's.

Some states were more severe. For example, by 1837, North Carolina required death for the crimes of murder, rape, statutory rape, slave-stealing, stealing bank notes, highway robbery, burglary, arson, castration, buggery, sodomy, bestiality, dueling where death occurs, hiding a slave with intent to free him, taking a free Negro out of state to sell him, bigamy, inciting slaves to rebel, circulating seditious literature among slaves, accessory to murder, robbery, burglary, arson, or mayhem and others. However, North Carolina did not have a state penitentiary and, many said, no suitable alternative to capital punishment.[10]

The first reforms of the death penalty occurred between 1776-1800. Thomas Jefferson and four others, authorized to undertake a complete revision of Virginia's laws, proposed a law that recommended the death penalty for only treason and murder. After a stormy debate the legislature defeated the bill by one vote. The writing of European theorists such as Montesquieu, Voltaire, and Bentham had a great effect on American intellectuals, as did English Quaker prison reformers John Bellers and John Howard.[11]

On Crimes and Punishment, published in English in 1767 by the Italian jurist Cesare Beccaria whose exposition on abolishing capital punishment was the most influential of the time, had an especially strong impact. He theorized that there was no justification for the taking of life by the state. He said that the death penalty was "a war of a whole nation against a citizen, whose destruction they consider as necessary, or useful to the general good." He asked the question what if it can be shown not to be necessary or useful? His essay contended that the only time a death was necessary was when only one's death could insure the security of a nation — which would be rare and only in cases of absolute anarchy or when a nation was on the verge of losing its liberty. He said that the history of using punishment by death (e.g., the Romans, 20 years of Czaress Elizabeth) had not prevented determined men from injuring society and that death was only a "momentary spectacle, and therefore a less efficacious method of deterring others, than the continued example of a man deprived of his liberty. . . ."[12]

Organizations were formed in different colonies for the abolition of the death penalty and to relieve poor prison conditions. Dr. Benjamin Rush, a renowned Philadelphia citizen, proposed the complete abolition of capital punishment. William Bradford, Attorney General of Pennsylvania, was ordered to investigate capital punishment. In 1793 he published *An Enquiry How Far the Punishment of Death is Necessary in Pennsylvania*. He strongly insisted that the death penalty be retained, but admitted it was useless in preventing certain crimes. In fact, he said the death penalty made convictions harder to obtain, because in Pennsylvania, and indeed in all states, the death penalty was mandatory and juries would often not return a guilty because of this fact. In response, in 1794, the Pennsylvania legislature abolished capital punishment for all crimes except murder "in the first degree," the first time murder had been broken down into "degrees." In New York, in 1796, the legislature authorized construction of the state's first penitentiary, abolished whipping, and reduced the number of capital offenses from thirteen to two. Virginia and Kentucky passed similar reform bills. Four more states reduced its capital crimes: Vermont in 1797, to three; Maryland in 1810, to four; New Hampshire in 1812, to two and Ohio in 1815, to two. Each of these states built state penitentiaries. A few states went the opposite direction. Rhode Island restored the death penalty for rape and arson; Massachusetts, New Jersey, and Connecticut raised death crimes from six to ten, including sodomy, maiming, robbery, and forgery. Many southern states made more crimes capital, especially for slaves.[13]

The first great reform era occurred between 1833-1853. Public executions were attacked as cruel. Sometimes tens of thousands of eager viewers would show up to view hangings; local merchants would sell souvenirs and alcohol. Fighting and pushing would often break out as people jockeyed for the best view of the hanging or the corpse! Onlookers often cursed the widow or the victim and would try to tear down the scaffold or the rope for keepsakes. Violence and drunkenness often ruled towns far into the night after "justice had been served." Many states enacted laws providing private hangings. Rhode Island (1833), Pennsylvania (1834), New York (1835), Massachusetts (1835), and New Jersey (1835) all abolished public hangings. By 1849, fifteen states were holding private hangings. This move was opposed by many death penalty abolitionists who thought public executions would eventually cause people to cry out against execution itself. For example, in 1835, Maine enacted what was in effect a moratorium on capital punishment after over ten thousand people who watched a hanging had to be restrained by police after they became unruly and began fighting. All felons sentenced to death would have to remain in prison at hard labor and could not be executed until one year had elapsed and then only on the governor's order. No governor ordered an execution under the "Maine Law" for

> twenty-seven years. Though many states argued the merits of the death penalty, no state went as far as Maine. The most influential reformers were the clergy. Ironically, the small but powerful group which opposed the abolitionists were also clergy. They were, almost to a person, members of the Calvinist clergy, especially the Congregationalists and Presbyterians who could be called the religious establishment of the time. They were led by George Cheever.[14]

Finally, in 1846, Michigan became the first state to abolish the death penalty (except for treason against the state), mostly because it had no long tradition of capital punishment (there had been no hanging since 1830, before statehood) and because frontier Michigan had few established religious groups to oppose it as was the case in the east. In 1852, Rhode Island abolished the death penalty led by Unitarians, Universalists, and especially Quakers. In the same year, Massachusetts limited its death penalty to first-degree murder. In 1853, Wisconsin abolished the death penalty after a gruesome execution in which the victim struggled for five minutes at the end of the rope, and a full eighteen minutes passed before his heart finally quit.[15]

During the last half of the century the death penalty abolition movement ground to a halt, with many members moving into the slavery abolition movement. At the same time, states began to pass laws against mandatory death sentences. Legislators in eighteen states shifted from mandatory to discretionary capital punishment by 1895, not to save lives, but to try to increase convictions and executions of murderers. Still, abolitionists gained a few victories. Maine abolished the death penalty, restored it, and then abolished it again between 1876-1887. Iowa abolished the death penalty for six years. Kansas passed a "Maine Law" in 1872 which operated as de facto abolition.[16]

Electrocution as a method of execution came onto the scene in an unlikely manner. Edison Company with its DC (direct current) electrical systems began attacking Westinghouse Company and its AC (alternating current) electrical systems as they were pressing for nationwide electrification with alternating current. To show how dangerous AC could be, Edison Company began holding public demonstrations by electrocuting animals. People reasoned that if electricity could kill animals, it could kill people. In 1888, New York approved the dismantling of its gallows and the building of the nation's first electric chair. It held its first victim, William Kemmler, in 1890, and even though the first electrocution was clumsy at best, other states soon followed the lead.[17]

The Second Great Reform era was 1895-1917. In 1897, U.S. Congress passed a bill reducing the number of federal death crimes. In 1907, Kansas took the "Maine Law" a step further and abolished all death penalties. Between 1911 and 1917, eight more states abolished capital punishment (Minnesota, North Dakota, South Dakota, Oregon, Arizona, Missouri and Tennessee — the latter in all cases but rape). Votes in other states came close to ending the death penalty.

However, between 1917 and 1955, the death penalty abolition movement again slowed. Washington, Arizona, Missouri, and Oregon in 1919-20 reinstated the death penalty. In 1924, the first execution by cyanide gas took place in Nevada, when Tong war gang murderer Gee Jon became its first victim. The state wanted to secretly pump cyanide gas into Jon's cell at night while he was asleep as a more humanitarian way of carrying out the penalty, but, technical difficulties prohibited this and a special "gas chamber" was hastily built. Other concerns developed when less "civilized" methods of execution failed. In 1930, Mrs. Eva Dugan became the first female to be executed by Arizona. The execution was botched when the hangman misjudged the drop and Mrs. Dugan's head was ripped from her body. More states converted to electric chairs and gas chambers. During this period of time, abolitionist organizations sprang up all across the country, but they had little effect. There were a number of stormy protests against the execution of certain convicted felons (e.g., Julius and Ethel Rosenberg), but little opposition against the death penalty itself. In fact, during the anti-Communist period with all its fears and hysteria, Texas Governor Allan Shivers seriously suggested that capital punishment be the penalty for membership in the Communist Party.[18]

The movement against capital punishment revived again between 1955 and 1972. England and Canada completed exhaustive studies which were largely critical of the death penalty and these were widely circulated in the U.S. Death row criminals gave their own moving accounts of capital punishment in books and film. Convicted kidnapper Caryl Chessman published *Cell 2455 Death Row and Trial by Ordeal.* Barbara Graham's story was utilized in book and film with *I Want to Live!* after her execution. Television shows were broadcast on the death penalty. Hawaii and Alaska ended capital punishment in 1957, and Delaware did so the next year. Controversy over the death penalty gripped the nation

> forcing politicians to take sides. Delaware restored the death penalty in 1961. Michigan abolished capital punishment for treason in 1963. Voters in 1964 abolished the death penalty in Oregon. In 1965 Iowa, New York, West Virginia, and Vermont ended the death penalty. New Mexico abolished the death penalty in 1969.[19]

Trying to end capital punishment state-by-state was difficult at best, so death penalty abolitionists turned much of their efforts to the courts. They finally succeeded on June 29, 1972 in the case *Furman v. Georgia.* In nine separate opinions, but with a majority of 5-4, the U.S. Supreme Court ruled that the way capital punishment laws were written, including discriminatory sentencing guidelines, capital punishment was cruel and unusual and violated the Eighth and Fourteenth Amendments. This effectively ended capital punishment in the United States. Advocates of capital punishment began proposing new capital statutes which they believed would end discrimination in capital sentencing, therefore satisfying a majority of the Court. By early 1975, thirty states had again passed death penalty laws and nearly two hundred prisoners were on death row. In *Gregg v. Georgia* (1976), the Supreme Court upheld Georgia's newly passed death penalty and said that the death penalty was not always cruel and unusual punishment. Death row executions could again begin. Another form of execution was soon found. Oklahoma passed the first death by lethal injection law, based on economics as much as on humanitarian reasons. The old electric chair that had not been used in eleven years would require expensive repairs. Estimates of over $200,000 were given to build a gas chamber, while lethal injection would cost no more than ten to fifteen dollars "per event."[20]

The controversy over the death penalty continues today. There is a strong movement against lawlessness propelled by citizens' fears for their security. Politicians at the national and state levels are taking the floor of legislatures and calling for more frequent death penalties, death penalties penalty for more crimes, and longer prison sentences. Those opposing these moves counter by arguing that tougher sentences do not slow crime and that crime is little or no worse than in the past. In fact, FBI statistics show murders are now up. (For example 9.3 persons per 100,000 population were murdered in 1973 and 9.4 persons per 100,000 were murdered in 1992). The battle lines are still drawn and the combat will probably always be fought.[21]

A number of important capital punishment decisions have been made by the Supreme Court. The following is a list of the more important ones along with their legal citations:

Wilkerson v. Utah 99 U.S. 130 (1878) — Court upheld execution by firing squad, but said that other types of torture such as "drawing and quartering, embowelling alive, beheading, public dissection, and burning alive and all other in the same line of . . . cruelty, are forbidden."

Weems v. U.S. 217 U.S. 349 (1910) — Court held that what constitutes cruel and unusual punishment had not been decided, but that it should not be confined to the "forms of evil" that framers of the Bill of Rights had experienced. Therefore, "cruel and unusual" definitions are subject to changing interpretations.

Louisiana ex rel. Francis v. Resweber 329 U.S. 459 (1947) — On May 3, 1946, convicted seventeen year old felon Willie Francis was placed in the electric chair and the switch was thrown. Due to faulty equipment, he survived (even though he was severely shocked), was removed from the chair and returned to his cell. A new death warrant was issued six days later. The Court ruled the 5-4 that it was not "cruel and unusual" to finish carrying out the sentence since the state acted in good faith in the first attempt. "The cruelty against which the

Constitution protects a convicted man is cruelty inherent in the method of punishment," said the Court, "not the necessary suffering involved in any method employed to extinguish life humanely." He was then executed.

Tropp v. Dulles 356 U.S. 86 (1958) — The Court ruled that punishment would be considered "cruel and unusual" if it was one of "tormenting severity," cruel in its excessiveness or unusual in punishment "must draw its meaning from the evolving standards of decency that mark the progress of a maturing society."

Furman v. Georgia 408 U.S. 238 (1972) — The Court looking at three cases struck down the death penalty in many states and set up the standard that punishment would be considered "cruel and unusual" if any of the following were present: 1) it was too severe for the crime; 2) it was arbitrary (some get the punishment and others do not, without guidelines); 3) it offends society's sense of justice: 4) it was not more effective than a less severe penalty.

Gregg v. Georgia 428 U.S. 153 (1976) — Court upheld Georgia's newly passed death penalty and said that the death penalty was not always cruel and unusual punishment.

Tison v. Arizona 481 U.S. 137 (1987) — Court upheld Arizona's death penalty for major participation in a felony with "reckless indifference to human life."

Thompson v. Oklahoma 108 S. Ct. 2687 (1988) — The Court considered the question of execution of minors under the age of 16 at the time of the murder. The victim was the brother-in-law, who he accused of beating his sister. He and three others beat the victim, shot him twice, cut his throat, chest, and abdomen, chained him to a concrete block and threw the body into a river where it remained for four weeks. Each of the four participants were tried separately and all were sentenced to death. In a 5-3 decision, four Justices ruled that Thompson's death sentence was cruel and unusual. The fifth, O'Connor, concurred but noted that a state must set a minimum age and held out the possibility that if a state lowers, by statute, the minimum death penalty age below sixteen, she might support it. She stated, "Although, I believe that a national consensus forbidding the execution of any person for a crime committed before the age of 16 very likely does exist, I am reluctant to adopt this conclusion as a matter of constitutional law without better evidence that we now possess." States with no minimum age have rushed to specify a statute age.

Penry v. Lynaugh 492 U.S. (1989) — Court held that persons considered retarded, but legally sane, could receive the death penalty. It was not cruel and unusual punishment under the Eighth Amendment if jurors were given the opportunity to consider mitigating circumstances. In this case, the defendant had the mental age of approximately a six-year old child.

Chapter 2

Administration of the Death Penalty Through the Courts: A Defense Attorney's Perspective

Kevin J. O'Connell

This is a two part essay written from my perspective as a defense attorney litigating capital cases. In the first part, I will attempt to give some overview of the capital case process. In the second part, I will share some of my thoughts as to why I feel that our system of capital punishment is inherently unfair.

I.

Essentially there are three stages to the litigation of a capital case: the initial trial/appeal stage; the state postconviction proceedings; and federal postconviction proceedings.

The trial of a capital case differs procedurally from the trial of other criminal cases in two major respects: the selection of the jury in a capital case includes questioning of jurors about their attitudes toward the sentence, i.e., the death penalty; and under current statutes, trials in capital cases are split in two — there is a guilt phase and a penalty phase.

In all but a handful of states the jury imposes sentence. In Delaware, Florida, Indiana and Alabama, the jury recommends the sentence, but the trial judge has the power to override that recommendation.

Almost all states have a mandatory appeal after trial in a capital case. After the direct appeal has made its way through all state appellate courts, the defendant is entitled to file a petition for writ of certiorari in the Supreme Court of the United States. Once the direct appeal has concluded, an indigent capitally sentenced defendant has no further constitutional right to counsel. At this stage, volunteer counsel must often be recruited.

The next avenue of appeal is state postconviction. In order to prepare the motion for postconviction relief, an extensive factual and legal investigation must be undertaken, usually by counsel who was not involved in the trial or direct appeal. The motion raises state law issues and federal constitutional issues relating to the fairness of the trial and appellate process. These claims may present the need for discovery, for evidentiary hearings and for expansion of the existing record.

Counsel representing a capitally sentenced defendant at the state postconviction level must not only be thoroughly familiar with the entire record below, including the transcripts and exhibits from trial as well as briefs on appeal, but she must also do a great deal of independent factual investigation outside the record. This is because, in a disturbingly large number of cases, the facts as presented at trial were incomplete or false. This may be because information was concealed by the state, because of witnesses who disappeared at the time of trial or who testified falsely at trial, because the defense attorney did not conduct an adequate investigation in the first instance into guilt or sentencing issues, or for a variety of other reasons. It is at this stage that the effectiveness of the representation of trial and appellate counsel will be scrutinized by the state courts.

In most states, the denial of postconviction relief can be appealed to the highest state appellate court. Barring relief from that court, the defendant can again file a petition for writ of certiorari to the United States Supreme Court to have any federal constitutional issues raised below reviewed by the United States Supreme Court.

The next stage is federal habeas corpus review. The federal petition for writ of habeas corpus must be filed with the federal district court with jurisdiction over the case. That petition usually parallels the state postconviction motion, although it normally also includes federal constitutional issues raised on the initial direct appeal which did not have to be raised again in state postconviction, and/or issues arising from the denial of rights in the state postconviction process itself. The federal district court's decision is reviewable by the United States court of appeals for the circuit in which that district court sits once a "certificate of probable cause to appeal" is issued by the district court or the court of appeals. This appeal is heard by a panel of three judges. In some cases, the appeal to the circuit court may be reheard by the full court (*en banc*) after a panel decision. Finally, the defendant is again entitled to a petition for writ of certiorari in the United States Supreme Court after a denial of relief by the federal appeals court.

Recently, Congress has enacted legislation severely curtailing the right of the capitally sentenced defendant to obtain review of his or her federal constitutional rights through the writ of habeas corpus. This new legislation imposes strict time limitations for the filing and consideration of such petitions, as well as many procedural barriers to the granting of relief, even in situations where a petitioner has meritorious, substantive claims or may be innocent.

The state/federal postconviction process may be repeated if a new issue arises, either because of the discovery of new facts or a change in the law. Nonetheless, courts are extremely harsh in their unwillingness to hear a successor petition. A person facing execution will be found to have "abused" the process his second time through, with extremely rare exception. Furthermore, the previously mentioned revisions to the federal habeas corpus statute place numerous procedural barriers to the filing and consideration of a subsequent petition.

In some jurisdictions, no execution date is set until the defendant finishes the first full round of postconviction proceedings. Delaware provides for automatic stays of execution through the first round of direct appeal and state postconviction review. Thereafter, stays of execution must be sought before additional review will be permitted.

Although capital appeals sometimes appear to languish in the courts for years (at least four cases in Delaware meandered through the courts for more than ten years), the process is becoming much more streamlined and expedited. Delaware has instituted an administrative directive giving time deadlines for completion of the capital trial, appellate and postconviction processes. The theory in Delaware is that all of these components of the capital case process should be completed within three years. Federal courts, likewise, have indicated a preference for expediting procedures in capital cases through their courts. As such, the federal postconviction process often takes place within a year. The entire federal postconviction review process for one individual executed by the State of Delaware in 1993 (Kenneth DeShields) took place over the course of one month.

The state and federal courts have generally attempted to portray an image that they believe that there is a heightened need for fairness in the administration of the death penalty. This unique need for a high level of fairness arises out of the simple fact that death truly is different from all other punishments a society inflicts upon its citizens. Because of this difference, there is a corresponding need for reliability in the determination of both guilt of the offense and the appropriateness of the punishment in a specific case.

When a prosecutor decides to seek the death penalty for an indigent defendant, the court appoints either a public defender or a local attorney to represent the defendant. Far too often these defense attorneys are inexperienced in the handling of death penalty cases. Those who do have adequate experience are often vastly overworked, underpaid and provided with little, if any, funding to investigate or to hire expert witnesses. Delaware is fortunate enough to have a well funded public defender system and pool of contract attorneys. Generally speaking, there is no cap on the amount that will be paid to a court-appointed attorney handling a capital case in Delaware; however, there is a limit ($50.00) on the hourly rate that the attorney can charge. While $50.00 may seem like a more than adequate hourly rate, in fact, it barely covers the cost of keeping a law office running, let alone paying the attorney a salary. The average hourly rate that a private attorney charges for work in Delaware ranges anywhere from $100.00 to $250.00 per hour.

In many states, only hard pressed county governments, rather than state governments, provide funds for the defense of indigents charged with capital crimes. Even where state governments do fund defense counsel, the money provided is generally grossly inadequate. The Alabama Supreme Court held in 1985 that the statutory limits of $1,000.00 for compensation and $500.00 for expenses does not deprive a capital defendant of any constitutional rights, because attorneys are "directed by their consciences and the ethical rules enforced by the State Bar Association" to serve their capital clients "well".[1]

Recognizing the inherent unfairness of having indigent defendants go to their death unrepresented, the United States federal government funded the creation of Capital Resource Centers in those regions of the country where the death penalty is imposed with greater frequency. These resource centers generally provided representation for individuals at the state and federal postconviction level, but they also provided much needed advice and counsel to inexperienced court-appointed attorneys at the trial and direct appeal stages. Despite the fact that an independent commission appointed by the federal government to study these resource centers found that they were a far more cost-effective means of providing indigent individuals representation in these latter stages of the process of administering the death penalty, Congress eliminated the funding for the resource centers in 1995. The resource centers ceased to exist on April 1, 1996.

The problems of inexperienced, overworked and inadequately funded defense counsel are often compounded by other factors. In many cases, the court appointed attorney representing a capital defendant lives in a community which is outraged about the heinous, violent crime. Unfortunately, some attorneys fear the reactions of the community or local judiciary and fail to protect their clients' legal rights. The United States Court of Appeals for the Eleventh Circuit found that the court-appointed Georgia defense counsel for Terry Lee Goodwin, fearing community reproach, did not challenge a jury selection method that discriminated against blacks and women. He even permitted the jury to learn that he was representing Goodwin only because he had to do so.[2]

Defense counsel often fail to recognize the importance of the additional preparation needed for the separate penalty phase of a capital trial. Indeed, some do not even know that there will be a separate penalty phase until they are in the middle of it. Many court-appointed attorneys, short on time and money, channel their energies into the first phase of the trial and often find themselves exhausted and without new witnesses or arguments when they reach the penalty phase. Often the determination of whether or not an individual charged with a capital offense receives the death penalty is dependent upon the financial wherewithal of that defendant, or, if indigent, whether or not that individual lives in a state that adequately funds the defense of those accused of capital crimes.

Race also plays a strong role in both the decision to charge individuals with capital offenses, as well as whether or not that individual will receive the death penalty. The significant impact that racism has upon who gets the death penalty was documented in *McCleskey v. Kemp*, 481 U.S. 271 (1987). Warren McCleskey, a black man, argued that the Georgia capital sentencing scheme was administered in a racially discriminatory manner, in violation of his constitutional rights. In support of his claim, he offered a highly reliable statistical study (The Baldus Study), which indicated that "after taking into account some 239 non-racial factors that might legitimately influence a sentencer, the jury, more likely than not, would have spared McCleskey's life had his victim been black."[3] The Baldus Study further demonstrated that "blacks who kill whites are sentenced to death at nearly twenty-two times the rate of blacks who kill blacks and more than seven times the rate of whites who kill blacks." *Id*, at 327. Despite this staggering evidence of racial prejudice infecting the Georgia capital sentencing scheme, the majority of the United States Supreme Court turned its back on Warren McCleskey's claims. Mr. McCleskey has since been executed by the State of Georgia.

Before his retirement in 1994, United States Supreme Court Justice Harry Blackmun wrote a thoroughly eloquent dissenting opinion in which he, once and for all, renounced his belief in the American system of capital justice administration. In *Callins v. Collins*, No. 93-7054 (1994) (Blackmun, J., dissenting from the denial of certiorari), Justice Blackmun wrote that he felt "morally and intellectually obligated to concede that the death penalty experiment has failed. It is virtually self-evident to me now that no combination of procedural rules or substantive regulations ever can save the death penalty from its inherent constitutional deficiencies."

In a scathing, highly critical concurring opinion, Justice Antonin Scalia took exception to Justice Blackmun's decision to renounce the death penalty. He went out of his way to point out that Justice Blackmun had chosen a relatively mild felony murder case as the vehicle for this decision, rather than a more violent crime.

> Justice Blackmun begins his statement by describing with poignancy the death of a convicted murderer by lethal injection. He chooses, as the case in which to make that statement, one of the less brutal of the murders that regularly comes before us — the murder of a man ripped by a bullet suddenly and unexpectedly, with no opportunity to prepare himself and his affairs, and left to bleed to death on the

floor of a tavern. The death-by-injection which Justice Blackmun describes looks pretty desirable next to that. It looks even better next to some of the other cases currently before us, which Justice Blackmun did not select as the vehicle for his announcement that the death penalty is always unconstitutional — for example, the case of the 11-year-old girl raped by four men and then killed by stuffing her panties down her throat.[4] How enviable a quiet death by lethal injection compared with that!

> *Callins v. Collins*, No. 93-7054,
> (Scalia, J., concurring in the denial of certiorari).

In one of the last opinions he would author as a Supreme Court Justice, Justice Blackmun had an opportunity to bring to light all of the facts (and the unfairness) of the case cited by Justice Scalia. In dissenting from the Court's denial of that certiorari petition, Justice Blackmun picked up the gauntlet previously thrown down by Justice Scalia in the *Callins* decision. While the crime in the *McCollum* case was truly "abhorrent, there [was] more to the story."

> Buddy McCollum is mentally retarded. He has an I.Q. between 60 and 69 and the mental age of a nine year old. He reads on a second grade level. . . .

> The sentencing jury found two aggravating circumstances: that the murder was committed to avoid arrest and that the murder was especially heinous, atrocious, or cruel. They found seven mitigating circumstances: that McCollum was mentally retarded, that he had difficulty thinking clearly under stress, that he was easily influenced by others, that he committed the felony murder under the influence of mental or emotional disturbance, that he had cooperated with the police, that he had no significant history of prior criminal activity, and that he had adapted well to prison. In addition, the trial judge concluded that "[a]ll of the evidence tends to show that [McCollum's] capacity . . . to appreciate the criminality of his conduct or to conform to the requirements of law was impaired." McCollum was 19 at the time of the crime. . . .

> Along with these compelling mitigating circumstances, the evidence at trial tended to show that Buddy McCollum was far from the most culpable of the four accomplices. He was not the one who initiated the rape, the one who proposed the murder, or the one who actually committed the murder. Nonetheless, he was the only one convicted of murder and the only one sentenced to die. . . .

That our system of capital punishment would single out Buddy
McCollum to die for this brutal crime only confirms my conclusion
that the death penalty experiment has failed. Our system of capital
punishment simply does not accurately and consistently determine
which defendants most "deserve" to die.[5]

II.

I have had occasion to represent seven individuals who were either
charged with or who had previously been convicted of capital offenses.
I currently represent four members of Delaware's "Death Row." One
of my clients, Andre Stanley Deputy, was executed by the State of
Delaware in June of 1994. Much of the Deputy case exemplifies the
injustices that occur, particularly to the indigent and those of color, in
capital cases.

Deputy was convicted by an all white jury. The State exercised
peremptory challenges, without defense counsel's objection, to remove
the only blacks selected to serve on Deputy's jury.

Andre Deputy came from a poor and unstable home environment.
He was raised primarily by an aunt and his older siblings. Early school
records noted that Andre "star-gazed", wet and soiled himself, did no
work, arrived at school late, showed no interest in school work, had
no friends, was retarded academically for his age and invoked pity and
perplexity from his teachers. Andre and two of his brothers were
examined at the Wilmington Mental Hygiene clinic after their school
filed a complaint of neglect against the parents. Andre was considered
to be the most disturbed of the three boys and was recommended for
admission to the Governor Bacon Health Center for residential treatment.
He stayed at the Governor Bacon Health Center for nearly two years,
demonstrating little improvement.

When Andre was twelve years old, he was witness to the brutal
shotgun slaying of his mother. Following his mother's murder, the
school psychologist wrote of Deputy, "Andre has exhibited quite
inconsistent behavior in recent weeks — aggressive and hostile at times
(but not openly), still at other times in a state of absolute lethargy.
With the recent death of his mother there may be some added emotional
problems and conflicts in need of urgent attention." It was the school
psychologist's judgment that Andre Deputy's behavior was part of "a
disguise for intense feelings in a hostility syndrome, and it may also

represent Andre's way of saying — 'if I don't want anything and don't do anything, I won't *feel* anything.'" Deputy was thereafter prescribed additional inpatient treatment at the Governor Bacon Health Center. During this admission, Andre's father never visited him, nor did he respond to a request for additional clothing. Andre's attitude while at the center was described as "poor". The treating psychologist noted "one never knows if he understands or even hears." Andre was considered functioning in the "borderline" range of intelligence (overall I.Q. scale of 74). After nearly a year of inpatient treatment, he was ultimately discharged.

Andre began drinking heavily at age fifteen. At age sixteen he was thrown out of his house by his father for good. A psychologist would opine of Deputy in 1979 that he was "a tragic picture of cultural deprivation and dysocial surroundings." The doctor went on to characterize Andre Deputy as an "untalented black man growing up in — probably — the worst family and the worst historical time that would have been possible for him." Andre's life had been ruled by an "overwhelming dependency on alcohol and the impulses of the atypical people with whom he has lived."

The foregoing is the type of mitigation evidence which should have been presented to the jury which considered whether or not Andre Deputy was an appropriate person to be put to death. Unfortunately, Deputy's trial counsel failed to conduct any investigation as to his background. Trial counsel knew so little about his client's personal life that, when asked at a postconviction relief hearing if he had interviewed any family member prior to trial, trial counsel stated that he thought he may have spoken with Deputy's mother in the courthouse during trial. Andre Deputy's trial counsel is now a diving instructor in the Virgin Islands. Prior to Deputy's case, this attorney had never handled a capital murder trial.

Despite the apparent grossly ineffective assistance Deputy received from his attorney at trial and his penalty hearing, all reviewing courts determined that counsel's performance satisfied the United States Constitution and that Deputy had received a fair trial.

Notwithstanding a horrible past, Deputy underwent an incredible transformation while in prison in 1981. He turned his life over to God, and thereafter was a changed man. Deputy maintained an almost spotless conduct record while housed at Sussex Correctional Institution; acquired his high school equivalency diploma; was trained and began working in the food service department of the prison; participated in the "Scared Straight" program for teenagers to help them keep their lives on a positive track; became a founding and active member of the Lifer's Group at the prison; was a speaker to high school students visiting the prison in connection with criminal justice courses; and, most importantly, was a regular participant in a variety of religious activities, including attendance at chapel each week, handling all special music for the church choir and providing religious counseling to other inmates, as well as Bible study.

At the Pardon Board Hearing, we had to limit the number of people who could speak on Andre Deputy's behalf. Various representatives from Prison Ministry, the Department of Correction and students who had come in contact with Deputy spoke at length as to the tremendous positive impact Andre had on their lives. The State was unable to present any evidence to discredit this substantial transformation, which had now lasted for more than thirteen years. All the State could do was point to the heinous nature of the offense for which he had been found guilty (Deputy was convicted of the 1979 stabbing of the aunt and uncle of William Flamer — his co-defendant — in order to obtain money to continue a drinking binge). Until his death, Deputy maintained that he had neither intended to kill the victims in this case, nor had he participated in their killing in any way.

Notwithstanding his exemplary prison record, the Pardon Board determined that commutation of his sentence from death to life in prison without hope of parole was inappropriate for Andre Deputy. If ever there was a case that warranted commutation, Andre Deputy's was it. The State of Delaware executed Andre Deputy on June 23, 1994.

Delaware's death row has nearly quadrupled since 1991, when the system for determining who received the death penalty was changed from having a jury unanimously recommend the sentence to giving that power to the trial judge. Delaware has executed eight individuals in less than four years. This number is likely to increase in the near future. All those who have been executed and who await execution are indigent. Half of those executed so far have been minorities. Half of the remaining members of our death row are black, despite the fact that African-Americans represent approximately eighteen percent of Delaware's population.

Despite having the highest per capita rate of administering the death penalty in the United States, the Delaware violent crime rate has not gone down. In fact, no study has ever demonstrated that the death penalty has a deterrent impact on the violent crime and murder rate.

The F.B.I. Uniform Crime Reports Division publication "Crime in the U.S.A." shows that murder rates in states which have abolished the death penalty average 5.1 murders per 100,000 population, while states still using the death penalty average 9.1 murders per 100,000 population. A Congressional Staff Report, issued on October 21, 1993 by the Subcommittee on Civil and Constitutional Rights to the Committee on the Judiciary, describes forty-eight cases in the past twenty years where a convicted person has been released from death row because of actual innocence. A recent study published by the Stanford Law Review found that at least 350 persons have been mistakenly convicted of potentially capital crimes from 1900 to 1985. Of these innocent people, 139 were sentenced to death and 23 were executed.

The only conclusion one can reach when the facts are reviewed is that this crude expression of societal vengeance that we call capital punishment is administered unfairly and must be abolished. The focus of our criminal justice system should not be hatred and vengeance, but instead healing and reconciliation. Until we acknowledge this and do away with this barbaric form of punishment, we should not consider ourselves a civilized society.

Chapter 3

Great Ideas in the Law: Due Process in Law

Isidore Starr

Due Process Guidelines for Imposing the Death Penalty

T he shock of the ruling in *Furman v. Georgia* reverberated throughout the halls of state legislatures. Thirty-five states rushed through new capital punishment legislation to conform to the principles stated in the Court's opinions. But what did that decision really say? The nine opinions had revealed a variety of points of view. Should the new laws mandate death in certain cases? Certainly this would remove the objection of wanton, capricious, freakish, and unpredictable behavior by judges and juries. How specific must the new legislation be to meet the objections of the Court?

Furman v. Georgia had been decided by a vote of five to four. Now there was a new justice on the Supreme Court: Justice Stevens had replaced Justice Douglas, who had retired. Would this make a difference?

On June, 2, 1976, the Court handed down five decisions in cases challenging recently-enacted capital punishment laws. The Justices upheld the laws of Georgia, Florida, and Texas, while invalidating those of North Carolina and Louisiana. The judicial lineup now stood as follows: Justices Brennan and Marshall continued their attack on the constitutionality of capital punishment by dissenting in the three cases where capital punishment laws were upheld and joining Justices Stewart, Powell, and Stevens to make a majority in the other two cases. The latter three justices sided with each other in all five cases, upholding three and condemning two of the state laws. Justices White and Rehnquist and Chief Justice Burger teamed up to support all five state laws. Justice Blackmun, standing on his dissent in the Furman case, also supported all five laws. The cases that so divided the Court follow.

Troy Leon Gregg and a companion were picked up by two drunk men. When their car broke down, one of the men purchased a new car, using part of a large roll of cash, which Gregg saw. Subsequently when the men stopped the car and got out to relieve themselves, Gregg also got out and shot the two as they returned to the car. Gregg then took $400 and the car from the men. When Gregg was asked why he shot them, he said, while in custody, "By God, I wanted them dead."

Gregg was convicted of armed robbery and murder and was sentenced to death. The Georgia Supreme Court affirmed the victims and upheld the death sentence for the murders but vacated the armed robbery sentences on the grounds that the death sentence had rarely been imposed for that offense.

The new Georgia law provided for a bifurcated trial wherein the jury first determines the guilt or innocence of the accused; followed by another proceeding in which the same jury decides the sentence. In arriving at the guilty verdict and the death sentence, the jury had to consider aggravating and mitigating circumstances and find that at least one of the following aggravating circumstances existed beyond a reasonable doubt before the death penalty could be imposed:

1. The offense of murder, rape, armed robbery, or kidnapping was committed by a person with a prior record of conviction for a capital felony; or the offense of murder was committed by a person who has a substantial history of serious assaultive criminal convictions.
2. The offense of murder, rape, armed robbery, or kidnapping was committed while the offender was engaged

in the commission of another capital felony or aggravated battery, or the offense of murder was committed while the offender was engaged in the commission of burglary or arson in the first degree.

3. The offender by his act of murder, armed robbery, or kidnapping knowingly created a great risk of death to more than one person in a public place by means of a weapon or device which would normally be hazardous to the lives of more than one person.

4. The offender committed the offense of murder for himself or another for the purpose of receiving money or any other thing of monetary value.

5. The murder (was) of a judicial officer, former judicial officer, district attorney or solicitor, former district attorney or solicitor during or because of the exercise of his official duty.

6. The offender caused or directed another to commit murder or committed murder as an agent or employee of another person.

7. The offense of murder, rape, armed robbery, or kidnapping was outrageously or wantonly vile, horrible or inhuman in that it involved torture, depravity of mind or an aggravated battery to the victim.

8. The offense of murder was committed against any peace officer, corrections employee or fireman while engaged in the performance of his official duties.

9. The offense of murder was committed by a person in, or who has escaped from, the lawful custody of a peace officer or place of lawful confinement.

10. The murder was committed for the purpose of avoiding, interfering with or preventing a lawful arrest or custody in a place of lawful confinement, of himself or another.

In this case, the jury, found that Gregg's criminal conduct (armed robbery and murder) included two of the above listed aggravating circumstances: sections (2) and (4).

In deciding whether to impose the death sentence, the jury may consider any mitigating circumstances that would make them judge the defendant less harshly. Although the Georgia statute did not specify mitigating circumstances, those factors that are usually considered mitigating circumstances are the defendant's age, prior record, emotional state at the time of the crime, and willingness to cooperate with the police.

To make certain that the judge and jury do not act unreasonably or with prejudice, the Georgia statute requires an automatic appeal to the Georgia Supreme Court, where the sentence is examined against the following three criteria: 1. whether the sentence was imposed on the basis of prejudice or any other arbitrary, factor; 2. whether the evidence supported a finding of an aggravating circumstance; 3. whether the penalty in the case was excessive compared to penalties which had been imposed in similar cases.

The Georgia Supreme Court affirmed the death sentence in Gregg's case. Gregg based his appeal of that decision on a number of grounds, including the claim that the death penalty is cruel and unusual punishment. Justice Stewart announced the judgment of the Court and "wrote the opinion in which only Justices Powell and Stevens concurred. Although this represents a plurality opinion, four other Justices joined in the judgment to make it a seven to two ruling."

Justice Stewart, who had condemned the imposition of capital punishment as "wanton" and "freakish" in the *Furman* case found the new statute constitutional. The Georgia law, he concluded, is carefully drawn, provides specific instructions to judge and jury and mandates an automatic appeal to the state's highest court. The death penalty, he stated, is not necessarily cruel and unusual punishment. In this case, he concluded that the penalty for the murders cannot be considered excessive.

What Justice Stewart found especially relevant in influencing his change of mind on the death penalty were the events that followed the *Furman* ruling.

The most marked indication of society's endorsement of the death penalty for murder is the legislative response to *Furman*. The legislatures of at least thirty five states have enacted new statutes that provide for the death penalty for at least some crimes that result in the death of another person. And, the Congress of the United States, in 1974, enacted a statute providing the death penalty for aircraft piracy that results in death. These recently adopted statutes have attempted to address the concerns expressed by the Court in *Furman* primarily (i) by specifying the factors to be weighed and the procedures to be followed in deciding when to impose a capital sentence, or (ii) by making the death penalty mandatory for specified crimes. But all of the post-

Furman statutes make clear that capital punishment itself has not been rejected by the elected representatives of the people.

In the only statewide referendum occurring since *Furman* brought to our attention, the people of California adopted a constitutional amendment that authorized capital punishment, in effect negating a prior ruling by the Supreme Court of California.

There is a saying which states that the Supreme Court follows the election returns. Do you think Justice Stewart was basing his decision on popular opinion rather than constitutional principles? Justice Stewart summarized his position as follows:

"In sum, we cannot say that the judgment of the Georgia Legislature that capital punishment may be necessary in some cases is clearly wrong. Considerations of federalism, as well as respect for the ability of a legislature to evaluate, in terms of its particular state, the moral consensus concerning the death penalty and its social utility as a sanction, require us to conclude, in the absence of more convincing evidence, that the infliction of death as a punishment for murder is not without justification and thus is not unconstitutionally severe."

Justice White, speaking for Chief Justice Burger and Justice Rehnquist, agreed with the decision, saving that Georgia law meets the criticism he and Justices Stewart and Douglas had expressed in the Furman case. The new arrangement prevents the imposition of the death penalty in a "discriminatory, standardless, or rare fashion."

Justice Blackmun, standing on his *Furman* dissent, concurred in the judgment. The dissenting opinions of Justices Brennan and Marshall appear on page 33.

Jerry Lane Jurek was found guilty of killing a ten-year-old girl. While attempting to kidnap and forcibly rape her, he strangled her and threw her unconscious body in a river. The issue was the constitutionality of the death penalty imposed on him by the jury.

After the decision in *Branch v. Texas*, decided with Furman, the Texas legislature rewrote its laws relating to capital punishment. The new law limited capital punishment to five situations: murder of a peace officer or fireman; murder committed in the course of kidnapping, burglary, robbery, forcible rape, or arson; murder committed for hire; murder committed while escaping or attempting to escape from prison; and murder committed by an inmate when the victim is a prison employee.

As in Georgia, the trial is bifurcated, with the jury first determining guilt and then, in a separate proceeding, deciding the sentence. In the second proceeding in which the jury decides "whether the death sentence should be imposed," they are required to answer three questions:

1. Whether the defendant's conduct was committed deliberately and with reasonable expectation that death would result.
2. Whether there was a probability that the defendant would commit acts of criminal violence that would constitute a continuing threat to society.
3. Whether the defendant's conduct in killing the victim was unreasonable in response to provocation, if any, by the victim.

In the Jurek case, only the first two questions were regarded as relevant, and the jury answered each in the affirmative.

The issue here is whether the Texas law provides for the jury's consideration of aggravating and mitigating circumstances, as well as for appellate review to rule out arbitrary and capricious sentencing. Here the Court was confronted with a problem. Unlike the Georgia statute, the Texas law made no mention of mitigating circumstances.

Justice Stevens delivered the judgment and opinion of the Court, in which Justices Powell and Stewart joined. The opinion concluded that the aggravating circumstances could be inferred in the five crimes that were designated as capital offenses. Similarly, although mitigating circumstances are not stated, the three questions which the jury must consider before imposing the death sentence permit the defendant to bring before the members of the jury such relevant data as age, prior record, employment, duress, mental or emotional pressure, psychiatric records, and remorse. In addition, the Texas law, like the Georgia statute, provides for prompt review of the jury's verdict by a court of statewide jurisdiction. This allows for the Texas Court of Criminal Appeals to focus on the matter of mitigating circumstances in reviewing the case.

Jurek had argued that the second of the three questions which the jury had to answer was so vague that a lay person could not possibly handle it. How can the average juror, the defense counsel asked, predict the future behavior of a convicted person? Justice Stevens answered that "any sentencing authority must predict a convicted person's probable future conduct." A jury, he said, can make a reasonable prediction when presented with all possible relevant information. Texas law assured the presentation of such evidence.

Justices White and Rehnquist, joined by Chief Justice Burger, concurred in the decision. Justice White repeated his view that the Eighth Amendment does not forbid the death penalty. He also agreed that the new Texas statute eliminated the discretion of the Court, jury and law enforcement officers, so that the death penalty would not be "seldom" or "arbitrarily" imposed. Justices Brennan and Marshall dissented. (See pp. 111-112).

The third capital punishment case was somewhat different from the first two and raised an interesting issue. Under the new Florida law, after the jury's verdict, a separate hearing is required to determine whether a death sentence or life imprisonment should be imposed. This responsibility rests with the judge, rather than with the jury as in the Georgia and Texas procedures. In arriving at his judgment, the judge has to determine whether statutory mitigating circumstances outweigh statutory aggravating circumstances. These circumstances are set forth in Florida law.

The aggravating circumstances are:

a. The capital felony was committed by a person under sentence of imprisonment.
b. The defendant was previously convicted of another capital felony or of a felony involving the use or threat of violence to the person.
c. The defendant knowingly created a great risk of death to many persons.
d. The capital felony was committed while the defendant was engaged, or was an accomplice, in the commission of, or an attempt to commit, or flight after committing or attempting to commit, any robbery, rape, arson, burglary, kidnapping, or aircraft piracy or the unlawful throwing, placing, or discharging of a destructive device or bomb.
e. The capital felony was committed for the purpose of avoiding or preventing a lawful arrest or effecting an escape from custody,
f. The capital felony was committed for pecuniary gain.
g. The capital felony was committed to disrupt or hinder the lawful exercise of any governmental function or the enforcement of laws.
h. The capital felony was especially heinous, atrocious, or cruel.

The mitigating circumstances are:

a. The defendant was an accomplice in the capital felony committed by another person and his participation was relatively minor.
b. The defendant acted under extreme duress or under the substantial domination of another person.
c. The capacity of the defendant to appreciate the criminality of his conduct or to conform his conduct to the requirements of law was substantially impaired.
d. The age of the defendant at the time of the crime.

Charles William Proffitt was tried and found guilty of first degree murder. After weighing the relevant aggravating and mitigating circumstances, the judge imposed the death sentence. The Florida law also required an automatic review by the state Supreme Court, and that court affirmed the death sentence.

This case raised the issue of whether sentencing by the judge rather than by the jury makes a critical difference.

What do you think? Would you prefer the sentencing authority to be the judge or the jury?

Justice Powell spoke for the Court, with the concurrence of only Justices Stevens and Stewart. They stated that the Florida law is constitutional because it clearly specifies mitigating and aggravating circumstances as well as automatic appeals. Judges are given specific and detailed guidance in deciding on the sentence. If they impose the death penalty they must state in writing the facts on which they based their decision. Justice Powell saw a possible advantage in having judges do the sentencing because . . . judicial sentencing should lead, to even greater consistency in the imposition at the trial court level of capital punishment, since a trial judge is more experienced in sentencing than a jury, and therefore is better able to impose sentences similar to those imposed in analogous cases.

Once again, Justice White spoke for Chief Justice Burger and Justice Rehnquist in an opinion concurring with the judgment of the Court. He reaffirmed his position that the death penalty is constitutional when it is imposed under procedures which regularize the deliberations of judge and jury. Justice Blackmun concurred in the judgment, citing his dissenting opinion in Furman.

The Dissenting Opinions of Justices Brennan and Marshall

Justices Brennan and Marshall, whose opposition to capital punishment had put them on the side of the majority in the Furman case, now found themselves the only dissenters. They disagreed with the majority in the Gregg, Jurek, and Proffitt cases and each wrote a dissenting opinion in which he addressed all three cases together. In these dissents they continued their assault on the constitutionality of capital punishment as cruel and unusual.

Justice Brennan accused the majority of being more concerned with the procedures employed by the states to impose death than with the very essence of the penalty. He declared that the court, as the ultimate arbiter of the meaning of the Constitution, has the duty to speak out when punishments are "no longer morally tolerable in our civilized society." He stated that the death penalty is "degrading to human dignity, . . . treats individuals as "nonhumans" and borders on "official murder."

Justice Marshall repeated two arguments he had made in his Furman opinion: that the death penalty is excessive and the American people if "fully informed as to the purposes of the death penalty and its liabilities, would reject it as "morally unacceptable;" and that retribution and deterrence do not justify a punishment that degrades the victim and violates the substance and spirit of the Eighth Amendment.

Different issues and a Court divided along different lines appear in the fourth and fifth cases which follow. Some of the states, in enacting new capital punishment laws to conform with the suggestions mentioned in the Furman opinions, made obvious attempts to escape any criticism that their new laws might be discriminatory or wantonly, freakishly, and infrequently imposed. To overcome these conditions, North Carolina enacted the following statute:

> Murder in the first and second degree defined: punishment — A murder which shall be perpetrated by means of poison, lying in wait, imprisonment, starving, torture, or by any other kind of willful, deliberate and premeditated killing, or which shall be committed in the perpetration or attempt to perpetrate any arson, rape, robbery, kidnapping, burglary or other felony, shall be deemed to be murder in the first degree and shall be punished with death. All other kinds of murder shall be deemed murder in the second degree, and shall

be punished by imprisonment for a term of not less than two years
nor more than life imprisonment in the State's prison. [emphasis
added]

Prior to the Furman decision, North Carolina had allowed the jury
to chose whether or not to impose capital punishment for first degree
murder. James Tyrone Woodson and Luby Waxton were convicted of
first-degree murder and sentenced to death. The statute required the
death penalty in all first-degree murder cases. The Supreme Court
stated the issue which was raised in the case as follows:

> The Court now addresses for the first time the question whether a
> death sentence returned pursuant to a law imposing a mandatory
> death penalty for a broad category of homicidal offenses constitutes
> cruel and unusual punishment within the meaning of the Eighth and
> Fourteenth Amendments.

Do you think that it is fair to require the death penalty for certain
crimes such as first degree murder? It puts everyone in the state on
notice that courts and juries have no choice in the matter. It does away
with the "unbridled discretion" which makes it possible for juries to
give some defendants life imprisonment, while others are put to death.
If you were a Supreme Court justice who had participated in the Court
rulings up to this time, what would be your decision?

The judgment of the Court was delivered in an opinion announced
by Justice Stewart and concurred in by Justices Stevens and Powell.
The opinion began by tracing the history of mandatory punishment in
this country.

In order to provide a frame for assessing the relevancy of these
factors in this case we begin by sketching the history of mandatory
death penalty statutes in the United States. At the time the Eighth
Amendment was adopted in 1791, the States uniformly followed the
common-law practice of making death the exclusive and mandatory
sentence for certain specified offenses. Although the range of capital
offenses in the American Colonies was quite limited in comparison to
the more than 200 offenses then punishable by death in England, the
Colonies at the time of the Revolution imposed death sentences on all
persons convicted of any of a considerable number of crimes, typically
including at a minimum, murder, treason, piracy, arson, rape, robbery,
burglary, and sodomy. As at common law, all homicides that were
not involuntary, provoked, justified or excused, constituted murder

and were automatically punished by death. Almost from the outset jurors reacted unfavorably to the harshness of mandatory death sentences.

The reluctance of juries to return verdicts in mandatory death sentence cases led states to grant juries discretion in capital cases. The first states to abandon mandatory death sentences in favor of discretionary death sentences were Tennessee, in 1838, Alabama, in 1841, and Louisiana, in 1846. Congress acted in this area in 1897.

If you were a member of a jury in a mandatory death sentence case, would you feel comfortable with a situation in which your only choice was guilty or not guilty? Why do juries seem to be reluctant to impose mandatory death sentences?

The Court found that two criticisms of mandatory death sentences are that they are "unduly harsh and unworkably rigid." In the eyes of Justice Stewart and his two colleagues, the reluctance of juries to sentence and the legislative approval of discretionary jury sentencing by Congress and many of the states are evidence of " contemporary standards of justice" which the Court cannot disregard. And, in their view, it is the jury which remains the link between "contemporary community values and the penal system." It is for this very reason that the justices concluded that the North Carolina law must be struck down.

North Carolina's mandatory death penalty statute for first-degree murder departs markedly from contemporary standards respecting the imposition of the punishment of death and thus cannot be applied consistently with the Eighth and Fourteenth Amendments' requirement that the State' power to punish "be exercised within the limits of civilized standards."

The opinion also cites the lack of standards to guide sentencing in the statute, the lack of a procedure for appellate review and the failure of the statute to provide for consideration of individual circumstances surrounding the crime as reasons for finding that the North Carolina law violated the Eighth and Fourteenth Amendments. Another reason is given in the opinion for striking down the North Carolina law.

A third constitutional shortcoming of the North Carolina statute is its failure to allow the particularized consideration of relevant aspects of the character and record of each convicted defendant before the imposition upon him of a sentence of death. . . . A process that accords no significance to relevant facets of the character and record of the individual offender or the circumstances of the particular offense, excludes from consideration, in fixing the ultimate punishment of death, the possibility of compassionate or mitigating factors stemming from the diverse frailties of humankind. It treats all persons convicted of a designated offense not as uniquely individual human beings, but as members of a faceless, undifferentiated mass to be subjected to the blind infliction of the penalty of death . . . "we believe that in capital cases the fundamental respect for humanity underlying the Eighth Amendment . . . requires consideration of the character and record of the individual offender and the circumstances of the particular offense as a constitutionally indispensable part of the process of inflicting the penalty of death." [emphasis added]

Justices Brennan and Marshall joined Justices Stewart, Stevens, and Powell in the Court's decision but not in the reasoning of the Court's opinion. They reaffirmed their opposition to capital punishment and therefore found the North Carolina law unconstitutional.

The four dissenters were Chief Justice Burger and Justices White Blackmun, and Rehnquist. Justice Rehnquist wrote a separate dissenting opinion in which he disagreed with practically everything in the Court's opinion. He concluded that there was little difference between the North Carolina statute, which the Court condemned, and the Texas and Georgia laws, which the Court approved. Louisiana also enacted a new capital punishment law designed to meet the objections voiced by the Court in the Furman case. The statute at that time read:

First degree murder

First degree murder is the killing of a human being:

1. When the offender has a specific intent to kill or to inflict great bodily harm and is engaged in the perpetration or attempted perpetration of aggravated kidnapping, aggravated rape or armed robbery, — or
2. when the offender has a specific intent to kill, or to inflict great bodily harm upon, a fireman or a peace officer who was engaged in the performance of his lawful duties, — or
3. where the offender has a specific intent to kill or to inflict great bodily harm and has previously been convicted of an unrelated murder or is serving a life sentence, — or
4. when the offender has a specific intent to kill or to inflict great bodily harm upon more than one person, — or
5. when the offender has specific intent to commit murder and has been offered or has received anything of value for committing the murder.

For the purposes of Paragraph (2) herein, the term peace officer shall be defined and include any constable, sheriff, deputy sheriff, local or state policeman, game warden, federal law enforcement officer, jail or prison guard, parole officer, probation officer, judge, district attorney, assistant district attorney or district attorneys' investigator. Whoever commits the crime of first degree murder shall be punished by death. [In 1975, (1) was amended to add the crime of aggravated burglary as a predicate felony for first-degree murder.]

Stanislaus Roberts was found guilty of first-degree murder and the death sentence was imposed under the new Louisiana law. He appealed on the grounds that capital punishment was cruel and unusual under the Eighth and Fourteenth Amendments and that the Louisiana law was similar to the legislation condemned in the *Furman* case.

Again there was a five to four decision, and again it was announced in an opinion by Justice Stevens and concurred in by Justices Stewart and Powell. They found the mandatory death penalty as dictated by Louisiana law unconstitutional under the Eighth and Fourteenth Amendments because it lacked a "meaningful opportunity for consideration of mitigating factors presented by the circumstances of the particular crime or by the attributes of the individual offender." The Court compared the North Carolina and Louisiana statutes.

The Louisiana statute thus suffers from constitutional deficiencies similar to those identified in the North Carolina statute in *Woodson v. North Carolina*. . . . As in North Carolina, there are no standards provided to guide the jury in the exercise of Its power to select those first-degree murderers who will receive death sentences, and there is no meaningful appellate review of the jury's decision. As in North Carolina, death sentences are mandatory upon conviction for first degree murder. Louisiana's mandatory death sentence law employs a procedure that was rejected by that State's legislature 130 years ago and that subsequently has been renounced by legislatures and juries in every jurisdiction in this Nation. . . . The Eighth Amendment, which draws much of its meaning from "the evolving standards of decency that mark the progress of a maturing society" . . . simply cannot tolerate the reintroduction of a practice so thoroughly discredited.

Accordingly, we find that the death sentence imposed upon the petitioner under Louisiana's mandatory death sentence statute violates the Eighth and Fourteenth Amendments and must be set aside. [emphasis added]

Observe that the opinion again emphasizes standards for guiding the jury and a procedure for appellate review of the decision to impose the death sentence.

As could be expected, Justices Brennan and Marshall joined in the judgment of the Court, but their reasoning differed from that of the opinion of the Court because they consistently maintained that capital punishment per se was a violation of the Eighth and Fourteenth Amendments.

Justices White, Rehnquist, and Blackmun and Chief Justice Burger dissented. Justice White's dissenting opinion again emphasized that contemporary community standards, to which the Court's opinion continually refers, seem to accept capital punishment for at least some offenses.

Since the judgment in *Furman*, Congress and thirty five state legislatures re-enacted the death penalty for one or more crimes. All of these States authorize the death penalty for murder of one kind or another. With these profound developments in mind, I cannot say that capital punishment has been rejected by or is offensive to the prevailing attitudes and moral presuppositions in the United States or that it is always an excessively cruel or severe punishment or always a disproportionate punishment for any crime for which it might be imposed. These grounds for invalidating the death penalty are foreclosed by recent events, which this Court must accept as demonstrating the capital punishment is acceptable to the contemporary community as just punishment for at least some intentional killings.

And, the dissenters were saying in their opinion, that the Louisiana law brought certainty into an area previously dominated by capricious, arbitrary, and freakish jury judgments, by eliminating the "guilty without capital punishment" verdict provision which had existed in the prior Louisiana statute, and making a verdict of "guilty of first degree murder" carry a mandatory death sentence. Justice White made it clear that he did not think it a proper exercise of the court's power of review to overturn the conclusions of Congress and thirty five state legislatures, who found that there are circumstances in which the death penalty can serve as a deterrent of crime. Justice White rebuked the Justices, showing his annoyance with their reasoning.

Indeed, the more fundamental objection than the plurality's muddled reasoning is that in *Gregg v. Georgia* . . . it lectures us at length about the role and place of the judiciary and then proceeds to ignore its own advice, the net effect being to suggest that observers of this institution should pay more attention to what they do than what they say. The plurality claims that it has not forgotten what the past has taught about the limits of judicial review, but I fear that it has again surrendered to the temptation to make policy for, and to attempt to govern the country through a misuse of the powers given this court under the Constitution. One might have thought that the capital punishment controversy had been resolved by the Court's prior rulings. But this was not so. In 1978, two cases reached the Court from the State of Ohio, and the issues posed brought forth a new ruling which divided the Justices again and in different ways.

Sandra Lockett was accused of driving the getaway car for a robbery during which the victim was killed. She was charged with aggravated robbery and aggravated murder, convicted, and sentenced to death under the Ohio capital punishment statute. The individual who actually committed the murder turned state's evidence and testified against her. Under Ohio law at the time, the death sentence was mandatory in this type of case unless the judge, considering "the nature and circumstances of the offense and the history, character, and conditions of the offender," determines that at least one of the following mitigating circumstances is established by a preponderance of the evidence:

1. The victim of the offense induced or facilitated it.
2. It is unlikely that the offense would have been committed but for the fact that the offender was under duress, coercion, or strong provocation.
3. The offense was primarily the product of the offender's psychosis or mental deficiency, though such condition is insufficient to establish the defense of insanity.

In accordance with Ohio law, the judge requested a pre-sentence report, as well as psychiatric and psychological tests. The reports concluded that Lockett did not suffer from any psychoses and was not mentally deficient. Without specifically addressing the first two mitigating circumstances, the judge declared that he had "no alternative whether [he] like[d] the law or not" but to impose the death sentence.

Lockett challenged the trial and sentence on various grounds. The one which the Court considered crucial was her contention that her death sentence was invalid because the Ohio statute did not permit the judge to consider as mitigating circumstances such matters as age, character, prior record, her minor role in the crime, and the absence of specific intent to cause death.

What do you think of Lockett's argument? Does it seem to be based on the North Carolina and Louisiana cases? How would you expect the Justices to divide on this issue?

Chief Justice Burger delivered the opinion of the Court, and Justices Stewart, Powell, and Stevens agreed with his conclusion that the Ohio law was unconstitutional. Acknowledging that the prior opinions of the Court had been anything but crystal clear, the Chief Justice reassured the states that an attempt would be made in this opinion to clarify the Court's position, stating: In the last decade, many of the States have been obliged to revise their death penalty statutes in response to the various opinions supporting judgments in *Furman* . . . and its companion cases. The signals from this Court have not, however, always been easy to decipher. The States now deserve the clearest guidance that the Court can provide — we have an obligation to reconcile previously differing views In order to provide that guidance [emphasis added]. The Chief Justice then announced the principle that would serve as the guide.

> We conclude that the Eighth and Fourteenth Amendments require that the sentencer, in all but the rarest kind of capital cases, not be precluded from considering as a mitigating factor [emphasis in original], any aspect of a defendant's character or record and any of the circumstances of the offense that the defendant proffers as a basis for a sentence less than death. . . . Given that the imposition of death by public authority is so profoundly different from all other penalties, we cannot avoid the conclusion that an individualized decision is essential in capital cases. . . .

> There is no perfect procedure for deciding in which cases governmental authority should be used to impose death. But a statute that prevents the sentencer In a// capital cases from giving independent mitigating weight to aspects of the defendant's character and record and to circumstances of the offense proffered in mitigation creates the risk that the death penalty will be imposed in spite of factors which may call for a less severe penalty. When the choice is between life and death, that risk is unacceptable and incompatible with the commands of the Eighth and Fourteenth Amendments. [emphasis added]

Since the Ohio statute did not permit "individualized consideration of mitigating factors," it failed to meet the standards required by the Eighth and Fourteenth Amendments in capital cases and was held unconstitutional.

Justice Brennan did not take part in the case, while Justice Marshall repeated his position that the Eighth and Fourteenth Amendments outlaw capital punishment.

Justice Blackmun agreed that the law was unconstitutional, but he offered two reasons which were not considered by the Court's ruling. He pointed out that the Ohio law provides the death penalty for a defendant who aids and abets a murder without allowing the sentencing authority to consider the extent of the defendant's actual involvement. His second objection was that while the Ohio law gave the sentencing judge full discretion to impose less than the death sentence on a defendant who pleaded guilty or no contest, it required the death penalty for one who insists on the right to a trial and is found guilty. It was this provision that had allowed the defendant who pulled the trigger to avoid the death sentence by pleading guilty, while Lockett, who was less involved in the crime, was sentenced to death.

Justice White also concurred in the Court's ruling but differed in his reasoning. Justice Rehnquist concurred in part and dissented in part. He responded to the principle of law announced in the Court's opinion with the warning:

> If a defendant as a matter of constitutional law is to be permitted to offer as evidence in the sentencing hearing any fact, however bizarre, which he wishes, even though the most sympathetically disposed trial judge could conceive of no basis upon which the jury might take it into account in imposing a sentence, the new constitutional doctrine will not eliminate arbitrariness or freakishness in the imposition of sentences, but will codify and institutionalize it. By encouraging defendants in capital cases, and presumably sentencing judges and juries, to take into consideration anything under the sun as a "mitigating circumstance," it will not guide sentencing discretion but will totally unleash it. . . . I do not think Ohio was required to receive any sort of mitigating evidence which an accused or his lawyer wishes to offer.

Sixteen-year-old Willie Lee Bell was charged with aggravated murder which occurred in the course of a kidnapping. He waived his right to trial by jury and was convicted before a three-judge panel. In his statement to the police, Bell denied he had done the actual killing. He said his companion, eighteen-year-old Samuel Hall, had pulled the trigger and that he had not been aware of Hall's intention. Under Ohio law, the judges ordered a pre-sentence investigation and psychiatric examination of Bell. The report of the psychiatrist concluded that none of the three mitigating factors mentioned in the statute were present in Bell's case (refer to the Lockett case beginning on page 31 for the three factors). The pre-sentence report supplied the judges with information regarding the offense, as well as Bell's background, intelligence, prior record, character, and habits. It described his intellectual capacity as low average or dull normal and noted that he had allegedly been using mescaline on the night of the crime.

Before sentencing, Bell's attorney was permitted to present evidence that Bell had a drug problem, that he regarded his accomplice as a "big brother" and had followed his instructions because he was afraid, and that he was emotionally unstable and mentally deficient. The lawyer brought out the fact that Bell had cooperated with the police and that there was a lack of proof that he had participated in the actual killing.

After considering the reports and the evidence, the judges first decided that none of the three mitigating factors defined by Ohio law were present and then imposed the death sentence. The Ohio supreme court held that the evidence that Bell had aided and abetted was enough to sustain the conviction and the death penalty because under Ohio law, an aider and abettor could be prosecuted as if he or she were the principal offender.

Chief Justice Burger again delivered the opinion of the Court in which Justices Stewart, Powell, and Stevens concurred. The opinion repeated the position taken by the four Justices in the Lockett case: The Eighth and Fourteenth Amendments require that sentencing judges and juries take into consideration all mitigating circumstances reflect to the defendant's character, record, and any other evidence that the defendant wants to offer. Since the Ohio law did not permit "individualized consideration of mitigating factors," it was declared unconstitutional.

Justice Brennan did not take part in the case. Justice Marshall concurred but repeated his position stated in Furman that the death penalty is under all circumstances cruel and unusual punishment. Justice Rehnquist stood on his dissent in the Lockett case. Justice White concurred in the judgment of the Court that the Ohio law was unconstitutional but dissented from the reasoning of the Court's opinion. In an opinion dissenting in part from the Court's opinion in both Lockett and Bell, he said that the death sentences in both cases should be set aside because there was no finding that the defendants engaged in conduct "with the conscious purpose of producing death." Without a finding that a defendant possesses a purpose to cause the death of a victim, he said, the imposition of the death penalty violates the Eighth Amendment.

Chapter 4

A Judge's View of the Death Penalty

Judge Richard S. Gebelein

A s a judge, and before that as an attorney involved in the criminal justice system, I have followed the debate over capital punishment with a great deal of interest for about twenty years. There are sound arguments on both sides of the philosophical debate. However, on March 14, 1992 the death penalty was transformed from a mere philosophical debate to a reality in Delaware. On that Saturday, Delaware executed its first defendant since 1946, Steven B. Pennell. After a substantial period when no one was executed in America, people are now being executed across the nation in growing numbers. In Delaware, we have executed three people in the past two years.

The law in Delaware places the actual decision on whether a defendant will serve life in prison or die upon the trial judge. The jury, by statute, makes a "recommendation" to the Judge which he or she is not bound to follow. This law was enacted late in 1991 because under previous Delaware law a defendant could not be executed unless the entire jury of twelve agreed that the death penalty was the appropriate punishment. In a number of outrageous murder cases the jury simply could not reach the unanimous decision necessary for the death penalty to be imposed. The General Assembly apparently believed that it was more likely that a trial judge could and would reach the decision necessary to put those to death, whose crimes and criminal history indicate it as appropriate, than a unanimous jury. This belief is evident from the legislative debates on this law.

As a trial judge, I have been placed in the position to make this decision on three separate occasions; twice I decided the death penalty was required and once that life in prison was appropriate. One of those individuals has been executed, and the other is on so-called "death row."

On a philosophical level, it is easy to reach the decision that a defendant in a case of brutal murder deserves to die. That defendant has committed first degree murder, the intentional killing of another human being, and the murder has been committed in a way that causes the death penalty to be involved, i.e., the defendant committed one or more aggravating factors that the General Assembly has decided justifies the death penalty. Indeed, under the new statute, the Court is required to impose death if it finds that the aggravating factors outweigh any mitigating factors.

Some of those aggravating factors, such as the killing of more than one person, the use of torture, and the commission of the murder while committing another felony, were the issues in the cases I had to decide. Likewise, I was required to consider mitigating factors in each case, such as the family situation of the defendants, the defendants' psychological condition, and potential to do beneficial acts in the future. Legally speaking there is no doubt that the sentence of death was justified by the wanton acts of these defendants; and in two cases I found that the aggravating factors outweighed any mitigating factors.

There is, however, another side to this decision process. Call it the emotional side or the human side. This aspect of this truly unique decision is probably the reason why it has been hard to obtain unanimous votes for the death penalty from juries in the past several years. All of those juries were "death qualified,", i.e., those prospective jurors who for moral or religious grounds declared that they could not impose the death penalty were excluded from service in these cases. In spite of this, the twelve citizens picked to serve were rarely able to vote 12-0 for imposition of the death penalty. After being called upon to make this decision myself, I believe I know why the required unanimity was difficult to obtain.

The jurors, just as the judge, live through a murder trial for several weeks or perhaps even months. They get to know the defendant as a human being in the courtroom; they may get to see the family of the defendant as those family members attend the daily trial. It is not then a natural human occurrence to decide in a cold, logical, deductive process to kill an individual whom you have come to know as a human being. You may not like that person, you most likely loath what the defendant has done; but, it is still difficult to be the deciding factor causing that person's death. I find it impossible to criticize jurors, average citizens who have been brought by the criminal justice system into the courtroom and away from their familiar life for a brief period of time, who then simply cannot vote to kill someone they have come to know.

Since the law was changed to make the juries decision merely a recommendation, it has become more frequent that juries return an unanimous verdict. They are now called upon to answer the antiseptic question, whether the aggravating factors outweigh the mitigating factors. They are told their decision is merely a recommendation. They are no longer told that their decision will result in the defendant's death. I suggest that the removal of the ultimate responsibility for the final decision makes it much easier for the jurors to reach an unanimous decision.

As a judge, you are called upon to make difficult decisions all of the time. In many criminal cases, you must decide who goes to prison and for how long. You must consider the effects of these decisions on the defendant, the victims and their family members. You must decide who gets compensated for injuries and who does not. In Family Court, the Judge makes some of the toughest decisions of all relating to the custody of children. Fortunately, it is the rare day that you are called upon to decide if a defendant is to live or die. Fortunately, it is not an everyday occurrence that a defendant is strapped to a table on the basis of your order and injected with a series of poisons that cause almost instantaneous death.

Execution is not a natural process. It is a killing done not in the heat of passion, nor in the act of self-defense; it is rather a cold, logical, intentional killing. It is justified by the facts of the crime and the background and propensities of the murderer, but it is not nice. It affects the correctional workers and court personnel. It affects the judge as well. The actual execution is an event that touches all of those involved in the case leading to the result. It profoundly affects the lawyers who prosecuted the case and those who defended the murderer. On the day of execution those involved in the process feel sorrow, not sympathy for the defendant who well deserved this punishment. The sorrow of being part of the intentional killing of another human being.

As an individual, I support the death penalty. I believe it is justified for some murders and for some murderers. As a human being, I do not enjoy making this decision and feel no satisfaction at the execution being fulfilled.

Chapter 5

The Role of a Prosecutor in a Death Penalty Case

Steven P. Wood, Esquire

One of the most powerful and important people in our criminal justice system is the prosecutor, who is the lawyer for the people of his or her county or state (including the victim) in every criminal trial. It is the prosecutor who, along with his or her fellow prosecutors, decides whether or not to formally charge a defendant with a crime. It is the prosecutor who decides which particular charge or charges to file against the defendant. In Delaware, prosecutors are called Deputy Attorneys General because they work in the Office of the Attorney General. In other states, prosecutors may be called Assistant District Attorneys (as they are in Pennsylvania and New Jersey), or Assistant State's Attorneys (as they are in Maryland).

Because prosecutors are lawyers, and not police officers, homicides are investigated by the police, who are responsible for discovering and interviewing witnesses, collecting and analyzing physical evidence, and locating, apprehending and interviewing the suspect. However, prosecutors are often involved in homicide investigations from their earliest stages. In Delaware, as soon as a homicide is reported to the police, they in turn notify the Attorney General's Office, and a Deputy Attorney General is sent immediately to the crime scene. Once the prosecutor arrives and is briefed on the case by the police, he or she remains available to answer any legal questions which may arise, and to offer suggestions for investigative strategies and evidence collection.

Once the police have learned enough about the crime to determine how the homicide happened (and why), it is the prosecutor's responsibility to decide with which particular homicide offense to charge the suspect. In Delaware, and all other States, there are a number of crimes which can be prosecuted when one person kills another. In Delaware, only Murder First Degree can be punishable by death, so the prosecutor's charging decision makes the death penalty a possibility or an impossibility. The prosecutor and his or her colleagues must also decide whether or not to seek the death penalty in a Murder First Degree case, since the death penalty is not applicable in all Murder First Degree cases, and may not be a just penalty even in those cases where it is a legal option.

Under Delaware law, in order for a Murder First Degree case to be a capital case (one in which the death penalty, which is also called capital punishment, is available), the State must prove beyond a reasonable doubt that what are called "statutory aggravating circumstances" are present. There are currently twenty-two such circumstances which are explicitly listed in Delaware's Criminal code, and they fall generally into one of three types: the nature of the murder, the character of the murderer, and the identity of the victim. If the murder was committed during the commission of another felony (like robbery, burglary, or rape) , or in order to further the killer's escape from custody, or if the murderer was paid in or ordered to commit the crime, the nature of the murder may make the death penalty legally available. If the murderer had previously been convicted of murder or another crime of violence, or if the murderer was serving a life prison sentence at the time of the crime, the background of the murderer may constitute a statutory aggravating circumstance. If the victim was a police officer, or a hostage, or was pregnant, or elderly, or if there were two or more victims, then these facts may also make the death penalty possible. If one or more statutory aggravating circumstances are present in a Murder First Degree case, the State will normally seek the death penalty. However, from time to time the prosecutor may feel that justice requires something less than a death sentence. In other cases, the prosecutor may be forced into a plea bargain in which the State agrees not to seek the death penalty because the case is a weak one, and a conviction may not be possible should the case proceed to trial. In any case where a prosecutor feels the death penalty is not appropriate, the case will be extensively discussed by all of the senior prosecutors in the Attorney General's Office, and the Attorney General himself or herself is frequently involved in the discussions.

Once these decisions are made, the prosecutor will file the appropriate charges in Superior Court. Many months of pre-trial preparation then begin. The prosecutor must interview the witnesses, ensure that any appropriate scientific analysis of the physical evidence is performed. He or she must use his or her experience and knowledge to anticipate any likely legal issues so that pre-trial legal research can be done. These preparations are much more intense in a death penalty case than in any other, not only because of the stakes involved, but because the prosecutor knows that if the defendant is convicted and a death sentence is imposed the case will spend years in both State and Federal appeals court under intense scrutiny. Every prosecutor is fully aware of many convictions which were overturned years after the original guilty verdict because of a minor technical error wholly unrelated to the defendant's guilt or innocence, so every possible step is taken to ensure that no such mistakes are made.

Within a few days or weeks of the crime, the prosecutor will meet with the victim's family. Because the victim's family has no formal standing in a criminal case, they are not represented by an attorney. It is thus the prosecutor's responsibility to act as an advocate for the rights of the victim's family, to explain the criminal justice process to them, and to keep them informed of all significant developments in the case. The victim's family often has a strong (and understandable) interest in ensuring that justice is done for their murdered loved one. Many families feel that securing a conviction and death sentence is the last thing they can do for the deceased family member, so the criminal case frequently assumes a special kind of emotional importance for them. Frequently, the family will be frustrated by the exceedingly slow pace of prosecution, and they will often feel anger at the various procedural safeguards which are afforded to the defendant — from their perspective, the defendant gets all the breaks. The prosecutor, who is usually assisted by social workers who are experts in dealing with the victims of crime, must be able to address and assuage the victim's family's concerns with patience and compassion.

As the trial date approaches, many of the legal issues discussed earlier will be resolved in pre-trial hearings. This is especially so if the defense is seeking to prevent the State from using either statements to the police made by the defendant, or particular items of physical evidence. (The defense will usually claim that some sort of procedural or constitutional error occurred when the statement was taken or the evidence was gathered.) The defendant may also attempt to stop the trial by claiming to suffer from a mental illness so severe that he or she does not understand what is happening in court, and therefore cannot assist his or her lawyer in preparing a defense. Such a claim of "incompetence to stand trial" will also be resolved in the pre-trial hearing.

The prosecutor must approach these pre-trial hearings with the same degree of diligence and preparation afforded the trial itself. He or she must become an expert in any relevant areas of constitutional law, psychology or psychiatry, and locate any necessary expert witnesses in these fields. Because the outcome of the pre-trial hearing will often determine the outcome of the trial, it is a vitally important step in the prosecution.

Once the pre-trial hearings are concluded, the prosecutor is free to concentrate on the preparation for the trial itself. As is the case with every trial, the prosecutor must become completely familiar with every fact and detail present in the case, no matter how small or (seemingly) trivial. Every witness must be interviewed, every police report must be read and studied, and the scientific evidence must be understood. The prosecutor must know about the case, as it is only then that he or she can begin the process of deciding how best to present the evidence and the case to a jury in a way that will be easily understood — and convincing. The final and intense phase of pre-trial preparation will typically consume several weeks, and the prosecutor will focus exclusively on the case during this time, putting all of his or her other cases on hold.

Before the trial can start, the jury must be selected. Each of the jurors is asked a specific set of questions by the judge in the presence of the prosecutor, defense attorney, and defendant. These questions are designed to uncover any biases, prejudices, or preconceived notions held by the juror that might make it difficult for him or her to fairly judge the case. Any juror who is identified as a potential problem during this process, referred to as "voir dire," may be removed from the jury by the judge. In addition, each side has a limited number of so-called preemptory challenges, which it can use to remove a juror for any reason whatsoever. However, the juror's race, ethnic origin, or sex may not be the primary reason for dismissal. The prosecutor will use preemptory challenges to help ensure a jury that will carefully listen to the evidence, and which does not contain members who are biased against the death penalty. At the conclusion of this process, which often takes several days, a jury comprised of twelve jurors and several alternates is selected.

The trial then begins. In Delaware, our death penalty law mandates that the trial occurs in two stages. First, the jury hears evidence on the issue of whether the defendant is guilty or not guilty. This portion of the trial is called the "guilt phase." During the guilt phase, the prosecutor must convince the jury that the defendant is guilty of Murder First Degree, and he or she must also begin the process of convincing the jury that the crime was so terrible that death is the only appropriate penalty. If the jury unanimously agrees to convict the defendant of Murder First Degree, the same jury will then hear evidence relating to whether or not the death penalty shall be imposed. This portion of the trial is known as the "sentencing phase." In cases where the defendant has pleaded guilty to Murder First Degree, the sentencing phase becomes the first — and only — part of the trial. During the sentencing phase , the role of the jury changes. While it is the jury's sole responsibility to determine the guilt or innocence, in Delaware both the judge and jury play a part in the decision whether to impose the death penalty. Ultimately, the decision is the judge's, but by law the jury performs an important advisory role in the process. Both the judge and jury will hear evidence relating to either the "circumstances and details of the crime" or the "character and propensities" of the defendant. The prosecutor will present evidence highlighting not only the terrible nature of the crime, but also the bad character of the defendant. Both the judge and the jury must use this evidence to answer questions which are specified by Delaware's death penalty law. First, the jury must decide whether the State has proven the existence of at least one statutory aggravating circumstance. Then, the jury must decide if all aggravating circumstances (statutory and non-statutory) outweigh all of the mitigating circumstances, if any are found to exist. A non-statutory aggravating circumstance is *any fact* which makes the imposition of the death penalty more appropriate, while a mitigating circumstance is any fact which makes the imposition of the death penalty *less* appropriate.

Once the jury votes on its answers to these two questions, the vote tally as to each is reported to the judge, who must then answer the same questions. The jury's answers are not binding upon the judge, although they are afforded "great weight" by him or her. The answers of the judge are official. If he or she answers *no* to the first question (has a statutory aggravating circumstance been proven beyond a reasonable doubt?), then the death penalty cannot be imposed, and the defendant must be sentenced to life imprisonment. If the judge finds a statutory aggravating circumstance, he or she must then decide whether all the aggravating circumstances outweigh all of the mitigating circumstances, he or she *must* impose the death penalty. Thus, the only discretion afforded to the judge by Delaware's death penalty law relates to factual determinations which, once made, determine the sentence to be imposed.

Should the judge decide to impose the death penalty, he or she must announce, in detail, the reasons for doing so. The factual findings supporting the death sentence are outlined in exhaustive detail in a written opinion, which the judge will also read in open court. Once the opinion is read, the judge will set a date for execution. However, the first execution date is almost always meaningless, as it will automatically be postponed once the appeals process begins.

The many years of delay between the imposition of most death sentences and the eventual execution are the result of the lengthy and complex appeals process. Unlike the trial process, which is fundamentally about determining guilt or innocence, the appellate process is focused on assessing whether any constitutional or procedural errors were made during the trial. Guilt or innocence is not usually at issue during the appellate process — instead, the defendant attacks his or her conviction by contending that errors occurred which unfairly affected the outcome. Depending on the case, the original trial prosecutor may continue to handle the case during the appellate process, or he or she may turn the case over to another prosecutor who specializes in appellate law.

The process begins in the State court (in Delaware, all death penalty cases are automatically appealed to the Delaware Supreme Court), where all issues relating to the fairness of the trial are addressed. If the defendant claims that his or her rights as guaranteed by the United States constitution were violated during the investigation or trial, once the first round of appeals are finished, he or she may appeal to the Federal District Court, and then to the Federal Court of Appeals and finally to the United States Supreme Court (an appeal to our nation's highest court may always be requested, but the chance to pursue the appeal is seldom granted). Once this first round of appeals is finished, the defendant may elect to start all over again by making a "collateral attack" on the conviction. During this round of appeals, the defendant will frequently claim that errors made by his or her lawyer resulted in a deprivation of his or her constitutional rights to an attorney. Again, this round of appeals must work its way up and through the State courts, and it may then be continued up and through the various levels of the Federal Court system.

Given the time it takes to litigate each issue in each court, it is not surprising that the process can take years. The seemingly-endless round of appeals and delays can be brought to a halt only when the State is able to convince the various State and Federal courts that the defendant has had a competent attorney *and* the opportunity to raise each and every important legal issue which might be present in the case. Frequently, the appellate process ends in a last-minute frenzy of activity, with motions being filed and decided on a daily basis. Typically, teams are involved in each case on both sides.

The appeals process in a death penalty case is unique not only because of the ultimately high stakes, but because the State and the defendant disagree about the legitimacy and morality of the penalty to be imposed. In every death penalty appeal, the issue of whether or not the death penalty should be used by our society is at issue, and often times the argument is overtly raised. Our legal system is designed to enforce ideas and values which are widely held by our society, and when it focuses on an issue about which our society is split, the system is robbed of some of its legitimacy, and therefore its efficiency. This is exactly the case when the death penalty is at issue, as our society, and the legal community, do not agree about its fundamental moral underpinnings.

As these issues are played out in the lengthy appellate process, the various rationales for the death penalty often come into play. The defense will often argue that the man or woman who is about to be executed is a very different person than the one who committed the horrible murder many years before. This argument is designed to meet what is perhaps the strongest argument for the death penalty — specific deterrence. This concept embodies the reality that an executed person will (of course) be perfectly prevented from committing additional crimes in the future; thus, a specific person (the executed defendant) is *deterred* from future criminal conduct. The State will also argue that the death penalty is the appropriate and just punishment for the taking of a human life. This notion, which can be expressed by the maxim "an eye for an eye, a tooth for a tooth" is deeply embedded in Judeo-Christian thought, and also finds expression in many of the world's older belief systems. Some advocates of the death penalty also believe that it serves a *general* deterrent function, in that the execution of one person will stop other people from committing similar crimes for fear of being subjected to the same punishment. Opponents of the death penalty hotly dispute the existence of a general deterrent effect, and most prudent scholars have concluded that neither side has proved its case scientifically.

Eventually, all of these legal and moral issues move from the theoretical to the real, as the execution date approaches. The attempts to stop the execution through last minute appeal often continue up until the very end. The original trial personnel express obligation to their own convictions, and as representatives of the victim and his or her family. The actual execution is a sobering and powerful experience. It represents the end of many years of hard work for the prosecutor. It provides a kind of closure to a terrible period in the life of the victim's family. For our society, the death penalty speaks to the many fundamentals issues that deal with fairness, justice and morality, as each execution provides another forum for these important issues to be considered and debated.

Chapter 6

Silent Voices: If Only These Murdered Women Could Speak — A Perspective of the Death Penalty

Colonel Thomas P. Gordon

A s convicted murderer Steven Pennell lay motionless before me, I considered the irony of the situation. Here I stood, once the commander of this investigation and now a police chief, serving as a witness to the execution of this violent criminal. The death of Steven Pennell was a peaceful one, in comparison to the gruesome torture and painful deaths he inflicted upon his female victims.

One young woman actually died of a heart attack during her severe torture; the other four helpless women were beaten to death after being tortured by Pennell. These women were methodically stalked and viciously killed by this remorseless predator; the man who lay dying from a state-administered injection of lethal drugs. Even the death penalty of Steven Pennell, however, received its share of conscientious objectors.

The national debate about the legitimate use of the death penalty in the American criminal justice system has escalated to lofty heights.

To some philosophically inclined, the death penalty should be eliminated because it is useless since murders still occur, undeterred by the possibility of this ultimate sanction. To many civil rights activists, the death penalty should be eliminated because statistically it is argued to have been imposed upon a disproportionately higher number of non-white criminals, as compared to white criminals. To many moral theorists, the death penalty should be eliminated because the deliberate taking of any human life should never occur, and, therefore, may not be sanctioned by our government. These meritorious perspectives miss their mark, however nobly-intentioned their genesis.

The death penalty serves two vital purposes in American society. First, it is the appropriate cost to be paid for the murder of another person. In every other crime, victim compensation is court ordered against the guilty offender. What about the victim of the murderer? Who speaks for the dead person who was deprived of the most precious possession of all — life? What about justice for the victim? Is our system only concerned exclusively for criminal justice? Surely, it is no longer relevant to the once alive, now murdered victim whether their murderer was white or non-white. The victim is still dead. Nor is it relevant to the unfortunate dead victim that the murderer was not deterred by past executions of convicted murderers. The victim is still dead. As to the last argument, ultimately, the dead victim will not lose any sleep about the propriety of a government which authorizes the death penalty for murderers.

During the two long years of the Pennell investigation, the badly beaten bodies of his young victims were discovered throughout New Castle County. To humiliate his victims further, these women had their nude bodies dumped during the darkness of night in very public places. For example, early one morning, construction workers reported to work to find one woman's naked body spread upon their construction site for all to see. The most experienced detective was sickened at the brutal deaths of these women, followed by such public mockery of their fate.

Our community was frozen in terror. Our state had never been subjected to a serial killer, let alone the residents of our suburban county. Women's fear increased with every new body discovered. Panic struck entire families if a female relative was late, or God forbid, reported missing, as Pennell's victims were. Women were forced to think of themselves in terms of potential prey, and adjust their lives to accommodate the rising chill of terror.

The second reason the death penalty is a necessary sanction is for the protection of the community. Government has a responsibility to protect its people from known, convicted murderers. There should be no chance that this deadly criminal could ever be allowed to prey upon another human being. Recidivism — the rate of repeat crimes by the same offender — is notoriously high. Only one guarantee exists to ensure a murderer will not strike again: the permanent elimination of the murderer. Murder is the one crime against both society and the individual so malicious that it must never be permitted to reoccur. The death penalty eliminates recidivism.

The second victim of a murderer will not care if the murderer was white or non-white, nor care if the murderer was undeterred by past executions, nor care about the impropriety of a government-sanctioned death penalty. The only thing important to the second murder victim is that the second death should never have occurred. There simply is no justification for allowing the selection of yet another helpless victim, knowing that it could have been prevented.

As I watched Steven Pennell dying, the son of saddened parents, I felt for those who loved him. Then the faces of parents and children of all his victims came to mind. Their faces were filled with grief and horror. Finally, the images of those savagely murdered women flashed into focus. Those images were of faces bloodied beyond recognition. I knew then with certainty that all such lofty, intellectual debate was purely academic. Pennell the murderer had to be permanently stopped, as did Ted Bundy and other notorious anomalies of human origin.

It is for the community I have sworn to protect that I express my beliefs with reasonable, rational pragmatism. It is, however, for the murdered victims whose voices have been forever silenced that I speak with deep emotion and utmost dedication.

Chapter 7

Tracking a Death Penalty Case

Jim Courtney

It's a call I make almost every weekday to the U.S. Third Circuit Court of Appeals in Philadelphia:

"Hello. This is Jim Courtney of WBOC-TV in Dover, Delaware. Is there anything new in the cases of . . . ? and then I fill in the blank.

These days, it's Billie Bailey, William Flamer, and James Riley. For many months it included Kenneth DeShields and Andre Deputy. This call is so much a part of my routine that I know the phone number by heart, and am on a first name basis with several workers in the office.

I make similar calls to other offices, tracking the status of other cases. Regulars include the Kent County Superior Court, Delaware Supreme Court, the U.S. District Court in Wilmington and about a half dozen lawyers' offices. For a while, the U.S. Supreme Court was also on my list.

Unlike journalists, judges aren't constrained by deadlines. A case will be before a particular court for weeks, and even months, before a decision is made. Since that decision can come at any time, I make that phone call everyday.

I make these phone calls to ensure our station is on top of the cases with which our viewers are familiar. These are cases where the crime, or at least part of it, was committed in Kent or Sussex County, Delaware. As with any story, we want to report it while it is still news. Ideally, that means before it is in the newspapers; certainly before the decision is several days old.

Four men have died by lethal injection since Delaware began executions again in 1992. The first two, Steven Pennell and James Red Dog, asked for no appeals. Subsequently, their cases went from trial to sentence to actual execution in roughly three years. Most viewers were familiar with the cases from the outset. But Kenneth DeShields, executed September 1, 1993, had been on death row since 1986. Andre Deputy, executed June 23, 1994, committed his capital crime in 1979.

The slow nature of the appeals process actually poses more than one challenge to the video-journalist. Unless one is a relative of the criminal or the victim, you would probably forget the guy is still around, if you are familiar with the case at all! So, with these cases, we must review the crime as well as update the status of the case. From a video standpoint, this can be difficult.

Pictures are the lifeblood of television news. There's a saying in some news rooms: "If you don't have the pictures, it didn't happen." I do not agree with that statement completely. But it is certainly difficult to tell the story of a person on death row for murder appealing his sentence without having any video of the person appealing the sentence, any video of the original crime scene, any video of the crime you're talking about—including pictures of the victims, any video of the original trial this person is appealing, etc. Clearly, the story can still be told. It just becomes a story the anchor reads from the set, and is written short because there are no pictures.

Pictures of the crime scene transport the viewer back to the place where the incident occurred. Immediately, everyone sees the house, or the yard, or the field as it looked then. Older viewers suddenly remember seeing that place years ago, and recall the first time they heard about the crime. Newer viewers are instantly up to speed on what everyone else already knew.

Pictures of the victim put a human face on the tragedy. Unfortunately, in our society, we hear about violence and death all the time. It takes the picture of a horrendous car wreck, followed by the yearbook picture of a smiling high school junior to illustrate the senselessness of drinking and driving. Similarly, there is no better way to humanize the murder of a defenseless old lady than to show a picture of the sixty five-year woman who was murdered. (I don't mean after she was murdered, of course, but in a family picture.) Likewise, video of the condemned person humanizes the story. It puts a face on the otherwise sterile details of a legal appeal. It shows the viewer who the state is planning to put to death.

The office I work in, WBOC's Dover Bureau, did not open until 1986. Finding video, or film, of any Delaware event that occurred previous to that is a challenge, because the filing system in our Salisbury office is incomplete. It's not their fault. Finding sixty seconds of videotape shot nearly a decade ago is probably a lot like being audited for a really old tax return. Sometimes too much time has elapsed.

We were able to locate file video of Kenneth DeShields' trial in Georgetown. He was on crutches at the time. Ironically, showing that video of him hobbling into court generated sympathy from some, who called in to complain about the state executing such a defenseless creature. We got new video of the defendant during his appearance before the Board of Pardons, no longer on crutches, and the calls stopped.

We were able to locate original video of the investigation showing police cars outside the Sussex County Landfill, where the murder occurred. The son of the murdered victim was kind enough to show us a picture of his mother. He also talked to us about the effect the loss still has on him and his family, providing balance to the defendant's story that he had since changed, and deserved mercy.

Other cases are so old, people involved in the original investigation and trial are no longer around. Police have retired, lawyers have moved away, family members have moved away or passed away. Those that remain have dealt with their feelings already and no longer see a need, or want to dredge up the past.

In the case of Andre Deputy, time may have healed many old wounds. At his Board of Pardons hearing, two family members of the people he once admitted to helping kill came forward to say they didn't favor execution. Fifteen years had passed since their parents were killed, and since nothing could bring them back, life in jail for Deputy was fine with them. The Board of Pardons rejected Deputy's plea anyway.

The days and hours leading up to an execution are a spectacle all their own. Lawyers file last minute appeals with any court that will accept them. We, as journalists, must make constant calls to see if a decision is made.

The closer the time to execution, the more unlikely it would be for a judge, or the governor, to halt it. With the first three men executed, there was little doubt they were guilty. Despite DNA evidence to the contrary, Pennell swore he did not commit the murders. Still, he wanted to die rather than spend his life in jail. Though he pled "no contest," Red Dog never denied his crimes, and believed there was honor in being executed. DeShields fought his death sentence to the bitter end, but never denied he was guilty of the crime. Andre Deputy unsuccessfully fought to stay alive, proclaiming his innocence to the very end.

I know execution is near when other stations call requesting our video of the prisoner, scripts to use for background, names and phone numbers we have for relatives of the victim and the name and number of the convict's lawyer.

On the day of an execution, each reporter realizes he or she is not the only one following the story. This case that you have so meticulously followed — developed a personal interest in, and worked hard to beat everyone to the punch to be the first to report new developments in — is suddenly crowded with reporters from everywhere.

Rarely do we see Philadelphia reporters cover stories in Kent County. All the major television stations sent reporters and live trucks to the past executions. We never see Baltimore reporters cover any Delaware stories. Several stations sent their people to Red Dog's execution.

For better or worse, there have been enough executions recently to make covering them routine. There's always an anti-death penalty rally the day before the execution at Rodney Square in Wilmington. The day of the execution, opponents gather at the Smyrna Rest Area a few hours early and then head up to the prison to begin their vigil.

The reporter and camera person must report to the prison training center at least two hours before the scheduled execution. We must show up that early to be eligible for the witness lottery, but it helps to get there even earlier to assure ourselves a good spot for the post-execution press conference. Then, all media sit around, waiting for things to happen.

About an hour and a half before the execution, Corrections releases what the condemned person ate for their last meal. A half hour later, Corrections announces who the four lottery media witnesses are. Everyone waits around for this since eligibility requires that the reporter must be present when his or her name is called.

The system for witnessing executions favors print reporters. Reporters from the Associated Press, News Journal and Delaware State News are automatically witnesses. Everyone else must enter the lottery for the four remaining seats. Not that anyone I know is really eager to watch someone die. But if one must cover story, the best way to do it is through one's own eyes.

Those reporters not chosen for the lottery head up to the prison to get their interviews and pictures of the protesters, who begin their vigil about a half hour before the execution is scheduled to start. Soon the announcement of the inmate's time of death is made outside the prison. Reporters head back to the prison training center for the post-execution press conference, where witnesses describe what they saw.

Generally the stories of the witnesses are about the same, as they were for the first three executions. They say watching someone die by lethal injection is a lot like watching someone go to sleep.

Probably the most colorful story to come from witnesses is the story of James Red Dog's last words. When the warden asked Red Dog if he had any last words, he thanked his lawyer, and his wife and other supporters, and then turned to those there to watch him die and said: "As for the rest of you all, you can kiss my ass."

After the media briefing, television reporters usually head back to the prison grounds to shoot their "stand up," the portion of the story where the viewer sees the reporter standing in front of the camera speaking. If it is close to a show time, reporters from WBOC usually file a live report from the prison grounds. I did a live report for our noon show after the Red Dog execution, and repeated the story of Red Dog's last words. We received two phone calls complaining about the "vulgar language."

I have been told prison officials in Texas have a hard time getting the media to come and cover executions because they happen so often. This has not happened in Delaware yet. We covered Pennell because he was the first executed in over 40 years. Red Dog, DeShields and Deputy had down state Delaware connections, as do Flamer, Bailey, Riley, Dawson, Sullivan and Lawrie.

I have noticed less public reaction to executions in the two years since Delaware has reinstated them.

We received many calls from people wanting to voice their opposition to the death penalty before the state executed Pennell. We received fewer calls for Red Dog, and none for DeShields or Deputy.

Even our own station's treatment of the event has lessened. The day the state executed DeShields was the same day Hurricane Emily threatened the Delaware and Maryland coastlines. We led our 6 p.m. broadcast with storm-related preparation stories and an expanded weather segment. Those tuning in to hear about DeShields execution had to wait until 6:15.

The decision to structure the broadcast that way was made by our producer and our news director in Salisbury. They reasoned, correctly, severe weather directly affected more viewers that evening than the execution.

I do not often stop to ponder whether public interest in capital punishment is rising or falling. As long as cases are pending before one court or another, I (or whoever takes my place) will be there to track its course all the way to the end.

Chapter 8

Racist Beliefs and Organizational Affiliation: Can They Be Taken into Account in a Capital Sentencing Proceeding?

L. Anita Richardson

David Dawson v. State of Delaware
112 S. Ct. 1093 (1992)

The Eighth Amendment prohibits cruel and unusual punishment. The U.S. Supreme Court has held that the death penalty is not cruel and unusual punishment for certain categories of murder so long as it is imposed as a reasoned moral response to circumstances of the capital offense and the character and background of the offender.[1]

No capital offender can be sentenced to death unless the state proves at least one statutory aggravating factor beyond a reasonable doubt.[2] Among the factors deemed aggravating in most capital-sentencing statutes are: 1) killing someone in the course of committing a felony such as armed robbery; and 2) killing someone after the perpetrator has escaped from prison.

Many states also permit the sentencing authority to consider non-statutory aggravating factors in determining if a sentence of death is warranted. Among the non-statutory aggravating factors routinely considered are: 1) resistance to rehabilitation; 2) prior criminal history; and 3) a history of disciplinary infractions during prior incarcerations.

The First Amendment protects various rights that are central to a democratic society: the right to speak freely on matters of political or social concern; the right to express ideas through symbols or passive conduct, the right to associate.[3,4,5] Ordinarily, the First Amendment plays no role in the capital sentencing process. However, the two amendments can come together when a state attempts to use a capital offender's political views or organizational membership as an aggravating factor supporting imposition of the death penalty. In *Zant v. Stephens*, the Supreme Court assumed, but did not hold, that the death penalty could not be imposed on the basis of beliefs or conduct protected by the First Amendment.[6] *Dawson v. Delaware* asks the Supreme Court to hold expressly that such factors cannot be used in determining whether or not death is the appropriated penalty in a capital case.

Issue

Can membership in the Aryan Brotherhood, a white racist prison organization, and the display of tattoos emblematic of membership in the Aryan Brotherhood be used as non-statutory aggravating factors justifying a sentence of death?

Facts

David Dawson and three fellow inmates escaped from a Delaware Correctional Center located near Smyrna, Delaware in the early morning hours of December 1, 1986. Soon after the escape, Dawson separated from the others and embarked on a course of criminal activity that included robbery and burglary, and culminated in the fatal stabbing of Madeline Kisner. Dawson was white, as was Kisner.

Dawson was apprehended and indicted for multiple offenses, including capital murder. He was tried before a jury and convicted on all counts charged. The same jury sentenced Dawson to death, after concluding that the state of Delaware had proved the following statutory aggravating factors beyond a reasonable doubt: 1) the murder was committed by Dawson after he had escaped from a lawful place of confinement; 2) the murder was committed in the course of committing another felony; and 3) the murder was committed for pecuniary gain. The state also introduced evidence in support of a non-statutory aggravating factor — Dawson's "bad character." Evidence in support of this non-statutory aggravating factor included Dawson's extensive criminal history and his membership in the Aryan Brotherhood, a Nazi-oriented white race, prison organization.

Dawson sought to exclude the Aryan Brotherhood evidence, arguing that it was not relevant and inflammatory under the Eighth Amendment. He also argued that admission of evidence would violate his First Amendment rights of free association, expressive speech and, in addition, would amount to a violation of substantive due process under the Fourteenth Amendment.

The trial judge ruled that the Aryan Brotherhood evidence was relevant to Dawson's character. As a result, the following evidence was admitted: 1) a stipulated explanation of the origin and purpose of the Aryan Brotherhood; 2) testimony and a photograph showing that Dawson had a tattoo on his right hand bearing the name Aryan Brotherhood; and 3) testimony that Dawson used the moniker Abaddon, meaning "one of Satan's angels" or "angel of the bottomless pit" and that Dawson had the name Abaddon tattooed across his stomach. However, before this evidence was admitted, Dawson was permitted to ask the jurors the following question:

In this case there will be evidence relating to membership in an organization called the Aryan Brotherhood, a white supremacist group. Would this affect your ability to serve as a fair and impartial juror in this case?

Dawson did not testify at the sentencing proceeding but he did introduce evidence in mitigation. Relatives testified that Dawson came from a broken family; that he was raised primarily by his grandmother and that he began getting into trouble at the age of 12, when his grandmother died. Dawson's aunt and half-sister testified that they loved Dawson despite his criminal activities and that they would continue visiting him as they had in the past. Dawson's aunt further testified that Dawson had volunteered to donate one of his kidneys to a dying cousin. Finally, Dawson introduced evidence that, during past incarcerations, he had accumulated good-time credits; joined various alcohol and drug treatment programs; attended group therapy; and worked in various prison industries.

The state stressed the connection between Dawson's bad character and his membership in the Aryan Brotherhood during closing argument and again in rebuttal. After deliberating for two hours, the jury imposed the death penalty which, under Delaware law, is a sentence binding on the court.

The Delaware Supreme Court affirmed Dawson's conviction and sentence against multiple challenges. In particular, the state high court rejected Dawson's contention that his sentence should be set aside because it as based, in part, on a constitutionally impermissible factor — his membership in the Aryan Brotherhood. On this point, the state supreme court concluded that the evidence was relevant to Dawson's character, reasoning that his "affiliation with this type of organization was not only indicative of how he identified himself and how he wanted to be identified by others, but again was characteristic of his lawless nature and rejection of rehabilitation during his incarceration."[7]

Dawson sought review in the U.S. Supreme Court on a petition for a writ of certiorari. The Court granted Dawson's petition to decide whether his death sentence was invalid because it was based, in part , on his personal ideology and organizational membership.

Background and Significance

Dawson advances three arguments in support of his position that his death sentence is invalid and should be vacated. Each of Dawson's arguments is premised on the proposition that the First Amendment protects: 1) his white racist beliefs;[8] 2) his membership in an organization espousing an unpopular ideology;[9] and 3) his use of symbols, here, tattoos, depicting those beliefs.[10] Dawson stresses that this is the law even if his views are offensive to others.[11]

Dawson maintains that the First Amendment categorically bars Delaware from punishing him for his beliefs, organizational membership, or expressive conduct. He contends that this is precisely what Delaware has done in introducing his white racist ideology, his Aryan Brotherhood membership and his tattoos and nickname as non-statutory aggravating factors supporting imposition of the death penalty in his case. Since his beliefs, membership and expressive conduct played a role in his sentencing in palpable violation of the First Amendment, Dawson concludes that his sentence is per se unconstitutional.

Dawson then advances a second argument — that the Court's Eighth Amendment jurisprudence bars the use of the Aryan Brotherhood evidence. Dawson acknowledges that, under the Eighth Amendment, the state, as well as the capital offender, can introduce all relevant evidence bearing on the nature of the offense and the character of the offender.[12] Dawson contends, however, that the Aryan Brotherhood evidence fails this test of relevance. Specifically, he argues that this evidence is not relevant to the circumstances of the offense. In this regard, he notes that the victim was white, as he is, and that there was absolutely no racial motivation for the murder.

Dawson also argues that the evidence is not relevant to his character. According to Dawson, his beliefs, membership, and expressive conduct would be relevant to his character for purposes of imposing the death penalty only if they were linked to actions that violated the law or, in his case, violated prison rules.

He stresses that there was no evidence at all that he ever acted on his white racist views, and also points out that neither his views nor his membership in the Aryan Brotherhood violated prison rules. He contends that absent harmful conduct motivated by his beliefs, the Aryan Brotherhood evidence was not only relevant but prejudicial under the Eighth Amendment.

Dawson's third argument asserts that Delaware's use of his white racist philosophy as an aggravating factor violates his substantive due process rights under the Fourteenth Amendment. Here, Dawson relies on dicta in *Zant*. Court observed that, if a state "attached the 'aggravating" label to factors that are constitutionally impermissible or totally irrelevant to the sentencing process, such as for example the race, religion, or political affiliation of the defendant... , due process of law would require that the jury's decision to impose the death penalty be set aside."[13]

Dawson maintains that Delaware has done exactly what *Zant* prohibits. The state has used constitutionally impermissible factors — his political, white racist ideology and his membership in the Aryan Brotherhood — as reasons to impose the death penalty, even though these factors do not relate in any way to his offense or his prison conduct in general. On authority of *Zant* and the Court's First and Eighth Amendment cases, Dawson concludes that his sentence is invalid. He asks the Court to vacate the sentence and remand for resentencing without the use of the Aryan Brotherhood as evidence.

Delaware responds by arguing, as a threshold manner, that neither Dawson's espousal of white racist beliefs nor his membership in the Aryan Brotherhood were factors in determining his eligibility for the death penalty. Delaware points out that these factors came into play only after the jury found that the state had proved three statutory aggravating factors beyond a reasonable doubt. Thus, the state argues that Dawson cannot complain that his personal beliefs or his membership in the Aryan Brotherhood, even if protected by the First Amendment, served as an independent basis for imposing the death penalty. Delaware then proceeds to its central argument, an argument that focuses on the unique role accorded the offender's character in a capital-sentencing proceeding.

Delaware begins by observing that from *Gregg* , in 1976, to *Payne v. Tennessee*, 111 S.Ct. 2597, in 1991, capital sentencing is individualized sentencing, and individualized sentencing requires a close examination of the defendant's character to ensure that the death penalty will be imposed, if at all, only as a reasoned moral response to the capital offender as a unique person. Delaware maintains that, in introducing evidence of Dawson's ideology and his membership in the Aryan Brotherhood, it was fulfilling the Court's mandate of individualized sentencing.

Delaware also contends that a capital offender's beliefs and associations, as a reflection of his character, are introduced routinely by capital offenders as mitigating factors. Indeed, Delaware points out that Dawson did exactly that at his sentencing hearing when he introduced evidence of his participation in counseling groups and in alcohol and drug rehabilitation groups, along with evidence of his offer to donate a kidney to a relative.

Delaware contends that, in essence, Dawson is seeking to extract the benefit of character evidence for purposes of mitigation while denying the state the opportunity to use character evidence in aggravation. Because such a one-sided rule is not supported by the Court's Eighth Amendment decisions and, in fact, undermines the mandate of individualized sentencing, Delaware concludes that the First Amendment does not bar use of the Aryan Brotherhood evidence at issue in this case.

Delaware next argues that the Aryan Brotherhood evidence was relevant to the jury's sentencing determination. According to Delaware, this evidence indicated that Dawson's enthusiasm for the Aryan Brotherhood was far more significant than his occasional participation in groups that might facilitate his rehabilitation. According to the state, the sentencing jury was entitled to draw this inference and to sentence Dawson accordingly.

Dawson v. Delaware will be an important case regardless of the outcome. If Dawson prevails and the Court holds that political beliefs and organizational affiliation cannot be used as aggravating factors in capital sentencing, it will have established a bright-line rule that will be easy to administer. If Delaware prevails, the Court will be sending a strong signal, initiated in *Payne v. Tennessee*, that it believes capital sentencing proceedings have been giving an unfair advantage to capital offenders. Thus, this case could be a barometer of the Court's future decisions in capital cases, in particular, and in criminal cases in general.

The Supreme Court's Decision

The Court ruled in favor of Dawson, accepting his argument that the Aryan Brotherhood evidence was irrelevant. First, the Court concluded that the Dawson's racist beliefs, inferred from his membership in the Aryan Brotherhood, were irrelevant to the murder of Madeline Kisner because the murder was not motivated by the race. Next, the Court concluded that Dawson's Aryan Brotherhood beliefs and membership were irrelevant to such legitimate sentencing issues as Dawson's future dangerousness because the state had not established any connection between the Aryan Brotherhood and specific patterns or acts of violence. Finally, the Court concluded that the Aryan Brotherhood evidence was not relevant to rebutting Dawson's mitigating evidence because the state failed to prove a connection between Dawson's racists beliefs or organizational affiliation and his "bad" character. In other words, the Court reasoned that holding racists beliefs is not enough to prove bad character for purposes of imposing the death penalty.

The Court made it clear in its decision that the state's Aryan Brotherhood evidence simply did not go beyond proving that Dawson held racist views. In other words, the state failed to connect Dawson's racist views with any of the well-recognized factors that are relevant imposing the death penalty.

The Court's decision in *Dawson* establishes that a capital offender's beliefs and organizational membership are protected by the First Amendment to the extent that they are just that—beliefs. To the extent that a capital offender's beliefs relate to the motive for capital murder, to aggravating factors, or to rebutting the offender's mitigating evidence, evidence of those beliefs is admissible and would not be barred by the First Amendment.

Chapter 9

What I Will Not Tell You About the Death Penalty

Horacio D. Lewis

The debate on the death penalty has been around since the dawn of man. Indeed, both sides of this controversy are supported in the Bible with the passages: ". . . life for life, eye for eye, tooth for tooth, . . ."[1] and "If someone strikes you on the right cheek, turn to him the other also."[2] Yes, death penalty arguments will thrive at least throughout my lifetime. Hence, you will have probably heard the arguments I am about to present.

I think it is fair to say that at some time or another most of us feel angry enough to want to hurt or even kill someone, especially if they are trying to hurt or kill us or what's precious to us. However, the death penalty is not about self-defense, it is instead about the state or a government taking it upon itself the right to judge who should live and who should die.

Therefore, it is no coincidence that in Furman Vs. Georgia the United States Supreme Court ruled that the death penalty had often been used in an arbitrary, capricious, and discriminatory manner, thereby violating Eighth Amendment guarantees against cruel and unusual punishment. Of course, most likely, you already know that. You probably also know that is why the death penalty was struck down in 1972 (Unfortunately it was reinstated in 1976).

I am also not going to tell you that non-whites and the poor have been executed in disproportionate numbers since records on executions were kept in 1930. For example, of the some 3,868 persons executed in the U.S. from 1930 to 1983, 53% were Black or five times the proportion of Blacks in the population at the time. Sadly, there have been an estimated total of over 20,000 executions during the past 300 years. Recent statistics reported by the NAACP Legal Defense and Educational Fund's "Death Row, USA," and by "K. William Hayes Capital Punishment Studies" reveal that of the estimated 354 executions (which includes one woman) occurring since 1976, roughly 44% represent Blacks, Latinos and other minorities; and that non-whites are more likely to be executed when their victims are whites. Moreover, most of these executions occurred in southern states.

The reports also estimate that of the 3,284 current death row inmates (including 51 women), 51% are non-whites and, as obvious, predominately male. Our own state of Delaware has already executed 21 non-whites (i.e., 20 Blacks and one Native American) and 12 whites (including one woman) since 1902, and is presently vying for the soul of yet another Black inmate of the 6 (and 5 whites) currently on death row. Delaware is among the very top in per capita death row inmates/ executions. Again, this is familiar to an unequal system of justice which penalizes non-whites, men, and the poor who can't afford the cost of equality. Yes, if you are the "wrong color," male, or can't buy the best defense, you are more likely to die at the hands of the government, the only developed western country with capital punishment.

Though most death row inmates plead and beg for their lives: "I am begging you to let me live . . . please," said Kenneth W. DeShields, a Delaware black inmate executed by lethal injection on August 23, 1993; the death penalty has also been increasingly used by others as an instrument of suicide, as was the case with the late Michael Alan Durocher, who rejected all appeals on his behalf and asked "that justice be served" to end his life. He was put to death on August 25, 1993 by electrocution in Florida. And, the slaughter continues.

Furthermore, I am not going to tell you that a system which says it is against the law to take a life unless it is the law that's doing the killing, is nothing but a hypocritical farce: no one should condone or model the taking of human life. Most likely, you also know that the death penalty is irreversible and that if there is an error, and there have been some, the finality of this mistake is obvious. Clearly, when any human life is taken , not only does the family suffer, but a little bit of each of us dies, since human life is interconnected. Let the state lead the way in breaking the cycle of murder. In fact, moments before he died, DeShields somnambulistically mumbled: "It ain't worth taking a life."

I am also not going to tell you that the death penalty does not rehabilitate anyone nor does it deter capital acts. On the contrary, studies reveal that murder rates increase following executions. Additionally, although most of the thirty eight jurisdictions/states with capital punishment statutes use lethal injection as their preferred method of execution, a surprising number still barbaricly execute by electrocution; while others use the gas chamber or offer an option of the firing squad or hanging in lieu of lethal injection.

What does all this get us? I assuredly differ with those who argue that our society is safer as a result of state sanctioned executions. Quite frankly, I feel no safer today than I felt before the last execution took place. As a society, we must find another way! We spend less time trying to understand each other than we spend with inanimate objects. Somehow I fail to see how building a spaceship or going to the moon is more important than valuing human life. And I am not going to tell you that what we need in our society is more people who care and more people who are fair to their fellow human beings regardless of race, ethnicity, age, gender, color, creed, handicap, or sexual orientation. This will serve as a greater deterrent to crime than any correctional facility or death penalty that may be devised.

Though individuals should be held responsible for their own actions, there is research correlating unfair treatment such as racism, child abuse, and societal ills such as substance abuse, irresponsible sexual activity, etc. with delinquency or criminal behavior. What we need are humanistic systemic changes which educate and rehabilitate those exhibiting unfair or destructive behavior in order to deter recidivism. This change would not exclude lifetime incarceration, with no parole when necessary, for those considered truly dangerous to society. Of course effective incarceration should include meaningful eight-hour a day jobs or education/self esteem rehabilitative activities in order to abolish the vast amount of idle time able-bodied inmates utilize to perfect their crime specialty or to learn and discuss new criminal behaviors. This reality makes them even more dangerous.

An effective and enforceable gun control law as well as the development of better alternatives to incarceration (e.g., required visits to prisons, community work, active mentoring, library research assignments and special projects), and diversionary/preventive programs such as required school curricula on prison and capital punishment issues, are necessary if we are to improve our correctional system and control criminal behavior. Further, I am not going to tell you about the need for fair and speedy trials and representative jury systems. Effective employment programs, which are less expensive than the more than $30,000 a year required to warehouse each inmate, offer yet another viable deterrence.

As an extension of God himself, human life is a precious gift which should not be destroyed by either a criminal citizen or a criminal government. Let it be equally against civilized law and ethical conscience for anyone or any government to put a human being to death. Human life should be treasured and nurtured, death does not a lost life restore. People change; none of us can claim to be exactly the way we were in the recent or distant past. In many respects, we have changed for the better, or have hopes to do just that. Significant contributions are made by the worst of us and by the best of us. Let us stop the reckless madness of snuffing out dreams and potential for making a difference and living out what may well be a divine plan.

Therefore, I am not going to tell you that I am strongly against the death penalty, because you now know that. Clearly, life and death should not be the business of the fallible. It should be left to powers higher than ourselves.

Chapter 10

Do Defendants Have a Right to Ask Prospective Jurors If They Would Automatically Impose the Death Penalty?

L. Anita Richardson

Derrick Morgan v. State of Illinois *(Docket No. 91-5118)* *Argument Date: January 21, 1992*

The Fourteenth Amendment's Due Process Clause guarantees the defendant in a criminal case the right to a trial that is fundamentally fair.[1] In addition, if the criminal defendant exercises his or her right to a jury trial, the Due Process Clause and the Sixth Amendment ensure that the jury will be impartial.[2]

The guarantee of fundamental fairness and the right to an impartial jury also apply to the jury's sentencing determination in a capital case.[3] Applying these principles, the United States Supreme Court, in *Witherspoon v. Illinois*, 391 U.S. 510 (1968), held that the prosecutor in a capital case cannot exclude prospective jurors "simply because they voice general objections to the death penalty or express conscientious or religious scruples against its infliction."

Morgan v. Illinois asks the Supreme Court to decide if the guarantee of fundamental fairness or the right to an impartial jury was violated because the defendant was not permitted to ask prospective jurors if they would impose the death penalty based solely on their determination that he was guilty of murder.

Issue

Does a capital defendant have a constitutional right to ask prospective jurors if they would impose the death penalty automatically on finding the defendant guilty of murder?

Facts

Derrick Morgan was charged with capital murder and armed violence in connection with the shooting death of David Smith. The prosecution dropped the armed-violence charge and proceeded to trial only on the murder charge.

Each prospective juror was asked by the trial judge if he or she could give both sides a fair trial. All jurors stated that they could. The judge also asked each prospective juror the following question: "Would you automatically vote against the death penalty no matter what the facts of the case revealed?" To this question, one juror, Stuart Ship, responded "I would not vote against it." The other jurors answered "no," either immediately or after additional inquiry by the judge.

Morgan wanted to ask each prospective juror a similar question to determine if the individual would impose the death penalty solely because he or she found Morgan guilty of murder. Specifically, Morgan wanted to pose the following question: "If you found Derrick Morgan guilty, would you automatically vote to impose the death penalty no matter what the facts are?" The trial judge refused to allow Morgan to impose this question.

The jury found Morgan guilty and, after a hearing, sentenced him to death. On automatic, direct appeal to the Illinois Supreme Court, Morgan's conviction and sentence were affirmed.[4] With respect to the question Morgan wanted to ask prospective jurors, the Illinois Supreme Court held that there is no constitutional right to "life qualify" a jury, i.e., to ask questions that would "exclude all jurors who believe that the death penalty should be imposed in every murder case." The Supreme Court granted Morgan's petition for writ of certiorari to review the Illinois Supreme Court's decision on the issue.

Background and Significance

Morgan's initial argument is premised on the right to an impartial jury guaranteed by both the Due Process Clause and the Sixth Amendment. Morgan, relying on *Ross v. Oklahoma*, 487 U.S. 81 (1988), contends that it is reversible error to permit a person to sit as a juror in a capital case if that person would impose the death penalty automatically on finding the defendant guilty.

Ross concerned a prospective juror, Darrell Huling, who stated explicitly that "if the jury found the defendant guilty, he would vote to impose the death penalty automatically." When the trial judge refused to remove Huling for cause, Ross removed him by using a peremptory challenge. In holding that the right to an impartial jury guaranteed by the Due Process Clause and the Sixth Amendment had not been violated, the Court acknowledged that, "had Huling sat on the jury that ultimately sentenced Ross, the sentence would have to be overturned."

Morgan argues that at least one juror in his case, Stuart Ship, indicated that he would vote to impose the death penalty automatically. In support of this contention, Morgan relies on the following exchange between the trial judge and Ship. The judge asked Ship if he "would automatically vote against the death penalty no matter what the facts of the case revealed." Ship answered that he "would not vote against it."

Morgan contends that Ship held the same views on automatically imposing the death penalty that Huling did in the *Ross* case. Morgan argues that Ross compels the Court to vacate his death sentence and remand for a new sentencing hearing at which he would be permitted to question prospective jurors about their automatic death-sentence views. Morgan finds additional support for his position in numerous state supreme court decisions holding that a capital defendant is entitled to ask prospective jurors if they would vote for a sentence of death solely and only because they found the defendant guilty.[5]

Morgan also advances a due process, fundamental fairness argument. Here, Morgan relies on *Wardius v. Oregon*, 412 U.S. 470 (1973), which held that it is fundamentally unfair to require a defendant in a criminal case to divulge to the prosecution the details of an alibi

defense when the prosecution is not required to divulge to the defendant
the evidence it expects to use to refute that defense. In reaching this
result, the Court observed that the Due Process Clause "speaks to the
balance of forces between the accused and his accuser" and that those
forces should be reciprocal.

Morgan insists that he was looking only for this reciprocal "balance
of forces" when he sought to ask prospective jurors if they would
impose the death penalty automatically on conviction. He contends
that there was reciprocal "balance of forces" in his sentencing hearing
because the state was permitted to question and remove for cause each
juror who would vote automatically against the death penalty and thus
prejudice the state's right to a fair sentencing determination, while he
was precluded from asking one simple question framed to ascertain
and remove any juror who would vote automatically for the death
penalty, thus prejudicing his right to a fair sentencing determination.

Morgan stresses that it is not sufficient to ask prospective jurors,
as the trial judge did in his case, whether or not they could give each
side a fair trial. He contends that a prospective juror could believe that
he or she was being fair in imposing the death penalty on each and
every capital defendant found guilty of murder. However, Morgan
insists that a juror who holds this view cannot be open and impartial in
considering, for example, mitigating evidence offered by the capital
offender in an effort to convince the jury that death is not the appropriate
penalty.

The real issue, argues Morgan, does not concern a prospective
juror's belief about his or her capacity to be fair; it concerns whether
or not a prospective juror has foreclosed a sentencing determination
other than death. Morgan contends that it is fundamentally unfair to
permit the state to ask a question framed to ascertain if a prospective
juror has closed his or her mind to the death penalty, while denying the
defendant the opportunity to ask a question framed to ascertain if the
individual has closed his or her mind to any penalty other than death.

The state of Illinois responds by agreeing that no person should
serve as a juror if that person cannot or will not follow the law.
However, Illinois insists that no such person sat as a juror in Morgan's
case.

Illinois challenges Morgan's claim that juror Ship would have voted
to impose the death penalty if he found Morgan guilty. First, Illinois
argues that Ship's response of "I would not vote against it," given
after being asked if he would vote automatically against the death penalty
regardless of the facts, does not support the inference that Ship believed

the death penalty must be applied to each and every defendant found guilty of capital murder. Moreover, Illinois points out that Morgan could not have believed that Ship would vote to impose the death penalty automatically, observing that Morgan never challenged Ship on this ground. Instead, notes Illinois, Morgan challenged Ship after Ship stated that he might be influenced adversely by a defendant's decision not to testify in his own defense.

Illinois next contends that general questioning of prospective jurors to determine their fairness and their willingness to follow the law is sufficient to detect and remove any individual who might automatically vote for the death penalty after finding a defendant guilty of capital murder. In this regard, Illinois points out that each juror who served in Morgan's case, including Ship, stated explicitly that he or she could give the defendant a fair trial. According to Illinois, this is all Morgan is entitled to under the specific right to an impartial jury or the more general guarantee of fundamental fairness.

The state also stresses that a capital defendant in Illinois is not prejudiced if, for some reason, an individual who believes in the automatic imposition of the death penalty actually sits on the jury. Under Illinois law, all twelve jurors must vote for the death penalty before that penalty can be imposed. Thus, argues Illinois, a juror who would impose the death penalty automatically would have no effect unless the other 11 jurors also believed that death was the proper penalty.

Illinois next argues that the general questioning of prospective jurors to determine their capacity to be fair is a matter best left to the sound discretion of the trial judge, to be disturbed only on a showing of manifest error.[6] According to Illinois, the trial judge in Morgan's case took all steps necessary to impanel an impartial jury and, in fact, impaneled such a jury. Under *Mu'min*, the state concludes that no further questioning of prospective jurors was warranted in this case, nor constitutionally required.

Illinois closes by arguing that Morgan is wrong in asserting that there is a state court consensus holding that a capital defendant has a constitutional right to ask prospective jurors if they would vote automatically to impose the death penalty after finding of guilt. Illinois points to two state supreme courts that have held that there is no such constitutional right, *Riley v. State*, 585 A.2d 719 (Del. 1990); *State v. Hyman*, 281 S.E.2d 209 (S.C. 1981).

Illinois also maintains that most state courts considering this issue have held that its resolution is best left to the sound discretion of the trial judge. Because there is no lower case consensus, because no juror actually sat in Morgan's case who would impose the death penalty automatically, and because Morgan's jury was impartial, Illinois asks the Court to reject Morgan's constitutional challenges and to affirm his sentence.

Morgan v. Illinois is an interesting case. On the one hand, Morgan is seeking only the right to ask one or two questions of prospective jurors in a capital case, questions that, in all likelihood, would not impede the progress of the trial. Furthermore, Morgan is seeking a reciprocal right. The state is permitted to give meaning to its right to remove for cause any prospective juror who automatically opposes the death penalty by asking appropriate questions. Morgan seeks to give meaning to his reciprocal right in the same way: by asking prospective jurors if they would impose the death penalty automatically. On the other hand, if Morgan received a fair trial, he has sustained no prejudice even if the question he sought to ask was proper and should have been posed. In other words, any constitutional error in this case may have been harmless.

Morgan v. Illinois has the look and feel of a close case. The Court's decision may well turn on the issue of fairness and the weight the Court gives to those state supreme court decisions that appear to support Morgan's position. Morgan will prevail if a majority concludes that fairness and impartiality were compromised because prospective jurors were asked only about one type of bias central to a capital case— automatic opposition to the death penalty—but not asked about another equally central bias—automatic imposition of the death penalty. Illinois will prevail if a majority concludes that Morgan's trial was fair and that any error was harmless.

The Supreme Court's Decision

The Court ruled in favor of Morgan, holding the Morgan was entitled to a fundamentally fair and impartial jury determination of whether or not death was the appropriate penalty in his case and that fundamentally fair determination required that Morgan be granted the same opportunity as the state to dismiss for cause any juror who would automatically vote one way or the other without regard to the evidence. Accordingly, the Court held that the requirement of impartiality embodied in the Due Process Clause entitled a capital offender to challenge and dismiss for cause any prospective juror who would vote to impose the death penalty automatically upon conviction without regard to any mitigating evidence the capital offender might introduce during the sentencing hearing.

The Court proceeded to hold that a capital offender is entitled to question prospective jurors to ascertain if they believe in the automatic imposition of the death penalty upon conviction of capital murder. On this point, the Court concluded that the trial judge's general fairness inquiry in Morgan's case was insufficient to vindicate his right to have his sentence determined by an open-minded jury which would weigh all the evidence, both aggravating and mitigating.

Chapter 11

Life or Death

Clifford Callaway

Cold blooded killers or caring men with a chance to help others. Who are these inmates that have been sentenced to death in Delaware?

Being incarcerated at Sussex Correctional (SCI) for the past several years has given me the opportunity to become friends with three of these men: Kenny DeShields, Andre Deputy, and Steven Pennell. All three have been executed for the crimes they committed.

I first became friends with Kenny DeShields in 1988. He was very friendly and likable. Other inmates would make comments about his pending death sentence, and how strong he was to handle the situation with such courage. In November of 1992, we took a Laubach training course together, with eight other inmates. It was during this time that I really became good friends with Kenny. After we completed our training, we were able to help other inmates learn to read and write. Kenny was a natural at this. A lot of the residents were young black men who were somewhat embarrassed at not knowing how to read. But when they heard Kenny was a Laubach tutor, many of them came to him to ask for help. One very shy student referred to him as his "big brother." No one else seemed to be able to reach him, except Kenny.

In July of 1993, Kenny was transferred to Delaware Correctional Center (DCC) in Smyrna because his execution date was approaching. I helped him carry his belongings to the receiving room, knowing that it might be the last time I would ever see him. In August, Kenny was scheduled to be put to death by lethal injection. With less than twenty four hours to go, he received a stay of execution. I felt relieved at first, but then I realized that I would only have to go through it again in a few weeks. Several weeks later, his execution date was rescheduled for August 31. This time he did not receive a stay of execution. The day Kenny was executed, there was an eerie silence cast over Sussex Correctional Institution. Ordinarily, the chow hall would be noisy, but on this day, you could have heard a pin drop. Several minutes past nine thirty, we received word that Kenny had been executed. After nine years of waiting, it was finally over for him. Kenny was convicted for one count of first degree murder, which occurred in August of 1984.

Kenny went through an exhaustive appeals process, including appeals to the Superior and Supreme Courts of Delaware, the United States District Court, the Third Circuit Court of Appeals, and the United States Supreme Court. A hearing before the Board of Pardons was held as a last attempt to have the death sentence commuted.

Another inmate facing death, Andre Deputy, and I became friends in 1988. Andre sang solos in church each week. He had a very gifted singing voice, and was a devoted Christian. In 1990, a chapel was completed at SCI. All the inmates housed in Maximum Security attended the services from the balcony in the chapel. Each week Andre would sing one or more selections from the balcony, his rich voice ringing throughout the chapel.

Like Kenny, Andre was very likable. We attended a lot of the church services and Bible studies together. Andre also was one of the first members of the Lifer's Group in November of 1992. He was a very active member, and was the chairman of the fund raising committee.

Andre had been facing his death penalty for more than fifteen years. Several times, over the past years, he has been transferred to DCC because of his approaching execution date. Each time he received a stay of execution. Once, in 1993, he came within thirteen hours of his execution, only to receive a stay at the last minute. Andre was convicted for two counts of first degree murder, which occurred in 1979. He was transferred for the final time on June 20, 1994, and was executed by lethal injection on June 23, 1994.

I had the chance to talk with Andre about his feelings toward the death penalty. When I asked him how he felt about the imposition of the death penalty, he replied, "I think it stinks, because it is not applied equally."

I also asked him if he could say something to the students that he had previously talked with, what would it be. His reply was, "obey your parents, and listen to them. Parents: talk with your children, not at them. My dad was a preacher and he tried to force his beliefs on me rather than talking with me."

When I asked him if the death penalty was a deterrent to crime, he replied, "no," the statistics prove it isn't, killing is rampant and getting worse. Andre's mother was murdered in front of him when he was very young. When I asked him to tell me about this, he became very sober and quiet. This is his account of what happened:

My sister had a boyfriend: they went together for a couple of years; they were on the verge of breaking up. He told her that if she left him, no one would have her. She left him anyway. Later that night he came in through our third floor window with a shotgun, walked down the steps with the gun. My mother got up off the couch and asked him for the gun, then he shot the gun and then he ran out the door. They caught him later that night hiding in a car.

It took Andre a while to get through telling this to me. He spoke in short choppy sentences, his voice very emotional.

The third inmate facing death I became friends with was Steven Pennell. Steve was very mysterious, and the way he would look at you with his dark eyes was very strange. I would play cards with him during evening yard. He was a good spades player, and we would win quite a few games. But then he would start talking about criminal law and certain issues involved in his case. His eyes would get very mysterious and he would no longer be interested in card playing.

There was something different about Steve's case, compared to Andre and Kenny's. While Andre and Kenny fought their death sentence, Steve wanted his to be carried out as quickly as possible.

Steve was convicted by a jury of two counts of first degree murder, for which he received two life sentences. In 1991, he was charged with two more murder charges. Instead of going through with a trial, he decided to plead guilty. He asked for the state to execute him, although he claimed he was innocent of the charges. I did not understand his reasoning for pleading guilty. His request to be executed was granted, and on March 14, 1992, Steve Pennell became the first person to be executed in Delaware in more than forty years. Although I was friends with Steve, it was not a close friendship like I had with Kenny and Andre. Steve was very difficult to get to know. Not many inmates wanted to socialize with him. He tried to commit suicide while housed at SCI, and I felt sad for him, knowing that he wanted to die so badly. I guess that I'll never understand why, or what drove him to his "death wish".

Is the death penalty cruel and unusual punishment? Some say yes, others say no. I think that keeping a man waiting to die, for more than fifteen years is cruel and unusual. Not knowing from one day to the next, when or even if you are going to die, has to have a very devastating effect on a man.

I know that the families of the victims of these crimes are also devastated, angry, and hurt. They have every right to be. Their loved one has been killed in a violent manner, and they certainly have the right to be angry, and to cry out for justice. Recently, a lot of articles have appeared in newspapers in support of the death penalty. Public opinion seems to be crying out for death sentences to be carried out quickly, instead of allowing the appellate process to drag on for years. Although I am not in favor of the death penalty in most cases, I feel that the waiting, the ups and downs when stays are granted, and the men with death sentences not knowing when or if they will die, violates the Constitution more that the death penalty itself.

In Andre and Kenny's case, I think that life in prison would have better served justice and the public. Several times, groups of students were brought in to SCI to talk with Andre and Kenny. They would tell them about prison, about how they did not want to come here. They talked about alcohol and drug abuse, and how it caused trouble for them. Who knows how many young people have been turned around because of something they may have said. How many inmates were inspired by Kenny to learn to read and write, and how many have changed their lives because of Andres' Christian testimony? These same inmates will be released someday, and they will be someone's next door neighbor. What does the public want, someone released from prison, worse than they were before, or someone who has learned to read and write, and maybe even learned a trade or something about themselves (like what caused them to get into trouble to start with). Both Kenny and Andre believed in education, and tried to persuade other inmates to better themselves. Some say that an inmate pays the ultimate price when he is executed. I disagree. Once he is executed, he no longer suffers. An inmate will pay a greater price if he has to live in prison and suffer for the rest of his life.

Chapter 12

A Family's Support of
the Death Penalty

Holly Wilson

O n February 10, 1991, my life changed forever. It was a beautiful,
sunny, almost warm winter day in St. Louis. I had decided to
hang some laundry out in the fresh air to dry. I came up the back stairs
and saw my husband talking intently on the phone. His head was bent
down and the back of his neck and ears were red. I remember thinking
something was wrong. My mind went into a red alert phase where the
body's adrenaline takes over, every corpuscle swells and your skin
tingles. He hung up the phone, turned around and saw me standing
there. "There is a problem" he said. "The police have found a body
in your sister's house and no one can find her."

I almost laughed that it sounded so ridiculous. A body? Whose?
And what was it doing in her basement? We didn't know it was our
beloved nephew Hugh; and that my sister had been kidnapped. That
would all come later as the police and our family traced the bizarre,
hideous world of James Allen Red Dog's trail of crimes.

We spent hours in agony, waiting to hear if the body was in fact
Hugh's. Anguished that I might lose my sister too, I was racked with

pain one moment and felt complete numbness the next as I reacted to phone calls from police and family.

After twenty four tortuous hours of repeated rapings and mental brainwashing, my sister escaped her captor. I will always consider her spared life a miracle. Red Dog remained at large four more terrifying days. He was finally captured on Valentines Day, a bitterly cold day with strong, howling winds. Valentines Day, the day we buried Hugh.

On February 9, 1991 James Red Dog calmly entered my nephew Hugh's home in Wilmington, Delaware and, for no apparent reason, bound him hand and foot. He then slit our defenseless Hugh's throat nearly to the point of decapitation. As Hugh's life slowly slipped away, our lives were changed forever. We became victims, a family reunited by tragedy to mourn Hugh's death. We were spread out in various parts of Wilmington behind closed and bolted doors for fear that the fugitive Red Dog would come back to Wilmington and try to kill us all. Our homes became prisons and our friendly neighborhoods now contained a certain horror and everyone, whether known to us or not, seemed to feel it. We were afraid, angry, despondent, and numb from the stress of the unfamiliar role as victims of a violent crime. I can remember saying it was like a bad television show that needed to be turned off. We wanted Red Dog captured quickly for everyday he was at large was a form of torture for the family. Red Dog had control of our lives and I had never even met him. I can remember planning Hugh's funeral with my sister. We had completed all the arrangements including his wish to be cremated, when the police detective called and told us Hugh would have to be buried in a special vault, elaborate and expensive, in order to preserve him in case he need to be exhumed later as evidence! Not only had Red Dog taken Hugh's right to life, he had taken his right to determine how he would be cared for after death.

Over the next few months we, and the police, were horrified as we learned of Red Dog's despicable, sordid past which included four previous murders, one while he was incarcerated. We learned the startling fact that he was never sentenced to any additional time in prison for any of his four murders. He was returned to prison only to finish a former sentencing for armed robbery. Our final and most incredible anguish came when we learned that the Federal Government had removed Red Dog from prison in Marian, Illinois under the "Federal Witness Protection Program." They had placed him in Delaware, where within the year, he murdered his fifth victim . . . Hugh.

Before February 10, 1991, we coped with life and death like most all our friends and family did: supportive of each other and understanding of God's caring and love for us all. I will admit that I was more prone to believe that all human life was precious, and violence should not beget violence. The death penalty seemed more wrong than right. After all, how could we determine who should live and who should die? That was God's responsibility. . . . Oh what innocence and naiveté to believe that we could hope to rehabilitate the hardened criminal. I am now definitely convinced that there are certain violent criminals who are completely without remorse and will consciously repeat a violent act upon their fellow man to quench their thrill of feeling 'high' from such violent acts.

As his penalty trial began in March of the following year, we realized there was a good chance that Red Dog could be given the death penalty. During that year I had become a student of crime, learning all I could about victim's and criminal's rights. I even attended a murder trial in Kansas to acquaint myself with courtroom proceedings, the media coverage, what the family did during testimony, where they sat, and what was expected of them. I watched a mother testify in Italian with a translator, telling, as a witness, of the cold-blooded shooting death of her son after they had pulled over following a minor fender bender accident. As she walked by the accused, her anguish and pain were so intense she spewed forth tormented Italian as she tried in vain to spit on him. He laughed and I felt my stomach turn into a twisted knot of misery as I felt all the pain that total stranger felt. Pain I had never felt before; a pain linked to this Italian mother who had lost her son to a senseless killing

Surely the court would sentence this remorseless killer to the death penalty? Then I learned that Kansas has no capital punishment law and this murderer would spend years behind bars, eventually receiving a parole hearing. My opinion of the death penalty changed dramatically after that. I was forever grateful that Red Dog would be tried in Delaware, a state with capital punishment. The penalty hearing concluded and Red Dog received his sentence by Judge Barron. It was Maundy Thursday. Red Dog was to die by lethal injection and that day I made up my mind I wanted to be back in Delaware for the execution. There really is no peace for the living victims throughout the trial, throughout the time for required appeals. You live with the harrowing knowledge that, at any time, Red Dog could ask for an appeal and the sentence might be overthrown on a technicality. We worried that momentum might start to stay execution and delay our hope to end Red Dog's crime spree, forever. Somehow I equated being near the source of Hugh's "terminator" (as Red Dog once called himself) with an opportunity to send altruistic messages to Red Dog not to appeal but to end his incorrigible life. For us, the death penalty became the only justifiable end. It was the only way to stop Red Dog from torturing and killing another helpless victim.

Executions are to rid our country of one criminal's ability to repeat any crime. If revenge were our sole reason for capital punishment, then as victims we would certainly not choose painless injection as a means of death. Should not the criminal die as he choose to inflict death to his victim? The death penalty is about saving lives and sparing the victim's family endless years of torment while the prisoner lives at the taxpayers expense, serving no useful purpose to society. Meanwhile, a loved one has been buried, taking with them a family's future hopes and dreams. It is incongruous for society or the judicial system to think we can both punish and protect a violent criminal.

Execution dates came and went as various tactics to stay the execution were taken on Red Dog's behalf. He sought no appeals and stated that he wanted to die and thus become "a warrior and soar like an eagle." This was not remorse, only grandiosity. The automatic appeal to the Delaware State Supreme Court came in August. My family was present that day. The justices heard both the prosecutor and the defense review the case. Once again I sat there knowing that Red Dog's fate was not in our hands. It is difficult to sit facing six justices and not be allowed to interject any personal feelings about the death penalty or tell the justices that to give Red Dog a life in prison would really be sentencing the victim's family to a life fearing Red Dog. After a few months, our questions were answered; the death penalty was upheld.

Red Dog was sentenced to die on March 3, 1993 between 10:00 a.m. and noon. My request was granted to be allowed to be inside the Symrna Correctional facility during those hours. It was important to me to find some kind of inner peace, and I thought that by being around the intensity of the prison I might feel closer to Hugh. I had no doubt Hugh was spiritually leading me there to face this execution. We were not present for Hugh's last moments but I very much wanted to be there for him, the innocent victim, who, with his death, gave Red Dog his last chance to murder. As the minutes slipped by I waited alone, except for the female prison employee assigned to stay with me.

I began to pace the room to relieve some of my tension. I prayed that Red Dog would not appeal. I thought of his painless, sterile death in the presence of his medicine man, compared to Hugh's painful last lonely moments, lying on a cold basement floor.

I wanted to scream out for the inequity of it all. I walked over to some high windows and on tiptoes, watched the prison guards patrol the grounds two by two. The minutes passed and I kept returning to the window to absorb this strange environment. I noticed a guard coming around the corner by himself carrying something under his arm. I asked the attendant why he was by himself.

She looked out and said that the guards were supposed to be in pairs and that he shouldn't be carrying a newspaper. I peered out again and exclaimed a breathless shrill of delight at what I saw. The guard was carrying the morning paper folded in such a way that Hugh's picture was the only part visible to me. It seemed like Hugh was telling me everything was going to be all right. I accepted the calmness that permeated my tension. I immediately asked for the time and soon learned that I had seen the newspaper the guard carried at the very same moment that Red Dog had received his fatal injection.

Shortly after, a state official came into the room and read the official proclamation. My knees buckled. I cried. I gave thanks that no more humans would suffer at the merciless hands of James Allen Red Dog.

I now firmly believe the death penalty, does indeed, save lives.

Chapter 13

Innocence & the Death Penalty: Assessing The Danger of Mistaken Executions

Staff Report issued on October 21, 1993 by the Subcommittee on Civil and Constitutional Rights Committee on the Judiciary
One Hundred Third Congress, First Session

C hairman Don Edwards of the House Judiciary Committee's Subcommittee on Civil and Constitutional Rights directed the subcommittee majority staff to prepare this report. This report has not been reviewed or approved by other members of the subcommittee.

Innocence and the Death Penalty: Assessing the Danger of Mistaken Executions

No matter how careful courts are, the possibility of perjured testimony, mistaken honest testimony and human error remain all

too real. We have no way of judging how many innocent persons
have been executed, but we can be certain that there were some.

                                        Furman v. *Georgia*,
                                   408 U.S. 238, 367-68 (1972)
                                      (Marshall, J., concurring).

I. Introduction

In 1972, when the Supreme Court ruled in *Furman* v. *Georgia*
that the death penalty as then applied was arbitrary and capricious and
therefore unconstitutional, a majority of the Justices expected that the
adoption of narrowly crafted sentencing procedures would protect
against innocent persons being sentenced to death. Yet the promise of
Furman has not been fulfilled: innocent persons are still being sentenced
to death, and the chances are high that innocent persons have been or
will be executed.

No issue posed by capital punishment is more disturbing to the
public than the prospect that the government might execute an innocent
person. A recent national poll found that the number one concern
raising doubts among voters regarding the death penalty is the danger
of a mistaken execution.[1] Fifty-eight percent of voters are disturbed
that the death penalty might allow an innocent person to be executed.
Earlier this year, the Subcommittee on Civil and Constitutional Rights
heard testimony from four men who were released from prison after
serving years on death row — living proof that innocent people are
sentenced to death.[2] The hearing raised two questions: (1) just how
frequently are innocent persons convicted and sentenced to death; and
(2) what flaws in the system allow these injustices to occur? In order to
answer these questions, Subcommittee Chairman Don Edwards called
upon the Death Penalty Information Center to compile information on
cases in the past twenty years where inmates had been released from
death row after their innocence had been acknowledged. This staff
report is based on the research of the Center.

Section II of the report briefly describes each of the forty eight
cases in the past twenty years where a convicted person has been released
from death row because of innocence. Sections III and IV examine
why the system of trials, appeals, and executive clemency fails to offer
sufficient safeguards in protecting the innocent from execution. The
role of current legal protections is addressed by looking closely at a
few of the cases where death row inmates were later found to be innocent

or were executed with their guilt still in doubt. The report concludes that there is a real danger of innocent people being executed in the United States.

II. Recent Cases Involving Innocent Persons Sentenced to Death

The most conclusive evidence that innocent people are condemned to death under modern death sentencing procedures comes from the surprisingly large number of people whose convictions have been overturned and who have been freed from death row. Four former death row inmates have been released from prison just this year after their innocence became apparent: Kirk Bloodsworth, Federico Macias, Walter McMillian, and Gregory Wilhoit.

At least forty eight people have been released from prison after serving time on death row since 1973 with significant evidence of their innocence.[3] In forty three of these cases, the defendant was subsequently acquitted, pardoned, or charges were dropped. In three of the cases, a compromise was reached and the defendants were immediately released upon pleading to a lesser offense. In the remaining two cases, one defendant was released when the parole board became convinced of his innocence, and the other was acquitted at a retrial of the capital charge but convicted of lesser related charges. These five cases are indicated with an asterisk.

Year of Release
1973

1. David Keaton   **Florida**   **Conviction: 1971**
Sentenced to death for murdering an off-duty deputy sheriff during a robbery. Charges were dropped and Keaton was released after the actual killer was convicted.

1975

2. Wilber Lee   **Florida**   **Conviction: 1963**
3. Freddie Pitts   **Florida**   **Conviction: 1963**
Lee and Pitts were convicted of a double murder and sentenced to death. They were released when they received a full pardon from Governor Askew because of their innocence. Another man had confessed to the killings.

1976

4.	**Thomas Gladish**	**New Mexico**	**Conviction: 1974**
5.	**Richard Greer**	**New Mexico**	**Conviction: 1974**
6.	**Ronald Kein**	**New Mexico**	**Conviction: 1974**
5.	**Clarence Smith**	**New Mexico**	**Conviction: 1974**

The four were convicted of murder, kidnapping, sodomy, and rape and were sentenced to death. They were released after a drifter admitted to the killings and a newspaper investigation uncovered lies by the prosecution's star witness.

1977

8. Delbert Tibbs   Florida   Conviction: 1974
Sentenced to death for the rape of a sixteen-year-old and the murder of her companion. The conviction was overturned by the Florida Supreme Court because the verdict was not supported by the weight of the evidence. Tibbs' former prosecutor said that the original investigation had been tainted from the beginning.

1978

9. Earl Charle   Georgia   Conviction: 1975
Convicted on two counts of murder and sentenced to death. Charles was released when evidence was found that substantiated his alibi. After an investigation, the district attorney announced that he would not retry the case. Charles won a substantial settlement from city officials for misconduct in the original investigation.

10. Jonathan Treadway   Arizona   Conviction: 1975
Convicted of sodomy and first degree murder of a six-year-old and sentenced to death. He was acquitted of all charges at retrial by the jury after 5 pathologists testified that the victim probably died of natural causes and that there was no evidence of sodomy.

1979

11. Gary Beeman   Ohio   Conviction: 1976
Convicted of aggravated murder and sentenced to death. Acquitted at the retrial when evidence showed that the true killer was the main prosecution witness at the first trial.

12. Jerry Banks   Georgia   Conviction: 1975
Sentenced to death for two counts of murder. The conviction was overturned because the prosecution knowingly withheld exculpatory evidence. Banks committed suicide after his wife divorced him. His estate won a settlement from the county for the benefit of his children.

13. Larry Hicks   Indiana   Conviction: 1978
Convicted on two counts of murder and sentenced to death, Hicks was acquitted at the retrial when witnesses confirmed his alibi and when the eyewitness testimony at the first trial was proved to have been perjured. The Playboy Foundation supplied funds for the reinvestigation.

1981

14. Charles Ray Giddens Oklahoma   Conviction: 1978
Conviction and death sentence reversed by the Oklahoma Court of Criminal Appeals on the grounds of insufficient evidence. Thereafter, the charges were dropped.

15. Michael Linder   South Carolina   Conviction: 1979
Linder was acquitted at retrial on the grounds of self-defense.

16. Johnny Ross   Louisiana   Conviction: 1975
Sentenced to death for rape, Ross was released when his blood type was found to be inconsistent with that of the rapist's.

1982

17. Anibal Jarramillo   Florida   Conviction: 1981
Sentenced to death for two counts of first degree murder; released when the Florida Supreme Court ruled the evidence did not sustain the conviction.

18. Lawyer Johnson   Massachusetts   Conviction: 1971
Sentenced to death for first degree murder. The charges were dropped when a previously silent eyewitness came forward and implicated the state's chief witness as the actual killer.

1986

19. Anthony Brown   Florida   Conviction: 1983
Convicted of first degree murder and sentenced to death. At the retrial, the state's chief witness admitted that his testimony at the first trial had been perjured and Brown was acquitted.

20. Neil Ferber   Pennsylvania   Conviction: 1982
Convicted of first degree murder and sentenced to death. He was released at the request of the state's attorney when new evidence showed that the conviction was based on the perjured testimony of a jail-house informant.

1987

21. Joseph Green Brown
   (Shabaka Waglini)   Florida   Conviction: 1974
Charges were dropped after the 11th Circuit Court of Appeals ruled that the prosecution had knowingly allowed false testimony to be introduced at trial. At one point, Brown came within 13 hours of execution.

22. Perry Cobb   Illinois   Conviction: 1979
23. Darby Williams   Illinois   Conviction: 1979
Cobb and Williams were convicted and sentenced to death for a double murder. They were acquitted at retrial when an assistant state attorney came forward and destroyed the credibility of the state's chief witness.

24. Henry Drake   Georgia   Conviction: 1977
Drake was re-sentenced to a life sentence at his second retrial. Six months later, the parole board freed him, convinced he was exonerated by his alleged accomplice and by

25. John Henry Knapp   Arizona   Conviction: 1974
Knapp was originally sentenced to death for the arson murder of his two children. He was released in 1987 after new evidence about the cause of the fire prompted a judge to order a new trial. In 1991, his third trial resulted in a hung jury. Knapp was again released in 1992 after an agreement with the prosecutors in which he pleaded no contest to second degree murder. He has steadfastly maintained his innocence.

26. Vernon McManus   **Texas**   **Conviction: 1977**
After a new trial was ordered, the prosecution dropped the charges when a key prosecution witness refused to testify.

27. Anthony Ray Peek   **Florida**   **Conviction: 1978**
Convicted of murder and sentenced to death. His conviction was overturned when expert testimony was shown to be false. He was acquitted at his second retrial.

28. Juan Ramos   **Florida**   **Conviction: 1983**
Sentenced to death for rape and murder. The decision was vacated by the Florida Supreme Court because of improper use of evidence. At his retrial, he was acquitted.

29. Robert Wallace   **Georgia**   **Conviction: 1980**
Sentenced to death for the slaying of a police officer. The 11th Circuit ordered a retrial because Wallace had not been competent to stand trial. He was acquitted at the retrial because it was found that the shooting was accidental.

1988

30. Jerry Bigelow   **California**   **Conviction: 1980**
Convicted of murder and sentenced to death after acting as his own attorney. His conviction was overturned by the California Supreme Court and he was acquitted at the retrial.

31. Willie Brown   **Florida**   **Conviction: 1983**
32. Larry Troy   **Florida**   **Conviction: 1983**
Originally sentenced to death after being accused of stabbing a fellow prisoner, Brown and Troy were released when the evidence showed that the main witness at the trial had perjured himself.

33. William Jent*   **Florida**   **Conviction: 1980**
34. Earnest Miller*   **Florida**   **Conviction: 1980**
A federal district court ordered a new trial because of suppression of exculpatory evidence. Jent and Miller were released immediately after agreeing to plead guilty to second degree murder. They repudiated their plea upon leaving the courtroom and were later awarded compensation by the Pasco County Sheriff's Dept. because of official errors.

1989

35. Randall Dale Adams   Texas   Conviction: 1977
Adams was ordered to be released pending a new trial by the
Texas Court of Appeals. The prosecutors did not seek a new trial
due to substantial evidence of Adam's innocence. Subject of the
movie The Thin Blue Line.

36. Jesse Keith Brown*   South Carolina   Conviction: 1983
The conviction was reversed twice by the state Supreme Court.
At the third trial, Brown was acquitted of the capital charge but
convicted of related robbery charges.

37. Robert Cox   Florida   Conviction: 1988
Released by a unanimous decision of the Florida Supreme Court
on the basis of insufficient evidence.

38. Timothy Hennis   North Carolina   Conviction: 1986
Convicted of three counts of murder and sentenced to death. The
State Supreme Court granted a retrial because of the use of
inflammatory evidence. At the retrial, Hennis was acquitted.

39. James Richardson   Florida   Conviction: 1988
Released after reexamination of the case by prosecutor Janet Reno,
who concluded Richardson was innocent.

1990

40. Clarence Brandley   Texas   Conviction: 1980
Awarded a new trial when evidence showed prosecutorial
suppression of exculpatory evidence and perjury by prosecution
witnesses. All charges were dropped. Brandley is the subject of
the book White Lies by Nick Davies.

41. Patrick Croy   California   Conviction: 1979
Conviction overturned by state Supreme Court because of improper
jury instructions. Acquitted at retrial after arguing self-defense.

42. John C. Skelton   Texas   Conviction: 1982
Convicted of killing a man by exploding dynamite in his pickup
truck. The conviction was overturned by the Texas Court of
Criminal Appeals due to insufficient evidence.

1991

43. Gary Nelson   Georgia   Conviction: 1980
Nelson was released after a review of the prosecutor's files revealed that material information had been improperly withheld from the defense. The district attorney acknowledged: "There is no material element of the state's case in the original trial which has not subsequently been determined to be impeached or contradicted."

44. Bradley P. Scott   Florida   Conviction: 1988
Convicted of murder ten years after the crime. On appeal, he was released by the Florida Supreme Court because of insufficient evidence.

1993

45. Kirk Bloodsworth   Maryland   Conviction: 1984
Convicted and sentenced to death for the rape and murder of a young girl. Bloodsworth was granted a new trial and given a life sentence. He was released after subsequent DNA testing confirmed his innocence.

46. Federico M. Macias   Texas   Conviction: 1984
Convicted of murder, Macias was granted a federal writ of habeas corpus because of ineffective assistance of counsel and possible innocence. A grand jury refused to re-indict because of lack of evidence.

47. Walter McMillian   Alabama   Conviction: 1988
McMillian's conviction was overturned by the Alabama Court of Criminal Appeals and he was freed after three witnesses recanted their testimony and prosecutors agreed case had been mishandled.

48. Gregory R. Wilhoit   Oklahoma   Conviction: 1987
Wilhoit was convicted of killing his estranged wife while she slept. He was acquitted at a retrial after 11 forensic experts testified that a bite mark found on his dead wife did not belong to him.

III. Where Did the System Break Down?

These forty eight cases illustrate the flaws inherent in the death sentencing systems used in the states. Some of these men were convicted on the basis of perjured testimony or because the prosecutor improperly withheld exculpatory evidence. In other cases, racial prejudice was a determining factor. In others, defense counsel failed to conduct the necessary investigation that would have disclosed exculpatory information.

Racial Prejudice: Clarence Brandley

> The court unequivocally concludes that the color of Clarence Brandley's skin was a substantial factor which pervaded all aspects of the State's capital prosecution of him.
>
> Judge Perry Pickett

Sometimes racial prejudice propels an innocent person into the role of despicable convict. In 1980, a sixteen year-old white girl named Cheryl Dee Ferguson was raped and murdered at a Texas high school. Suspicion turned to the school's five janitors. One of the janitors later testified that the police looked at Clarence Brandley, the only black in the group, and said, "Since you're the nigger, you're elected."[4]

Brandley was convicted and sentenced to death by an all-white jury after two trials. The prosecutor used his peremptory strikes to eliminate all blacks in the jury pool.[5] Eleven months after the conviction, Brandley's attorneys learned that 166 of the 309 exhibits used at trial, many of which offered grounds for appeal, had vanished.

After six years of fruitless appeals and civil rights demonstrations in support of Brandley, the Texas Court of Criminal Appeals ordered an evidentiary hearing to investigate all the allegations that had come to light. The presiding judge wrote a stinging condemnation of the procedures used in Brandley's case, and stated that "The court unequivocally concludes that the color of Clarence Brandley's skin was a substantial factor which pervaded all aspects of the State's capital prosecution of him."[6] Brandley was eventually released in 1990 and all charges were dismissed.[7]

It took many years and a tremendous effort by outside counsel, civil rights organizers, special investigators, and the media to save Brandley's life. For others on death row, it is nearly impossible to even get a hearing on a claim of innocence.

The Pressure to Prosecute: Walter McMillian

> I was wrenched from my family, from my children, from my grandchildren, from my friends, from my work that I loved, and was placed in an isolation cell, the size of a shoe box, with no sunlight, no companionship, and no work for nearly six years. Every minute of every day, I knew I was innocent.
>
> Walter McMillian,
> Written testimony at Subcommittee Hearing,
> July 23, 1993

In 1986, in the small town of Monroeville, Alabama, an eighteen-year-old white woman was shot to death in the dry cleaners around 10 AM. Although the town was shocked by the murder, no one was arrested for eight months. Johnny D. (Walter) McMillian was a black man who lived in the next town. He had been dating a white woman and his son had married a white woman, none of which made McMillian popular in Monroeville.[8]

On the day of the murder, McMillian was at a fish fry with his friends and relatives. Many of these people gave testimony at trial that McMillian could not have committed the murder of Ronda Morrison because he was with them all day. Nevertheless, he was arrested, tried and convicted of the murder. Indeed, McMillian was placed on death row upon his arrest, well before his trial. No physical evidence linked him to the crime, but three people testifying at his trial connected him with the murder. All three witnesses received favors from the state for their incriminating testimony.[9] All three later recanted their testimony, including the only eyewitness, who stated that he was pressured by the prosecutors to implicate McMillian in the crime.

The jury in the trial recommended a life sentence for McMillian but the judge overruled this recommendation and sentenced him to death. His case went through four rounds of appeal, all of which were denied. New attorneys, not paid by the State of Alabama, voluntarily took over the case and eventually found that the prosecutors had illegally withheld evidence which would have pointed to McMillian's innocence. A story about the case appeared on CBS-TV's program, 60 Minutes, on Nov. 22, 1992. Finally, the State agreed to investigate its earlier handling of the case and then admitted that a grave mistake had been made.[10] Mr. McMillian was freed into the welcoming arms of his family and friends on March 3, 1993.

Inadequate Counsel: Federico Macias

Federico Macias' court-appointed lawyer did virtually nothing to prepare the case for trial. Macias was sentenced to death in Texas in 1984. Two days before his scheduled execution, Macias received a stay. New counsel from the large Skadden, Arps law firm had entered the case and devoted to it the firm's considerable resources and expertise. Mr. Macias' conviction was overturned via a federal writ of habeas corpus, which was upheld by a unanimous panel of the U.S. Court of Appeals for the Fifth Circuit in December, 1992. The court found that not only was Macias' original counsel grossly ineffective, but also that he had missed considerable evidence pointing to Macias' innocence. The court concluded:

> "We are left with the firm conviction that Macias was denied his constitutional right to adequate counsel in a capital case in which actual innocence was a close question. The state paid defense counsel $11.84 per hour. Unfortunately, the justice system got only what it paid for."[11]

Thereafter, Macias was freed when the grand jury, which now had access to the evidence developed by the Skadden, Arps attorneys, refused to re-indict him.

There are many similar stories of defendants who have spent years on death row, some coming within hours of their execution, only to be released by the courts with all charges dropped.[12] What is noteworthy about the cases outlined above is that they are very recent examples which illustrate that mistaken death sentences are not a relic of the past.

Official Misconduct: Chance and Powell

While Clarence Chance and Benny Powell were not sentenced to death, their convictions for murder illustrate the dangers of overzealous police work. They were released from prison last year after Jim McCloskey of Centurion Ministries took on their case and demonstrated their innocence. The City of Los Angeles awarded them seven million and the judge termed the police department's conduct "reprehensible" while apologizing for the "gross injustices" that occurred.[13]

IV. Are the Protections in the Legal System Adequate to Prevent the Execution of Innocent Persons?

To some degree, the cases discussed in Section III illustrate the inherent fallibility of the criminal justice system. (Sensational murder cases often tend, however, to amplify the flaws of the system.) Mistakes and even occasional misconduct are to be expected. The cases outlined above might convey a reassuring impression that, although mistakes are made, the system of appeals and reviews will ferret out such cases prior to execution. In one sense, that is occasionally true: the system of appeals sometimes allows for correction of factual errors.

But there is another sense in which these cases illustrate the inadequacies of the system. These men were found innocent despite the system and only as a result of extraordinary efforts not generally available to death row defendants.

Indeed, in some cases, these men were found innocent as a result of sheer luck. In the case of Walter McMillian, his volunteer outside counsel had obtained from the prosecutors an audio tape of one of the key witnesses' statements incriminating Mr. McMillian. After listening to the statement, the attorney flipped the tape over to see if anything was on the other side. It was only then that he heard the same witness complaining that he was being pressured to frame Mr. McMillian.[14] With that fortuitous break, the whole case against McMillian began to fall apart.

Similarly, proving the innocence of Kirk Bloodsworth was more a matter of chance than the orderly working of the appeals process. Only a scientific breakthrough, and an appellate lawyer's initiative in trying it, after years of failed appeals, allowed Bloodsworth to prove his innocence. And even then, the prosecutor was not bound under Maryland law to admit this new evidence.[15]

Furthermore, not every death row inmate is afforded, after conviction, the quality of counsel and resources which Walter McMillian and Federico Macias were fortunate to have during their post-conviction proceedings. Many of those on death row go for years without any attorney at all.

Most of the releases from death row over the past twenty years came only after many years and many failed appeals. The average length of time between conviction and release was almost seven years for the forty eight death row inmates released since 1970.

Innocence is Not Generally Reviewed

Too often, the reviews afforded death row inmates on appeal and habeas corpus simply do not offer a meaningful opportunity to present claims of innocence. As will be discussed more fully below, in many states there simply is no formal procedure for hearing new evidence of a defendant's innocence prior to his execution date. After trial, the legal system becomes locked in a battle over procedural issues rather than a reexamination of guilt or innocence. The all night struggle to stay the execution of Leonel Herrera in 1992, even after the U.S. Supreme Court had agreed to hear his constitutional challenge, is an example of how much pressure is exerted to proceed with executions.[16]

Accounts which report that a particular case has been appealed numerous times before many judges may be misleading. In fact, most often, procedural issues, rather than the defendant's innocence, are being argued and reviewed in these appeals. For example, when Roger Keith Coleman was executed in Virginia last year, it was reported that his last appeal to the Supreme Court "was Coleman's 16th round in court."[17] However, the Supreme Court had earlier declared that Coleman's constitutional claims were barred from any review in federal court because his prior attorneys had filed an appeal too late in 1986.[18] His evidence was similarly excluded from review in state court as well. Instead, Coleman's innocence was debated only in the news media and considerable doubt concerning his guilt went with him to his execution.[19]

This section will examine some of the means, both extra-judicial and within the system, by which the cases of innocence are uncovered. But first, it is necessary to clarify what is meant in this report by the term "innocent."

Meaning of "Innocent"

In the criminal justice system, defendants are presumed to be innocent until proven guilty beyond a reasonable doubt. Thus, a person is fully entitled to a claim of innocence if charges are not brought against him or if the charges brought are not proven. A person may be guilty of other crimes or there may be some who still insist he is guilty, but with respect to the charge in question, he is innocent.

In some cases, the investigative process does conclusively determine innocence. A piece of evidence may demonstrate that a suspect or defendant could not have been the perpetrator, or someone else confesses, eliminating other suspects. Under the law, there is no distinction between the definitively innocent and those found innocent after a trial, but about whom there may remain a lingering doubt.

Extra-Judicial Redress

In the absence of adequate legal mechanisms, the most serious errors in the criminal justice system are sometimes uncovered as a result of such extra-judicial factors as the media and the development of new scientific techniques. These following cases illustrate the randomness of how the legal system works.

Role of the Media: Randall Dale Adams

One unpredictable element that can affect whether an innocent person is released is the involvement of the media. In Randall Dale Adams' case, film producer Errol Morris went to Texas to make a documentary on Dr. James Grigson, the notorious "Dr. Death."[20] Grigson would claim 100% certainty for his courtroom predictions that a particular defendant would kill again, and he made such a prediction about Randall Adams.

In the course of his investigation of Grigson, Morris became interested in Adams' plight and helped unearth layers of prosecutorial misconduct in that case. He also obtained on tape a virtual confession by another person. Morris' movie, *The Thin Blue Line*, told Randall Adams' story in a way no one had seen before. The movie was released in 1988 and Adams was freed the following year.

Role of the Media: Other Cases

Similarly, all charges and death sentences against Thomas Gladish, Richard Greer, Ronald Keine, and Clarence Smith were dropped in 1976 thanks, in part, to the Detroit News investigation of lies told by the prosecution's star witness.[21]

Walter McMillian's case was featured on 60 Minutes shortly before his release. So was the case of Clarence Brandley. Brandley was also aided by the civil rights community, which organized opposition to his execution. Supporters were able to raise $80,000 for his defense.[22] Obviously, these advantages are not available to everyone on death row who may have been wrongly convicted.

Unpredictable Emergence of New Scientific Tests: Kirk Bloodsworth

In 1984, a nine-year-old girl named Dawn Hamilton was raped and murdered in Baltimore County, Maryland. Two young boys and one adult said they had seen Dawn with a man prior to her death. They thought that Kirk Bloodsworth looked like the man who had been with her. Again, no physical evidence linked Bloodsworth to the crime. He was convicted and sentenced to death because he looked like someone who might have committed the crime.[23]

There was some evidence taken from the crime scene, but it gave the police no clue as to who the killer was. Tests were conducted on the girl's underwear, but the tests were not sophisticated enough at that time to detect and identify DNA material from the likely assailant. Fortunately for Mr. Bloodsworth, he was granted a new trial when a judge ruled that the state had withheld evidence from the defense attorneys about another suspect. This time he received a life sentence. Bloodsworth, however, continued to maintain his innocence and the life sentence gave him the time to prove it.[24]

When a new volunteer lawyer agreed to look into Bloodsworth's case, he decided to try one more time to have the evidence in the case tested. He sent the underwear to a laboratory in California that used newly developed DNA techniques. The defense attorney was astonished when he learned that there was testable DNA material. The tests showed that the semen stain on the underwear could not possibly have come from Mr. Bloodsworth. The prosecution then agreed that if these results could be duplicated by the FBI's crime laboratory, it would consent to Mr. Bloodsworth's release. On Friday, June 25, the FBI's results affirmed what Bloodsworth had been saying all along: he was innocent of all charges. On June 28, he was released by order of the court from the Maryland State Correctional facility in Jessup, after nine years in prison, two of which were on death row.

The next section of the report will look at the traditional avenues which an innocent defendant can use to prevent or overturn a sentence of death.

Trial Is Critical, but often Hampered by Poor Legal Representation

The trial is obviously the critical time for the defendant to make his or her case for innocence. Unfortunately, the manner in which defense counsel are selected and compensated for death penalty flaws does not always protect the defendant's rights at this pivotal time. Most defendants facing the death penalty cannot afford to hire their own attorney and so the state is required to provide them with one. Some states have public defender offices staffed by attorneys trained to handle such cases. In other states, attorneys are appointed from the local community and the quality of representation is spotty.[25]

Federico Macias is certainly not alone with respect to ineffective counsel. The stories regarding deficient representation in death penalty cases are rampant.[26] The Subcommittee has held several hearings documenting this problem.[27] Although death penalty law is a highly specialized and complex form of litigation, there is no guarantee that the attorney appointed to this critical role will have the necessary expertise. There is no independent appointing authority to select only qualified counsel for these cases and attorneys are frequently underpaid and understaffed, with few resources for this critical undertaking.

Proving Innocence After Trial: Defendant's Burden

Before trial, the arrested defendant need do nothing to prove his innocence. The burden is completely on the prosecution to prove that the individual is guilty of the crimes charged beyond a reasonable doubt. However, after someone has been found guilty, the presumption shifts in favor of the state. The burden is now on the defendant to prove to a court that something went wrong in arriving at the determination of guilt. It is no longer enough to raise a reasonable doubt. To overturn a conviction, the evidence must be compelling, and violations of Constitutional rights by the state will be forgiven as long as they were "harmless."[28]

The Appellate Process

If an innocent defendant is convicted, he generally has little time to collect and present new evidence which might reverse his conviction.

In Texas, for example, a defendant has only thirty days after his conviction to present new evidence, and the state strictly adheres to that rule. Sixteen other states also require that a new trial motion based on new evidence be filed within sixty days of judgment.[29] Eighteen jurisdictions have time limits between one and three years, and only nine states have no time limits.[30]

Thus, even a compelling claim of innocence, such as a videotape of someone else committing the crime (as recently hypothesized by Justice Anthony Kennedy in oral arguments of *Herrera*,[31] discussed below), does not guarantee a review in state or federal court.

All death row inmates are assured representation to make one direct appeal in their state courts. If that appeal is denied, representation is no longer assured.[32] In states like Texas and California with large death rows, many defendants sentenced to death are not currently being represented by any attorney.[33] Obviously, such a defendant's opportunity to uncover evidence to prove his innocence is greatly reduced, even assuming a court would hear the evidence if it was found.

Habeas Corpus: The Great Writ

When someone has been unjustly convicted under circumstances similar to those described above, he can challenge that conviction in federal court through the writ of habeas corpus. Although numerous legislative proposals to limit habeas corpus in the past few years have failed, the opportunity for using this writ has already been stringently narrowed by recent Supreme Court decisions. The following cases illustrate some of the barriers erected by the Court to claims of innocence in habeas cases.

Leonel Herrera

The Supreme Court has denied habeas review of claims from prisoners on death row with persuasive, newly discovered evidence of their innocence. Leonel Herrera presented affidavits and positive polygraph results from a variety of witnesses, including an eyewitness to the murder and a former Texas state judge, both of whom stated that someone else had committed the crime. However, the Supreme Court ruled that Herrera was not entitled to a federal hearing on this evidence and was told that his only recourse was the clemency process of the state of Texas.[34] Herrera was executed in May of this year.

Gary Graham

Death row inmates who claim their innocence are therefore often forced to rely on procedural claims. But those, too, are being foreclosed by the Supreme Court.

For example, Gary Graham's case has gained national attention because he has made a substantial claim of innocence. However, the barriers to getting such new evidence before the courts has necessitated that the defense pursue other claims which only affect his sentence. Death penalty attorneys realize that proving their client innocent after he is executed is of no value to him.

But when Gary Graham claimed that the Texas death penalty procedures did not allow consideration of his youth at the time of the crime, the U.S. Supreme Court refused to even consider the question. The Court said that even if he was right in his claim, ruling in his favor would create a "new rule" of law and no such rule could apply retroactively to his case.[35]

Another recent narrowing of the writ requires federal courts to reject all claims if the proper procedures were not followed by the defendant in state court. Roger Coleman, for example, filed his Virginia state appeal three days late and this error by his attorneys barred any consideration of his federal constitutional claims.[36] Coleman was executed without a federal court hearing his claim. Similarly, if a claim is not raised on a defendant's first habeas petition, the claim (with rare exceptions) is automatically rejected, even if the government withheld the very evidence the defendant would have needed to raise the claim in his first petition.[37]

Clemency

For the innocent defendant, the last avenue of relief is clemency from the executive branch. All death penalty states have some form of pardon power vested either in the governor or in a board of review.[38]

However, clemencies in death penalty cases are extremely rare. Since the death penalty was re-instated in 1976, 4,800 death sentences have been imposed but less than three dozen clemencies have been granted on defendants' petitions.[39] In Texas, the state with the greatest number of executions, no clemencies have been granted.

The procedures for clemency are as varied as the states. In many states the governor has the final say on granting a commutation of a death sentence. Since the governor is an elected official and since there is virtually no review of his or her decision, there is the danger that political motivations can influence the decisions.[40] Many of the commutations which have been granted in the past twenty years were granted by governors only as they were leaving office.

Other arrangements are also subject to political pressures. In Texas, a board must first recommend a clemency to the governor. However, the board is appointed by the governor and is not required to meet or hear testimony to review a case. Recently, a judge in Texas held that this lack of process violated Gary Graham's constitutional rights and ordered a hearing to review his claims of innocence.[41]

In Nebraska, Nevada and Florida, the chief state prosecutor sits on the clemency review board.[42] And generally, there are no procedural guarantees to assure that a claim of innocence which has been barred review by the courts will be fully aired for clemency. As Justice Blackmun recently pointed out:

> Whatever procedures a State might adopt to hear actual innocence claims, one thing is certain: The possibility of executive clemency is not sufficient to satisfy the requirements of the Eighth and Fourteenth Amendments.[43]

Thus, the prospect of clemency provides only the thinnest thread of hope and is certainly no guarantee against the execution of an innocent individual.

V. Conclusion

It is an inescapable fact of our criminal justice system that innocent people are too often convicted of crimes. Sometimes only many years later, in the course of a defendant's appeals, or as a result of extra-legal developments, new evidence will emerge which clearly demonstrates that the wrong person was prosecuted and convicted of a crime.

Americans are justifiably concerned about the possibility that an innocent person may be executed. Capital punishment in the United States today provides no reliable safeguards against this danger. Errors can and have been made repeatedly in the trial of death penalty cases because of poor representation, racial prejudice, prosecutorial misconduct, or simply the presentation of erroneous evidence. Once convicted, a death row inmate faces serious obstacles in convincing any tribunal that he is innocent.

The cases discussed in this report are the ones in which innocence was uncovered before execution. Once an execution occurs, the small group of lawyers who handle post-conviction proceedings in death penalty cases in the United States move on to the next crisis. Investigation of innocence ends after execution. If an innocent person was among the 222 people executed in the United States since *Furman*, nobody in the legal system is any longer paying attention.

Many death penalty convictions and sentences are overturned on appeal, but too frequently the discovery of error is the result of finding expert appellate counsel, a sympathetic judge willing to waive procedural barriers, and a compelling set of facts which can overcome the presumption of guilt. Not all of the convicted death row inmates are likely to have these opportunities.

Chapter 14

The Stars Fall on Texas

Ginny Carroll

Danny Glover and Bernadine Skillern have something in common. Both the actor, famous for cop roles, and Skillern, a Houston elementary-school aide, are opposed to the death penalty. But they're on opposite sides of the high-profile campaign to stop the August 17th execution of Texas death row inmate Gary Graham, a convicted murderer. Glover is one of the most prominent of a host of death-penalty opponents and celebrities — including Kenny Rogers, Ed Asner, Valerie Harper, and Mike Farrell — who have joined forces to portray Graham as the victim of a racist Texas justice system. Skillern was the key witness at Graham's 1981 trial.

While no one doubts the celebrities' sincerity (Rogers offered to foot the $250,000 tab for a new trial), the case raises troubling issues about what happens when celebrity activists take on a cause, without asking too many questions. "How can they hold rap concerts to raise money for a death-row inmate who is guilty of taking someone's life?" asks Skillern. "What effect does that have on children who look up to them?"

Graham, who was convicted of murdering fifty-three year old Bobby Lambert during a robbery in a parking lot, admits he's no choirboy. By the time he was seventeen, he had a record for robbery, burglary, and auto theft. In 1981, he embarked on a crime spree. He confessed to ten violent robberies during one week in May; in four of them, he shot his victims (none died). "I have a great deal of remorse, shame, and embarrassment," Graham, now twenty-nine, told Newsweek last week. "But we do not execute people for robbery." He claims he is innocent of murder and that new evidence would exonerate him.

'Next time': Larry Pollinger, a courtroom bailiff during Graham's trial, remembers when Graham spoke differently. After the death sentence was imposed, Pollinger handcuffed Graham and escorted him to a holding cell. En route, Graham said something that shocked Pollinger. "He said 'Next time, I'm not leaving any witnesses'," Pollinger told *Newsweek*. Pollinger reported the incident the same day to Assistant D.A. Carl Hobbs, who confirms his account. Prosecutors did not pursue it because Graham was already on his way to death row. Pollinger's evidence would be admissible at a new trial, they say. But Graham's lawyers say that testimony wouldn't be credible because it has been withheld for so long.

Graham languished on death row for twelve long years while his case ran the normal gamut of appeals. As he was nearing execution this spring, Amnesty International and the NAACP Legal Defense and Educational Fund stepped up publicity efforts, hoping to pressure Governor Ann Richards and Texas prison officials into commuting his sentence. They enlisted support from Glover, long a foe of the death penalty. Glover asked Graham's backers for more details. "The information provided me gave me the feeling that this man was innocent of this crime," he said last week.

Graham maintains that the celebrities got involved "primarily because of the injustices in my case, a case in which so much evidence of innocence has not been heard by any official body." There was no physical evidence — such as the gun used in the shooting — to link Graham to the murder. Skillern was the only witness who identified him during the trial, and Graham's lawyers say there are other witnesses who describe the shooter differently. After the conviction, friends and relatives of Graham claimed they could provide alibis.

Skillern, who is black, rejects the claim that the case is tainted by racism. "My seeing Gary Graham and coming forward was not a racist thing," she says. She has paid a price for testifying. This spring, when Graham's supporters began organizing marches, they circulated handbills in Skillern's neighborhood naming her. Vandals threw eggs at her house and car, and she received threatening phone calls.

Victim's side: Skillern is not the only one who resents the campaign to win a new trial. Several of Graham's victims have staged countermarches and rallies. Earlier this month, Rick Sanford, forty three, stomped on Glover videos and Rogers albums during a demonstration at the prison in Huntsville. He called for a boycott of both performers. "He was a real smooth-talking man when he kidnapped me," says Sanford, whom Graham robbed at gunpoint. "He kept bragging that he had killed six people and I would be number seven."

Greg Jones, thirty two, a Houston warehouse manager and another robbery victim, is also outraged. "I believe these Hollywood people have the right to speak their minds," he says, "but do they know what a violent person Graham is?" Graham told his victim: "I'm just a hustler." After pistol-whipping Jones, Graham held the gun to his throat. "I watched his muscles tighten as he pulled the trigger," Jones recalls, "and I saw him smile." The bullet went between his larynx and esophagus, the only path it could have taken without killing him, according to the doctors. "The day I was released out of the hospital," Jones says, "I went to a lineup and picked him out."

There are legal proceedings pending in both state and federal courts. If Graham gets a new trial, a jury will decide whether he is a victim — or a smooth-talking criminal who's hustling Hollywood.

Chapter 15

Capital Murder: The Trial and Appeal Process in Delaware

Joseph M. Asher, Esq.
Andrew McK. Jefferson, Esq.

Delaware, along with most states, will impose the ultimate sentence of death upon persons who have committed a capital murder. The focus of this essay will be the trial process in a capital murder case, and the appeals process which follows automatically when a person is convicted of first degree murder

Initially, a defendant will be arrested and charged with first degree murder. Generally, such person will not be considered eligible for bail due to the serious nature of the crime involved. Subsequently, assuming sufficient evidence of guilt, the State will seek an indictment of the defendant for the crime committed. Article I, §8 of the Delaware Constitution requires that a defendant be indicted by the Grand Jury before the State may proceed with the criminal process. The indictment is issued by the Grand Jury based on evidence of the crime which is presented during the Grand Jury proceedings. After the defendant has been indicted, then the pre-trial process begins. This process includes hearings to decide preliminary evidentiary issues. An example of this would be if the defendant felt that he had not properly been given his *Miranda* rights, (the right to remain silent, etc.), and therefore wants to challenge the introduction of any statements she or he might have made to the police.

Once the State and the defense have gone through all of the preliminary proceedings, it is time to begin the trial. It is at this stage of the process that the system devised for capital trials in Delaware becomes very different from that found in other states. Initially, before the trial ever begins, a jury must be selected. In all states, this is done by the respective attorneys in the case. However, before the jury is selected, the judge conducts a *voir dire* (questioning) of the potential jurors to determine if any have biases or predetermined ideas which would prevent them from giving the defendant a fair and impartial trial. The *voir dire* process in Delaware is distinguished from that found in most states in that it is conducted entirely by the judge presiding over the trial. This presents certain procedural and tactical problems for counsel in these cases, in that they do not get the opportunity to pose questions, nor are they ultimately entitled to choose what questions the judge asks. The attorneys are able to present written questions to the Court before the *voir dire* begins; however, this does not guarantee that those particular questions will be asked.

When, during questioning, a potential juror reveals any type of bias regarding some aspect of the case, that person will be discharged for cause by the Court. Once all the potential jurors have been questioned, those that have not been eliminated by the *voir dire* will, subsequently, be randomly selected to sit on the jury for the capital case in question. However, persons who have survived the *voir dire* stage still have another obstacle which may prevent their being included in a capital jury.

The attorneys have the ability to remove certain jurors from the panel using what are known as peremptory challenges. In capital cases, the State is entitled to twelve peremptory challenges and the defendant is entitled to a total of twenty peremptory challenges. The process of challenging jurors takes place at the conclusion of the *voir dire* examination of that individual juror. Generally, the defendant will have the first opportunity to challenge, and the State will follow, each side alternating as they proceed. No juror may be challenged during this process because of their race or gender.

Once the initial selection of twelve jurors is made, the Court may then select alternate jurors. It is within the Court's discretion to select up to six additional jurors who will hear the entire case. If one of the original twelve jurors must be excused for some reason, then the first of the six alternates chosen will take the departing juror's place. This process serves several functions, including the assurance of due process, and judicial economy.

After the jury and alternates have been impaneled, the trial will begin. In Delaware, this is actually a two part, or bifurcated, trial. The first part of the trial is known as the guilt phase. During this stage of the proceeding, the jury is presented with the substantive evidence of the offense. The State is afforded the opportunity to present evidence first during its case in chief. This is followed by the defendant's presentation of any evidence which challenges his or her guilt. The defendant is not required to present evidence, and may choose not to if it appears that the State has failed to meet its burden of proving guilt beyond a reasonable doubt.

The State has the burden of establishing, beyond a reasonable doubt, the guilt of the accused. The proof necessary to convict a defendant of capital murder is codified by statute. A person is guilty of murder in the first degree when:

1. He intentionally causes the death of another person;
2. In the course of, and in furtherance of, the commission of a felony or immediate flight therefrom, he recklessly causes the death of another person;
3. He intentionally causes another person to commit suicide by force or duress;
4. He recklessly causes the death of a law-enforcement officer, corrections employee or fireman while such officer is in the lawful performance of his duties;
5. He causes the death of another person by the use of or detonation of any bomb or similar destructive device;
6. He, with criminal negligence, causes the death of another person in the course of, and in furtherance of the commission or attempted commission of rape, unlawful sexual intercourse in the first or second degree, kidnapping, arson in the first degree, robbery in the first degree, burglary in the first degree, or immediate flight therefrom;

7. He causes the death of another person in order to avoid
    or prevent the lawful arrest of any person, or in the course
    of and in furtherance of, the commission or attempted
    commission of escape in the second degree or escape after
    conviction.

Generally speaking, the State is required to prove that a death
occurred, that the defendant had the intent to kill, and it was the
defendant's actions which brought about the death of the victim.

Once all of the evidence has been presented to the jury, the State
will make its closing argument followed by the defense's closing
argument. However, after the defense has made its closing, the State
gets the final word, in that they are allowed to offer rebuttal.
Subsequently, the judge presiding over the trial will give the jury
instructions to be used during the deliberative process. The jury
instructions include the appropriate law to be applied by the jury, conduct
of the jury during the deliberative process, and other information helpful
to reaching a fair and impartial verdict.

Once the jury has returned a verdict, one of two things happens.
If the verdict is not guilty, then the defendant will be released from
custody. If the jury returns a verdict of guilty, the trial then moves to
the sentencing phase, which will determine whether or not the defendant
will be sentenced to life in prison or death by lethal injection. The
other alternative is if the jury can not reach a unanimous verdict. If
this occurs, then the State must decide whether or not to retry the
defendant or drop the charges.

If a guilty verdict is returned by the jury, then the sentencing
phase begins. This phase underwent a dramatic change in 1991, when
the decision to impose the death penalty or life in prison was taken
away from the jury, and became the responsibility of the judge presiding
over the trial. The jury's role in the penalty phase is twofold. First, it
must determine whether the State has proven the existence of a statutory
aggravating circumstance. Some examples of statutory aggravating
circumstances are:

1. The murder was committed by a person in, or who has
    escaped from, the custody of a law enforcement officer
    or place of confinement.
2. The murder was committed for the purpose of avoiding
    or preventing an arrest or for the purpose of effecting an
    escape from custody.

3. The murder was committed against any law enforcement officer, corrections employee or fireman, while such victim was engaged in the performance of his official duties.
4. The murder was outrageously or wantonly vile, horrible or inhuman in that it involved torture, depravity of mind, use of an explosive device or poison or the defendant used such means on the victim prior to murdering him.
5. The victim was pregnant.
6. The victim was sixty two years of age or older.

This list is not exhaustive, but is representative of the type of conduct which will constitute an aggravating circumstance.

Next, the jury must determine whether the aggravating circumstances found to exist outweigh the mitigating circumstances present in the case. The trial judge must then answer the same two questions. If the answer to both is yes, the sentence is death. If not, the sentence is life imprisonment. The actual decision is made, in writing, by the judge, who considers the jury's answers to the questions in arriving at his conclusion. Thus, it is the judge who imposes the sentence, while the jury acts in an advisory capacity as the conscience of the community. If the judge has found the statutory aggravating circumstances outweigh the mitigating circumstances, then he or she will enter an order sentencing the defendant to death and set a date for execution.

The trial judge is required to notify in writing the Clerk of the Delaware Supreme Court that a death sentence has been imposed within five days of imposing the sentence. The letter from the trial judge constitutes an automatic appeal of the sentence to the Supreme Court. Immediately thereafter, the Court enters a stay of execution pending its review of the case.

By statute, the Court's review of the case pursuant to the automatic appeal is limited to the recommendation on and imposition of the death penalty. Following the submission of briefs by both the defendant and the State, and the presentation of oral argument by the parties, the Court commences its review by determining whether the evidence supports the judge's finding of a statutory aggravating circumstance. Secondly, the Court must determine, whether, considering all the evidence in aggravation and mitigation bearing upon the circumstances of the crime and character of the offender, the death penalty was imposed or recommended either arbitrarily or capriciously or was disproportionate to the penalty recommended or imposed in similar cases.

In determining whether the death penalty was imposed either arbitrarily or capriciously, the Supreme Court reviews the findings of the trial judge with respect to the aggravating and mitigating circumstances found to exist to determine if they are supported by the evidence. The Court further determines whether the Superior Court's decision to impose the death sentence was the product of a deliberate, rational and logical deductive process. The Superior Court's decision to impose the death penalty has never been reversed by the Supreme Court on the grounds that it was arbitrary or capricious, an obvious reflection of the care and thoroughness during the deliberations of the trial judges in their decisions regarding whether to impose the ultimate sentence on an individual.

When conducting its proportionality review, the Supreme Court compares the details and circumstances of the murder to the details and circumstances of other first degree murder cases that went to a penalty hearing to determine whether a death sentence is proportional in the instant case when compared to those other cases. Frequently, the Court will observe that the defendant, sentenced to death, committed a cold-blooded murder of a defenseless person, often for pecuniary gain. This is the most common factual murder scenario resulting in the imposition of the death penalty. Therefore, the imposition of the death penalty for such a crime will be proportional to the penalty imposed in other cases.

However, that does not mean that every murder of a defenseless person during a robbery or burglary results in the death penalty. Because of the unique circumstances of each case, discrepancies exist with respect to the penalty imposed. The decision to impose the death penalty reflects the individual judgment of jurors and judges and different results are a natural consequence of any justice system which permits for flexibility and equity in decision making.

The fact that one defendant may receive a death sentence while another receives life imprisonment for crimes which have many similarities does not mean that the penalty in either is disproportionate. However, if one person received the death penalty for a crime factually similar to numerous others for which the death penalty had never been imposed, a compelling proportionality argument could be made. The

Supreme Court has never reversed a death sentence on the grounds that it was disproportionate to the penalty imposed in similar capital cases.

The limited scope of the mandatory review does not prohibit a defendant from challenging his conviction and sentence on other grounds. A defendant may (and almost all do) file a separate appeal from his trial and sentencing hearing, raising any and all claims of error he chooses. Such claims of error are reviewed as they would be in any appeal, receiving the greatest care and consideration.

The mandatory review is just that — mandatory. Therefore, even if a defendant wishes to accept a death sentence, the Supreme Court must nonetheless conduct its mandatory review following the submission of briefs and the presentation of oral argument. Following the review, the Court may either affirm the death sentence or set it aside and remand the matter for correction of any errors which occurred during the sentencing hearing. Furthermore, the Court must set forth its findings as to the reasons for its actions, which is in a formal written opinion. In the event the death sentence is affirmed, the stay of execution terminates upon the issuance of the Court's mandate and the case is then remanded to the Superior Court for further proceedings, including the setting of a new date of execution.

Chapter 16

Board of Pardons: The Final Verdict

R. Thomas Wagner, Jr.

As Delaware's State Auditor, I am constitutionally charged with membership on the State Board of Pardons. The Board of Pardons traditionally offers the final verdict on death penalty cases on penalty cases in our state.

Delivering my vote on death penalty cases is one of the most difficult aspects of my job. It is probably the most important trust with which I am charged, in that the lives of the convicted, his or her families, as well as the lives of the victim's families are forever affected by my decisions and those of fellow members of the Board.

Delaware has a unique system by which it hears testimony to consider a stay of execution or the commutation of a death sentence. In many states, the Governor has the exclusive duty of considering requests for a stay or commutation; however, in Delaware, the Board of Pardons hears all testimony relative to a final request for commutation.

The Board of Pardons is comprised of five members. The membership consists of the Lieutenant Governor, Secretary of State,

Chancellor of the Court of Chancery, State Treasurer, and State Auditor, all of whom are elected officials, as well as the Secretary of State and Chancellor of the Court of Chancery.

Since taking office, three death penalty commutation cases have come before the Board. All of those men have been executed.

I am not opposed to the death penalty. Public opinion which has been expressed on the death penalty in Delaware indicates support for the ultimate punishment for those convicted of heinous and/or violent crimes. Once it is clear that all trials, convictions and sentences have been upheld by the Courts, it is likely that I would only yield with knowledge of irrefutable mitigating circumstances.

I personally place little credence in twelfth hour expressions of remorse or religious enlightenment. Although I would hope that these revelations offer comfort to the convicted and his or her family. I do not believe that a change of heart should have any bearing in consideration of commutation of a death penalty sentence. A murder victim has no second chance.

I carefully examine all of the case briefs which are submitted to the Board. I evaluate each application individually and objectively. Death penalty related petitions presented thus far have simply offered no mitigating information.

The debate as to whether or not the death penalty is a deterrent to heinous crimes will continue for as long as senseless acts of violence are committed. I believe that it is my duty to represent the people of Delaware. I am compelled to vote accordingly as a member of the Board of Pardons as long as the death penalty remains in effect in this State.

I know that in our nation, children are giving birth to children, children are killing children, and crime as a whole is on the rise in small towns as well as metropolitan areas. Getting tough on crime starts with saving our children. If our society can save its young people from gang lifestyles, drug abuse, inadequate education, and complete lack of self esteem by maintaining a strong family unit, we could possibly offer hope that a final verdict might never be required. A safe society truly starts with better parenting. Government should be far less participatory in the business of raising our nation's children.

Every parent must attempt to save his own child. Every parent must teach what is right and wrong, and must be responsible for his children's welfare. The time to commute a sentence is during childhood, before the seeds of desperation and contempt are planted.

Parents cannot guarantee success but must do their best to shape values and morals. I believe that the nurturing of goodness in our children is our greatest deterrent of crime. Parents are passing sentence on their children every day in America. Neglect, contempt, ignorance, and complacency shape the ultimate final verdict.

In the few years that I have served on the Board of Pardons, I have heard the cries for help, read the detailed accounts of the horrors of abuse negligence and I have seen the tears of anguish and loss of the faces of the victims friends and families.

Serving on the Board of Pardons is a very difficult job. I do my best to make fair and appropriate decisions. I know that all of my fellow members do so as well.

Chapter 17

Sentencing for Life: Americans Embrace Alternatives to the Death Penalty

The Death Penalty Information Center, Washington, D.C.

Public Opinion and the Death Penalty

In 1966, more Americans opposed the death penalty than favored it.[1] Executions were halted in 1967 and did not resume for ten years when support for the death penalty had grown. Today, a new phenomenon is emerging from the polls. Support for the death penalty drops precisely to the same low percentage as in 1966 when people are given the choice of stringent alternative sentences.

In March of this year, the polling firms of Greenberg/Lake and the Tarrance Group conducted a national survey of people's opinions about the death penalty. This poll revealed an increasing trend, first detected in a series of state polls on this issue, that Americans would favor certain alternative sentences over the death penalty. Although a majority of those interviewed said they favored capital punishment abstractly, that support is reversed when the sentence of life without parole, coupled with a requirement of restitution, is offered as an alternative. Forty-four percent favor that alternative, while only 41 % selected the death penalty. Even the choice of a sentence which guaranteed restitution and no release for at least twenty five years caused death penalty support to drop by 33%.

These results indicate a strong desire on the part of the public for protection from those who have committed society's worst crimes. There is also a preference for connecting punishment with restitution to those who have been hurt by crime. Support for the death penalty drops below 50% with a range of alternative sentences, especially those including restitution. Compared to the 77% who favor the death penalty in the abstract, support drops by 21 % when a sentence of life with no parole for twenty five years is considered; if a requirement of restitution is added to that sentence, support drops by 33%. And the sentence of life without parole plus restitution causes a support drop of 36% and relegates capital punishment to a minority position.

Recurrent Problems Erode Death Penalty Support

Why is it that people who appear to support the death penalty are willing to abandon that support in favor of alternative sentences? The answer may lie in the fact that people who support the death penalty nevertheless retain serious doubts about it which are triggered by some of capital punishment's recurrent problems. Also, people are unaware of the sweeping changes that have occurred in the actual amount of time which convicted murderers will have to serve for their crimes.

Doubts About the Death Penalty

Most people express doubts about the death penalty when presented with some of the problems which have plagued this ultimate punishment for years. Forty-eight percent responded that the issue of racism in the application of capital punishment raised some or serious doubts about the death penalty.

The perception of racial injustice within the criminal justice system, symbolized by the image of Rodney King in Los Angeles, is reinforced by the fact that Blacks are represented on death row three and half times their proportion in the population as a whole. And defendants who kill a white person in America are many times more likely to get the death penalty than those who kill a black person.[2] It is not surprising that almost three-fourths of Blacks believe that a black person is more likely than a white person to receive the death penalty for the same crime.[3] As these facts about capital punishment become more widely known, the enthusiasm for the death penalty may continue to wane.

Americans also expressed doubts about the death penalty after hearing information about the costs of the death penalty and the absence of any unique deterrent effect. The strongest doubts, however, were raised by the prospect that innocent people could be executed. Fifty-eight percent of those polled said the question of innocence raised doubts in them about the death penalty.

All of these issues are likely to cause further erosion in the public's support for the death penalty as new information buttresses people's concerns. Studies of the cost of the death penalty, for example, repeatedly show that it is much more expensive than the alternative of life in prison.[4] Reports on the death penalty's deterrent effect consistently conclude that it is no more a deterrent than lengthy prison terms.[5]

With all forms of government experiencing a need for streamlining expensive programs, the death penalty is ripe for a cost and benefit review.[6]

Other recent studies have confirmed that many who have been convicted of capital crimes, and even some who have been executed, were innocent.[7] In their recent book, *In Spite of Innocence*, the authors discuss over four hundred cases in which the defendant was wrongly convicted of a crime punishable by death. At least twenty three cases have resulted in the execution of innocent people.[8] The Supreme Court did little to dispel people's doubts with its recent ruling that new claims of innocence are almost never reviewable by the federal courts through habeas corpus petitions.[9]

It is sobering to recall that when the Supreme Court overturned all the existing death sentences in 1972 on constitutional grounds, a number of innocent lives were spared. Five of those who were on death row at the time went on to prove their innocence.[10] These innocent lives might well have been sacrificed and the same is undoubtedly true of some who are on death row today.

The recent release of Walter McMillian from Alabama's death row on March 2, 1993 illustrates this continuing danger.[11]

Mr. McMillian faced execution for six years. His appeals were turned down four times, despite the fact that no physical evidence held him with the crime and twelve witnesses placed him elsewhere at the time. Only the discovery by new attorneys of improper procedures used by the prosecutors and of witnesses who changed their stories allowed the conviction to be overturned and charges to be dropped.[12] Except for a series of fortuitous events, Mr. McMillian might have been executed while the courts refused to hear his valid claims of innocence.[13]

As the number of death row inmates across the country continues to reach record highs, and as the pace of executions accelerates, the probability of innocent people receiving the death penalty increases. This, too, will likely increase the doubts which people have about this ultimate punishment.

Awareness of Longer Sentences

Most Americans are poorly informed about the likely sentences which capital murderers would receive if not given the death penalty. Only 4% believed that those sentenced to life for first degree murder would be imprisoned for the rest of their lives. The average estimate of how long such a prisoner would serve was 15.6 years. Even when asked how long someone with a life without parole sentence would serve, only 11% believed that such a person would never be released. As discussed more fully below, those perceptions are far off the mark. Two-thirds of the states utilize sentences for first degree murder which guarantee that the inmate will never be eligible for release. (See Fig. 1) Most of the remaining states forbid considering parole for at least twenty five years. (See Fig. 2.)

Results From State Polls

Although the results from this latest poll may be surprising to those who believe that capital punishment has wide and unwavering support, they are consistent with a series of state polls which have explored some of the same issues over the past five years. These polls repeatedly showed that when people were presented with alternatives to the death penalty, their support for the death penalty dropped dramatically. Polls conducted in recent years in California, Florida, Georgia, Kentucky, Minnesota, Nebraska, New York, Oklahoma, Virginia and West Virginia all concluded that people prefer various alternative sentences to the death penalty.[14]

Another interesting finding reported consistently in the state polls, and confirmed by the national poll, is that death penalty support drops more with an alternative sentence of no parole for twenty five years than with a sentence mandating absolutely no parole, provided that the lesser sentence is combined with the requirement of restitution.[15] This result challenges the notion that people automatically favor the harshest of all possible sentences, such as the death penalty or life with no parole. Rather, people support reasonable alternatives which attempt to restore equilibrium and justice where it has been fractured in society.

These state polls also indicated the ambivalence which people have about capital punishment. People believe that the death penalty is arbitrary, that it is imposed in a racially discriminatory manner, and that there is a danger that innocent people may be executed by mistake. That ambivalence makes actual jurors hesitant to impose the death penalty when they are faced with the decision. It also leads people to readily prefer realistic alternatives, once they are given the choice.

Moreover, the support for alternatives to the death penalty appears to be growing. In a national poll in 1986, Gallup reported a 19% drop in support for the death penalty when life without parole was offered as an alternative.[16] The same question produced a 23% drop in 1991.[17] Now, in 1993, support for the death penalty dropped 28% when this same alternative was offered in the Greenberg/Lake poll. Similarly, a state poll conducted in New York in 1989 revealed that 62% of the people would prefer a sentence of life without parole plus mandatory restitution rather than the death penalty. In 1991, the same question was asked and 73% supported this alternative.[18]

The state polls reveal a number of other significant public perceptions on the death penalty. For example:

- When Nebraskans were asked which sentence would do the greatest good for all concerned, twice as many selected alternative sentences over the death penalty, and no parole for 30 years plus restitution was the first choice among the alternatives.[19]

- A majority of New Yorkers said they have moral doubts about the death penalty and are not really comfortable with capital punishment. Over 990% of New Yorkers agreed that the best way to reduce crime is to give disadvantaged people better education, job training, and equal employment opportunities.[20]

- Almost half of the respondents in Florida believed that the death penalty is racially and economically discriminatory.[21]

- In Oklahoma, only 5% of the people believe that the existence of the death penalty has definitely made the state a safer place to live. An additional 22% believe it probably has made it a safer place, but 62% of the people responded that it either probably not or definitely not made Oklahoma safer. Oklahomans would also prefer a sentence of life in prison over the death penalty by a margin of 56-35% if they were convinced that the death penalty discriminates against minorities.[22]

These and similar results from other states show the shallowness in the support for capital punishment. People are frustrated and frightened about violent crime. If they are offered no alternatives which reasonably meet their concerns for protection and punishment, then the death penalty seems attractive.

Jurors, too, look for alternatives. As many prosecutors who have brought "sure fire" death cases to juries know, there is often a reluctance by jurors to actually impose the death sentence on guilty murderers.[23] Jurors faced with making life and death decisions repeatedly inquire about the true meaning of a "life sentence," apparently hoping that this sentence will provide them with an acceptable alternative to sentencing someone to death.[24] When they are told that parole eligibility will not be explained, they incorrectly assume that the defendant will be out again in seven years. Faced with that alternative, jurors often choose death.

The Trend Toward Longer Incarceration

The development of prison sentences in which parole is restricted either for a substantial number of years or forever is a growing trend among states today. As a response to violent murders, almost every state, as well as the federal government, now uses a lengthy guaranteed minimum sentence before parole can even be considered.   The perception that a murderer convicted of a capital crime will be back on the streets in seven years if not given the death penalty is totally inaccurate.

This is a significant change from twenty years ago when the death penalty was temporarily suspended by the Supreme Court's ruling in *Furman v. Georgia*. Nearly 600 death sentences were commuted to life imprisonment by that decision, and almost every inmate has either been released or has an expected parole date set.[25]

Figure 1[26]
Life Without Parole States

Alabama	Idaho	Missouri	Rhode Island*
Arkansas	Illinois	Montana	South Dakota
California	Iowa*	Nebraska	Utah
Colorado	Louisiana	Nevada	Vermont*
Connecticut	Maine	New Hampshire	Washington
Delaware	Maryland	Oklahoma	West VA*
District of Col.*	Massachusetts*	Oregon	Wyoming
Hawaii*	Michigan*	Pennsylvania	

* States without the death penalty

In addition:
- Mississippi, Virginia, and South Carolina allow a sentence of life without parole for certain recidivists.
- Kentucky requires that a murderer serve half his term if sentenced for a number of years. Thus, a sentence equivalent to life without parole is available by sentencing the defendant to an exceedingly long term of years.
- In Wisconsin, the sentencing judge has the power to set the parole eligibility date which, in reality, could be longer than a person's natural life. A similar provision is in force in Alaska.
- The federal government employs life without parole for murders under certain statutes.

Figure 2
Restricted Parole: Years Before Parole Eligibility Under
Available Sentences for 1st Degree Murder Convictions

Alaska*	33 yr	Minnesota*	30 yr	Ohio	20 yr
Arizona	25 yr	New Jersey	30 yr	S. Carolina	30 yr
Florida	25 yr	New Mexico	30 yr	Tennessee#	25 yr
Indiana#	30 yr	New York*	25 yr	Texas	35 yr
Kansas*	40 yr	N. Carolina	20 yr	Virginia#	21 yr
Kentucky	25 yr	N. Dakota*	30 yr		

* States without the death penalty
\# Actual minimum sentence is longer, but inmates could be released after
the years stated if they received both parole and all possible "good time"
credit.

* Under Georgia law, anyone previously imprisoned under
    a life sentence must serve twenty five years before parole
    consideration.
* Canada requires that a convicted murderer serve twenty
    five years before being eligible for parole.

For defendants sentenced today, however, the prospects are quite
different. Thirty-three states (plus the District of Columbia and the
federal government) employ a sentence of life without parole in some
form. (See Fig. 1). A total of fourteen states call for the imposition
of a life sentence in which parole is not possible for at least twenty
years. Still others require that the inmate serve at least twenty years
before being considered for release. (See Fig. 2). And even in those
few states where parole is possible in under twenty five years, it is
very unlikely that those convicted of the worst crimes would be paroled
on their first try, if ever.

Effectiveness of Alternative Sentences

People are frightened by press accounts of parole consideration
for such notorious criminals as Charles Manson and Sirhan Sirhan.
No doubt, people believe that if these criminals are eligible for parole,
anyone would be. But neither of these men was sentenced under a life

without parole scheme, since that penalty had not been enacted when they had committed their crimes. The fact that these and similar cases receive consideration for parole, even though denied, tends to obscure the fact that today such offenders would not even be eligible for parole. In every state, the myth that if people are not given the death penalty they will be released in seven years is simply not true.

People are also disturbed by reports of prisoners who actually are released after a relatively short time, some of whom commit additional crimes. In Texas, for example, there is much confusion about sentencing. Prisoners, on the whole, are only serving 20% of their sentences and recidivism is a serious problem.[27] Typically, even those with a life sentence have been getting out in less than six years, partly due to the overcrowding in Texas' prisons.[28]

What is not widely known, however, is that for those convicted of capital murder, the reality is now quite different: a life sentence for them means they would not even be eligible for parole for thirty five years. However, Texas law forbids either side from informing the jury about the true meaning of a life sentence in a capital case, and so death sentences are being returned under a gross misperception. Jurors, and the public in general, mistakenly believe they must choose between releasing a violent murderer in six years or imposing the death penalty, even though the reality is quite different.

States that have used the sentence of life without parole say it works as promised. California has had a sentence of life without parole for over twenty five years and not one person sentenced under this law has been released from prison.[29] In Alabama, U.S. Court of Appeals Judge Edward Carnes, who headed the state's capital punishment division as assistant attorney general for many years, said that "life without parole in Alabama means just that—no parole, no commutation, no way out until the day you die, period."[30] Louisiana has perhaps the nation's toughest life sentence law. "Life in the state of Louisiana is just that—life," said a pardons board official in Baton Rouge. "There are no fifty year life sentences or twenty five year life sentences. Life means natural life." Nearly a hundred lifers have served twenty years or more at Louisiana's State Penitentiary in Angola.[31]

In South Dakota, all those given life sentences serve without possibility of parole. The only chance for release is through the commutation process requiring unanimous approval of the commutation board and the governor. No one convicted of homicide has been commuted since 1974.[32]

In Connecticut, assistant public defender Robert Gold described his state's recent experience with the life without parole alternative: "The sentence means what it says. You get carried out of the prison in a pine box as your only means of exit. Parole, good time, or other means of shortening the sentence are not available to people who have been convicted of [a] capital felony." [33]

Most of the states without the death penalty now utilize a sentence of life without parole for their worst offenders. Michigan, for example, has had a mandatory life law for first degree murder at least since 1931. It also bears the distinction of being the first English-speaking jurisdiction to permanently abolish the death penalty. For the past decade, the governor has averaged only one commutation per year of those sentenced to life for first degree murder. The time served for those few who were commuted between 1983 and 1990 averaged twenty seven years. [34]

In the District of Columbia, the voters overwhelmingly rejected the death penalty shortly after the city council passed legislation allowing for a sentence of life without parole for first degree murder. In New York, Governor Cuomo has also proposed this sentence as an alternative to reinstating the death penalty.

Commutation of Sentence

For those who would opt for a sentence under which prisoners could never be released, the theoretical possibility of executive clemency may appear to be a problem. In most states, either the governor or an appropriate board has the power to commute sentences. [35] Unless restricted by law, such a process could result in the reduction of a life without parole sentence to a simple life sentence where parole is possible.

In reality, however, this is a very remote possibility. Governors have the same power to grant clemency in death sentences but rarely do. On the average, there has only been 1 such commutation in twenty years for each state with the death penalty. [36] Presumably, if the same defendants had been given life without parole sentences, governors would have had even less incentive to commute them since the possibility of a mistaken execution would no longer be a motivation. This is borne out in states like Michigan, California and South Dakota which have had a life without parole sentence for some time and where commutations of those convicted of first degree murder are exceedingly rare or nonexistent. [37]

Moreover, the power to grant clemency is needed for those cases where evidence challenging the defendant's innocence or sentence arises only after the trial and appeals. The Supreme Court recently reinforced the need for such a safety valve when it refused to review the claims of innocence from a condemned Texas inmate, Leonel Herrera. "Clemency," said the Court, "is deeply rooted in our Anglo-American tradition of law, and is the historic remedy for preventing miscarriages of justice where judicial process has been exhausted."[38]

Some states have even gone so far as to restrict the executive's power of clemency in the worst cases. In California, for example, a prisoner serving life without parole cannot even apply for clemency for thirty years.[39] And in New York, Gov. Cuomo has proposed a constitutional amendment that would forbid anyone from granting clemency to those serving life without parole, should the legislature adopt such a sentence instead of the death penalty.[40] Thus, the possibility that dangerous criminals would be granted clemency is practically non-existent.

Juror Awareness of Alternative Sentencing

In America, juries are the voice of the people. As with the public at large, those who have served as jurors often prefer alternative sentences to the death penalty. A 1992 survey of nearly 800 jurors revealed that only 41% supported the death penalty if alternatives like life without parole were offered.[41] But just as the public is unaware of the fundamental changes in U.S. sentencing laws which have led to longer sentences, so, too, those with the responsibility for considering death sentences are without the correct information. Jurors in capital cases are particularly troubled because they believe they must choose between sentencing someone to death or allowing them to be released in a relatively short time. As the late Georgia Supreme Court Judge Charles Weltner said, "Everybody believes that a person sentenced to life for murder will be walking the streets in seven years." He went on to predict that the option of twenty to twenty five years parole ineligibility "would lower the number of death penalties that are given."[42]

The only problem with this prediction is that Georgia law (and the law of many other states) forbids the judge from explaining anything to the jury about parole possibilities, even if the judge receives a direct question from the panel while they are deliberating on a defendant's life or death sentence. In twenty three of the twenty nine states which utilize sentencing by the jury in capital cases, there is an absolute prohibition against any evidence or argument on parole.[43] As a result, jurors are left to their own misperceptions.

In one Georgia death penalty case, the jurors were interviewed after they returned their death sentence. Their comments clearly indicated that they were considering sparing the defendant's life but were swayed by the belief that he would be out in seven years:

> Some of the jurors were wanting to know would he get out in like seven years on good behavior. . . . If we were gonna' put him in prison, we wanted to make sure he would stay there. But . . . we didn't really feel like he would. . . . *We really felt like we didn't have any alternative.*[44]

The jurors in this case sent a note to the judge inquiring about the meaning of a life sentence: "Does life imprisonment mean Mr. Rogers (the defendant) would be eligible for parole in seven years or less on good behavior?" The Court replied: "You are not to concern yourself with the repercussions of either punishment that you fix. I cannot tell you as to the consequences of either of your sentences that you have for your consideration." After receiving this non-answer, the jurors returned a death sentence thirty four minutes later.[45]

Nor were this jury's concerns or final decision unique. A recent study looked at every Georgia trial in which a death penalty was returned by a jury since 1973. In seventy of the 280 cases, the jurors interrupted their deliberations to try to determine how soon the defendant might be released if he were given a life sentence. In all the cases, the jurors' inquiries were rebuffed by the court and a death sentence was returned.[46] According to the Prosecuting Attorney's Council of Georgia, the issue of parole "arises in almost every capital sentencing trial."[47]

Although Georgia does not have a life without parole sentence, some defendants, depending on their crime and prior history, may be sentenced so that they are not eligible for parole for twenty five to thirty years. That is significantly different from release after the presumed seven years and could clearly make a life or death difference in the jury's decision.

Interviews with jurors in other states reveal a similar pattern of concern about the likelihood of early release. In Virginia, those convicted of capital crimes must serve twenty five years before becoming eligible for parole and certain repeat offenders may never be considered for parole. However, Virginia law also forbids the jury from considering that information in deciding whether a defendant should be given a life or a death sentence. Jurors thus proceed on grave misperceptions when making their all-important determination. A study by the National Legal Research Group demonstrated the danger of uninformed jurors. The study found that prospective jurors in a sample Virginia county:

- Believed that a capital defendant sentenced to life imprisonment will likely serve only 10 years in prison;
- Believed that the length of time a capital defendant will actually serve when sentenced to life imprisonment is important to the penalty determination;
- Would disregard a judge's instruction not to consider parole when sentencing a capital defendant; and
- Would be influenced significantly in their sentencing decisions by information about Virginia's mandatory minimum sentence of twenty five years for capital defendants.[48]

From this and similar studies in other states,[49] it is clear that many jurors are sentencing people to death because they either lack adequate alternatives or because they are unaware that such alternatives exist." Executions based on such misinformation represent a travesty of justice. As the late U.S. Court of Appeals Judge Alvin B. Rubin noted, the "widely held misconceptions about the actual effect of imposing a life sentence raise an unacceptable risk that the death penalty may be imposed on some defendants largely on the basis of mistaken notions of parole law."[50]

Even when a state has incorporated a life without parole option into its choice of sentences, the jurors are likely to believe that the defendant will still be released and, therefore, are more likely to return a death verdict. In a survey of 250 potential jurors in Louisiana, an overwhelming 92% of those polled interpreted a "life sentence without the benefit of probation, parole or suspension of sentence" as meaning that the individual would still be eligible for release in a number of years.[51]

Politicians often add to these inaccurate perceptions when they use the death penalty to bolster their campaigns. For example, while running for governor of California as a pro-death penalty candidate, Dianne

Feinstein claimed: "You can't expect somebody to be deterred from committing murder if they know they will only serve four to five years."[52] What she neglected to say is that for those who face the death penalty, the only alternative sentence in California is life imprisonment with no possibility of parole. It is not surprising, then, that 64% of Californians erroneously believe that those sentenced under life without parole would nevertheless be released.[53]

Interestingly, politicians mistakenly believe that their constituents strongly prefer the death penalty over its alternatives. In New York, for example, 70% of the legislators polled thought their constituents would prefer the death penalty over a variety of alternatives. In fact, over 70% of the people would choose the alternative of life without parole plus restitution.[54]

This research implies that a sentence which eliminates parole for a substantial period, especially if coupled with a restitution requirement, is an appropriate alternative. It is appropriate because people prefer such an alternative to capital punishment and it protects society as effectively as the death penalty. Under the present system people are being sentenced to death under the erroneous assumption that, otherwise, the prisoner would be released early. To the extent that jurors have been choosing the death sentence in past cases based on this assumption, the executions which resulted are tragic mistakes.

The Effects of a Life Sentence

The existence of a stringent life sentence can either partially or completely eliminate the imagined need for the death penalty. In some states, a life without parole sentence is used as an option when the death penalty is not selected; in other states, like Michigan and Massachusetts, it exists as a complete replacement to capital punishment. In Maryland, for example, the state added the sentence of life without parole in 1987 as a choice for the jury in capital cases. Jurors are specifically instructed that they can choose a sentence of life without parole instead of the death penalty. In the five years since then, only eight new defendants have been added to the state's death row. A similar reduction in death sentences has resulted since Oklahoma introduced life without parole in 1988. That year, Oklahoma sentenced eighteen people to death. Last year, there were only five death sentences.[55] In contrast, Florida, which does not have life without parole, added forty five people to its death row in 1991.[56]

Sentences with significant minimum terms can also provide the public with the protection from repeat offenders that they want. An inmate released at the age of fifty five or sixty years old is statistically far less likely to engage in crime than someone in their late twenties. Violent crime arrest rates peak at age eighteen and then gradually decline to almost zero at age sixty and over.[57] As Louisiana's district attorney, Harry Connick, Sr., said: "When a guy gets to be sixty, he's not gonna rip and run a lot. Not like he used to."[58] In addition, convicted murderers are among the least likely offenders to repeat their crime, even if released.[59]

Thus, if the death penalty were eliminated tomorrow, the capital defendants of most states would face life sentences with no possibility of parole. In other states, they would have to serve lengthy minimum sentences before even being eligible for parole. By the time they were released, they would be in an age group where crime is at its lowest.[60]

Prisoners Serving Life

Inside prison, a number of wardens report that those serving life sentences are the best-behaved prisoners in their entire system. Leo Lalonde of the Michigan Department of Corrections says of those serving life without parole sentences: "After a few years, lifers become your better prisoners. They tend to adjust and just do their time. They tend to be a calming influence on the younger kids, and we have more problems with people serving short terms."[61] Similarly, Alabama officials noted that their life without parole inmates commit 50% fewer disciplinary offenses per capita than all other types of inmates combined.[62]

Lifers can also make a significant contribution to society in the time given them. For example, Craig Datesman at Graterford Prison in Pennsylvania coordinates a Lifers project to help young people who have had some trouble with the law to go straight. "We have taken a life and so we feel it's our responsibility to save a life now," said Datesman.[63] Executions, of course, cut off the possibility of any restitution to society or the family of the victim.

It is true that lengthier sentences can add to the costs of imprisonment. But as a replacement for the death penalty, even a sentence of life without parole would not add significantly to the prison population, and would, in fact, be cheaper than the prolonged litigation associated with a death sentence. Approximately 250 inmates are added to death rows around the country each year. Spread over the entire country, that is not a significant addition to a prison population which now numbers over one million.[64]

Restitution

Requiring those who have committed murder to make some monetary restitution to the family of the victim is strongly supported by those choosing alternatives to the death penalty. However, this sanction has not yet been widely employed by states. Inmates generally receive little in the way of remuneration for work performed in prison, usually barely enough for cigarettes or candy. A requirement of restitution might mean raising the pay for prison work. Nevertheless, the various opinion polls discussed above show that a requirement of restitution is one of the most consistent demands by those preferring alternatives to the death penalty.

One measure of what might be a feasible form of restitution was included in a New York opinion poll. New Yorkers were about evenly split in saying that $150,000 in restitution to the family of the victim would be either "about right" or "too little." The $150,000 restitution figure was derived from a requirement that the prisoner work forty hours per week, fifty weeks per year, over twenty five years at $3 per hour.[65] While the details of a restitution plan need to be worked out, polls show that the concept is extremely important to many people and could be incorporated further into the correctional system.

Many states are becoming more conscious of the needs of victims in their criminal justice systems.[66] Although funds for victim assistance are often provide directly from the state budget, some states are proposing restitution from the work of prisoners themselves. A bill before the 1993 Nebraska legislature would abolish the state's death penalty and instead impose a restitution requirement along with a sentence of life without parole. And in Arkansas, California, Wisconsin, Idaho, and Oregon, restitution to the victim's family can already be required of the offender in homicide cases.[67]

Other Alternatives: Decreasing the Amount of Crime

When considering the range of alternatives to the death penalty, the length of incarceration is not the only issue to be weighed. The discussion should also include alternatives which help reduce the risk of violence and murder. Crime prevention through community policing and gun control, employment opportunities, drug and alcohol rehabilitation programs, early intervention for abused and mentally handicapped children are all alternatives to capital punishment in that they lower the risk of crime in the first place.

Governments, of course, cannot fund every program that presents itself. Each program, including the death penalty, has its costs. If the death penalty were eliminated, there would be an immediate savings of millions of dollars for counties and states which could be transferred to other programs with proven records for reducing crime.[68] In the final analysis, it is these alternatives which actually address the rise in violence that prompted this country's return to the death penalty.

Families of Murder Victims

It is sometimes argued that the death penalty is necessary to assuage the grief suffered by the family of the murdered victim. For some families that may be true. However, in a country with 25,000 murders and twenty five executions per year, only one in a thousand families will actually receive such a "benefit." The rest may be left to wonder why their loss did not merit the same distinction. In fact, as many family members attest, neither the death penalty nor its alternatives can substitute for the tremendous loss of a loved one. A life sentence, on the other hand, does offer a sense of finality, rendered relatively quickly, as well as an opportunity for some restitution or reconciliation in the future.

Marietta Jaeger's seven year old daughter, Susie, was kidnapped and murdered, but she has never thought the death penalty offered any solace:

> The death penalty causes family members more pain than other sentences. The continuous sequence of courtroom scenes inherent in death penalty cases only serve to keep emotional wounds raw and in pain for years. . . . Actually, the memory of the victim is grossly insulted by the premise that the death of one malfunctioning person will be a just retribution for the inestimable loss of the beloved.
>
> In my case, my own daughter was such a gift of joy and sweetness and beauty, that to kill someone in her name would have been to violate and profane the goodness of her life; the idea is offensive and repulsive to me.[69]

In many ways, of course, the death penalty is no benefit at all: the threat of an execution means that there will almost always be a lengthy trial and years of appeals. Over 40% of death penalty cases are turned back for reconsideration.[70] Once a family becomes caught up in the quest for an execution, they are likely to follow a path of disappointment and failure.

Many families of victims are totally opposed to the death penalty. They echo the thoughts of Odine Stern, former director of Parents of Murdered Children, that no sentence can ever "equate to the loss of your child's life and the horrors of murder."[71] Frequently, victims' families recognize that the death penalty will inflict the same pain they have felt on the accused's family. As one mother replied when asked at the funeral of her murdered son if she wanted the death penalty: "No, there's been enough killing."[72]

Murder Victims Families for Reconciliation, another organization which deals with the grief of families, is planning a major national conference and educational program for June of 1993 around the theme of moving from violence to healing. As an organization, they are opposed to the death penalty. William Pelke, one of the organizers of the conference and the grandson of a murder victim, summed up his belief in alternative sentences:

> A simple life sentence without the possibility of parole can ease the pain much sooner and enable the victim's family to begin the process of healing. . . . As long as the thought remains that justice has not yet been carried out, the healing process that must take place is put on hold.[73]

The Politics of Death

In some states, politicians who favor the death penalty have resisted stiffer sentences which eliminate parole because they fear that with real alternatives in place there will be no more need for the death penalty. In New York, for example, the politicians who have succeeded in derailing Governor Cuomo's alternative of life without parole are those who favor the death penalty. They do not hide their manipulation of the issue: they would rather have criminals get out sooner than give up the death penalty as a cheap symbol for being tough on crime. This is what Governor Cuomo called "the politics of death."

> Life without parole is achievable immediately. The Legislature could enact it Monday. I would sign the measure Tuesday. It would apply to crimes committed the next day. In fact, the only thing preventing the next cop killer from spending every day of the rest of his life in jail is the politics of death.[74]

The perennial sponsor of the death penalty in New York, Vincent Graber, Democratic Assemblyman from Erie, admitted that his Senate colleagues opposed the life without parole bill because its passage would make the death penalty "less of a campaign issue."[75] The *New York Daily News*, long a supporter of the death penalty, became tired of this blatant manipulation and editorialized for a life without parole alternative:

> Why won't the Legislature adopt the obvious alternative—life without parole? Because polls would rather grandstand on the death penalty. It is cheap political expedience, not wise public policy.[76]

Recently, even Graber has acknowledged that he might have to accept the life without parole sanction as the New York legislature moves further away from overriding Cuomo's veto."[77]

As in New York, some South Carolina politicians are afraid that the passage of life without parole would result in less support for capital punishment. Death penalty advocate Senator John Drummond (D-Greenwood), for example, strongly opposed life without parole legislation:

If we pass this, you can't tell me that you will ever be able to seat a jury that will vote for the death penalty. In essence, what you're doing is asking us to vote against the death penalty.[78]

A similar scenario has been followed in Texas, where a number of state prosecutors have opposed Governor Richards' life without parole proposal. Harris County District Attorney John Holmes stated simply: "Those who ought to be confined forever ought to be executed."[79]

In the end, however, people will select politicians who conform to their opinions. For years, the myth that Americans love the death penalty has fueled an expansion of capital punishment and politicians' cry for more executions. But as the public's preference for alternative sentences becomes more widely known, and as those sentences become incorporated into law, the justifications for the death penalty will have finally disappeared.

Conclusion

America may now be ready to abandon the death penalty. People strongly prefer alternative sentences to the death penalty once they are given the choice. The lengthy sentences which people prefer and which guarantee that convicted murderers will stay behind bars are now in place in almost every state in the country. To the extent that support for the death penalty continues, it is because the public in general, and jurors in capital cases in particular, are still unaware of this fundamental change in U.S. sentencing practice.

Adequate alternatives are indeed in place throughout the country. Almost every state now severely restricts even the possibility of parole so that convicted murderers will not be released to the community for literally decades. The public wants to be sure that murderers will not, in fact, be released after a few years, and that the families of victims are compensated for their tragedy. As these ingredients become standard in the country's sentencing schemes, the death penalty may once again become a minority position in this country.

Chapter 18

Millions Misspent: What Politicians Don't Say About the High Costs of the Death Penalty

Richard C. Dieter

Executive Summary

A cross the country, police are being laid off, prisoners are being released early, the courts are clogged, and crime continues to rise. The economic recession has caused cutbacks in the backbone of the criminal justice system. In Florida, the budget crisis resulted in the early release of 3,000 prisoners. In Texas, prisoners are serving only 20% of their time and rearrests are common. Georgia is laying off 900 correctional personnel and New Jersey has had to dismiss 500 police officers. Yet these same states, and many others like them, are pouring millions of dollars into the death penalty with no resultant reduction in crime.

The exorbitant costs of capital punishment are actually making America less safe because badly needed financial and legal resources are being diverted from effective crime fighting strategies. Before the

Los Angeles riots, for example, California had little money for innovations like community policing, but was managing to spend an extra $90 million per year on capital punishment. Texas, with over 300 people on death row, is spending an estimated $2.3 million per case, but its murder rate remains one of the highest in the country.

The death penalty is escaping the decisive cost-benefit analysis to which every other program is being put in times of austerity. Rather than being posed as a single, but costly, alternative in a spectrum of approaches to crime, the death penalty operates at the extremes of political rhetoric. Candidates use the death penalty as a facile solution to crime which allows them to distinguish themselves by the toughness of their position rather than its effectiveness.

The death penalty is much more expensive than its closest alternative—life imprisonment with no parole. Capital trials are longer and more expensive at every step than other murder trials. Pre-trial motions, expert witness investigations, jury selection, and the necessity for two trials—one on guilt and one on sentencing—make capital cases extremely costly, even before the appeals process begins. Guilty pleas are almost unheard of when the punishment is death. In addition, many of these trials result in a life sentence rather than the death penalty, so the state pays the cost of life imprisonment on top of the expensive trial.

The high price of the death penalty is often most keenly felt in those counties responsible for both the prosecution and defense of capital defendants. A single trial can mean near bankruptcy, tax increases, and the laying off of vital personnel. Trials costing a small county $100,000 from unbudgeted funds are common and some officials have even gone to jail in resisting payment.

Nevertheless, politicians from prosecutors to presidents choose symbol over substance in their support of the death penalty. Campaign rhetoric becomes legislative policy with no analysis of whether the expense will produce any good for the people. The death penalty, in short, has been given a free ride. The expansion of the death penalty in America is on a collision course with a shrinking budget for crime prevention. It is time for politicians and the public to give this costly punishment a hard look.

Introduction

Death penalty cases are much more expensive than other criminal cases and cost more than imprisonment for life with no possibility of parole. In California, capital trials are six times more costly than other murder trials.[1] A study in Kansas indicated that a capital trial costs $116,700 more than an ordinary murder trial.[2]

Complex pre-trial motions, lengthy jury selections and expenses for expert witnesses are all likely to add to the costs in death penalty cases. The irreversibility of the death sentence requires courts to follow heightened due process in the preparation and course of the trial. The separate sentencing phase of the trial can take even longer than the guilt or innocence phase of the trial. And defendants are much more likely to insist on a trial when they are facing a possible death sentence. After conviction, there are constitutionally mandated appeals which involve both prosecution and defense costs.

Most of these costs occur in every case for which capital punishment is sought, regardless of the outcome. Thus, the true cost of the death penalty includes all the added expenses of the "unsuccessful" trials in which the death penalty is sought but not achieved. Moreover, if a defendant is convicted, but not given the death sentence, the state will still incur the costs of life imprisonment, in addition to the increased trial expenses.

For the states which employ the death penalty, this luxury comes at a high price. In Texas, a death penalty case costs taxpayers an average of $2.3 million, about three times the cost of imprisoning someone in a single cell at the highest security level for forty years.[3] In Florida, each execution is costing the state $3.2 million.[4] In financially strapped California, one report estimated that the state could save $90 million each year by abolishing capital punishments.[5]

The New York Department of Correctional Services estimated that implementing the death penalty would cost the state about $118 million annually.[6]

The Recession and the Death Penalty

The effects of the present financial crisis on the criminal justice system vary widely, but the common thread has been cutbacks in critical areas. In a report released in August of this year, the American Bar Association found that "the justice system in many parts of the United

States is on the verge of collapse due to inadequate funding and unbalanced funding." The report went on to state that "the very notion of justice in the United States is threatened by a lack of adequate resources to operate the very system which has protected our rights for more than two centuries."[7]

New Jersey, for example, laid off more than five hundred police officers in 1991.[8] At the same time, it was implementing a death penalty which would cost an estimated $16 million per year, more than enough to hire the same number of officers at a salary of $30,000 per year.[9]

In Florida, a mid-year budget cut of $45 million for the Department of Corrections forced the early release of 3,000 inmates.[10] Yet, by 1988 Florida had spent $57.2 million to accomplish the execution of eighteen people.[11] It costs six times more to execute a person in Florida than to incarcerate a prisoner for life with no parole.[12] In contrast, Professors Richard Moran and Joseph Ellis estimated that the money it would take to implement the death penalty in New York for just five years would be enough to fund two hundred and fifty additional police officers and build prisons for 6,000 inmates.[13]

Ten other states also reported early release of prisoners because of overcrowding and inadequate funding.[14] In Texas, the early release of prisoners has meant that inmates are serving only twenty percent of their sentences and re-arrests are common.[15] On the other hand, Texas spent an estimated $183.2 million in just six years on the death penalty.[16] Illinois built new prisons but does not have the funds to open them.[17] It does, however, have the fourth largest death row in the country. Georgia's Department of Corrections lost over nine hundred positions in the past year while local counties have had to raise taxes to pay for death penalty trials.[18]

Police officers on the beat, imprisonment of offenders, and a functioning criminal justice and correctional system form the heart of the nation's response to crime. Yet, in state after state, these programs are suffering drastic cuts while the death penalty absorbs time, money and political attention.

The Cost to Local Governments

An increasingly significant consequence of the death penalty in the United States is the crushing financial burden it places on local governments. The current economic recession has made it clear that there is no unlimited source of government largesse. Counties, which bear the brunt of the costs of death penalty trials, are also the primary deliverers of local health and human services in the public sector.[19] Hard choices have to be made among the demands of providing essential services, creative crime reduction programs such as community policing, and the vigorous pursuit of a few death penalty cases.

As Scott Harshbarger, Attorney General of Massachusetts, put it: "Virtually every major program designed to address the underlying causes of violence and to support the poor, vulnerable, powerless victims of crime is being cut even further to the bone. . . . In this context, the proposition that the death penalty is a needed addition to our arsenal of weapons lacks credibility and is, as a sheer matter of equity, morally irresponsible. If this is really the best we can do, then our public value system is bankrupt and we have truly lost our way."[20]

While state and national politicians promote the death penalty, the county government is typically responsible for the costs of prosecution and the costs of the criminal trial. In some cases, the county is also responsible for the costs of defending the indigent. Georgia, Alabama and Arkansas, for example, provide little or no funding for indigent defense from the state treasury.[21] In Lincoln County, Georgia, citizens have had to face repeated tax increases just to fund one capital case.

Even where the state provides some of the money for the counties to pursue the death penalty, the burden on the county can be crushing. California, for example, was spending $10 million a year reimbursing counties for expert witnesses, investigators and other death penalty defense costs, plus $2 million more to help pay for the overall cost of murder trials in smaller counties. (Now, even that reimbursement is being cut.) But many financially strapped smaller counties still could not afford to prosecute the complicated death-penalty cases. Some small counties have only one prosecutor with little or no experience in death-penalty cases, no investigators and only a single Superior Court judge.[22] In Sierra County, California authorities had to cut police services in 1988 to pick up the tab of pursuing death penalty prosecutions. The County's District Attorney, James Reichle, complained, "If we didn't have to pay $500,000 a pop for Sacramento's murders, I'd have an investigator and the sheriff would have a couple of extra deputies and we could do some lasting good for Sierra County law enforcement. The sewage system at the courthouse is failing, a bridge collapsed, there's no county library, no county park, and we have volunteer fire and volunteer search and rescue." The county's auditor, Don Hemphill, said that if death penalty expenses kept piling up, the county would soon be broke.[23] Just recently, Mr. Hemphill indicated that another death penalty case would likely require the county to lay off ten percent of its police and sheriff force.[24]

In Imperial County, California, the county supervisors refused to pay the bill for the defense of a man facing the death penalty because the case would bankrupt the county. The county budget officer spent three days in jail for refusing to pay the bill. A judge reviewing the case took away the county's right to seek the death penalty, thus costing the county the partial reimbursement which the state provided for capital cases. The County took the challenge all the way to the California Supreme Court and ended up costing the County half a million dollars.[25] In the criminal trial, the defendant was acquitted.

A similar incident occurred recently in Lincoln County, Georgia. The county commissioners also refused to pay the defense costs when the attorney won a new trial for a death row inmate Johnny Lee Jones. As in California, the commissioners were sent to jail. Walker Norman, chair of the County Commission explained: "We're a rural county of 7,500 people with a small tax base. We had to raise taxes once already for this case when it was originally tried, and now we are going to have to raise taxes again. It's not fair."[26] The first trial alone cost the county $125,000.[27] The second trial was completed in September and the defendant received a life sentence.

In Meriwether County, Georgia, a county of 21,000 residents and a $4 million annual budget, the prosecutor sought the death penalty three times for Eddie Lee Spraggins, a mentally retarded man. The case cost the county $84,000, not including the defense attorney's bill for appealing, and the third conviction was again overturned by the Georgia Supreme Court.[28] Spraggins was finally granted a plea and received a life sentence.

In Mississippi, Kemper and Lauderdale Counties recently conducted a border survey battle to avoid responsibility for a capital murder trial. Faced with a case that could cost the county $1,000,000, Kemper County wanted to show that the scene of the murder was outside their border and conducted two surveys of the site. County Supervisor Mike Luke explained, "As much as we were talking about the taxpayers of Kemper County having to pay out, we believed we needed to be sure." Luke said that the decision to seek the death penalty was not his: he only had to come up with the money. Lauderdale County, where the trial was originally scheduled, has now sent a bill to Kemper County for expenses incurred while holding the defendant in jail for nineteen months. Kemper County is considering how much it will have to raise taxes just to pay the twenty nine initial costs of the prosecution.[29]

In Yazoo City, Mississippi, the town is worried that it, too, might get stuck with an expensive death penalty case. "A capital murder trial is the worst financial nightmare any government body could envision," said the editor of the local paper.[30]

With more death row inmates and more executions than any other state, Texas is also experiencing the high costs of executions. Norman Kinne, Dallas County District Attorney, expressed his frustration at the expense: "Even though I'm a firm believer in the death penalty, I also understand what the cost is. If you can be satisfied with putting a person in the penitentiary for the rest of his life . . . I think maybe we have to be satisfied with that as opposed to spending one million to try and get them executed. . . . I think we could use (the money) better for additional penitentiary space, rehabilitation efforts, drug rehabilitation, education, (and) especially devote a lot of attention to juveniles."[31]

Vincent Perini of the Texas Bar Association, calls the death penalty a "luxury": "There's some things that a modem American city and state have got to have. You have to have police and fire and public safety protection. You have to have a criminal justice system. You do not have to have a death penalty. The death penalty in justice is kind of a luxury item. It's an add-on; it's an optional item when you buy your criminal justice vehicle."[32]

Chief Criminal Judge, James Ellis, came to a similar conclusion in Oregon: "Whether you're for it or against it, I think the fact is that Oregon simply can't afford it."[33] James Exum, Chief Justice of the North Carolina Supreme Court, agrees: "I, and those of us involved in prosecuting these (death penalty) cases, have this uneasy notion that . . . these cases are very time-consuming and very troublesome and take a lot of resources that might be better spent on other kinds of crimes.

Efforts are under way in both Congress and the Supreme Court to reduce the avenues of appeal available to death row inmates. But most of the costs associated with the death penalty occur at the trial level.[34] Whatever effect cutting back on the writ of habeas corpus may have on the time from trial to execution, it is not clear that the changes will make the death penalty any less expensive, and they may result in the execution of innocent people. With the number of people on death row growing each year, the overall costs of the death penalty are likely to increase.

Some state appeals courts are overwhelmed with death penalty cases. The California Supreme Court, for example, spends more than half its time reviewing death cases.[35] The Florida Supreme Court also spends about half its time on death penalty cases.[36] Many governors spend a significant percentage of their time reviewing clemency petitions and more will face this task as executions spread. As John Dixon, Chief Justice (Retired) of the Louisiana Supreme Court, said: "The people have a constitutional right to the death penalty and we'll do our best to make it work rationally. But you can see what it's doing. Capital punishment is destroying the system.[37]

Alternatives for Reducing Crime

New York does not have the death penalty. In the early 1980s, the New York State Defenders Association conducted a study to estimate how much the death penalty would cost if it were to be implemented in New York. The estimates were that each case would cost the state $1.8 million, just for the trial and the first stages of appeal.[38] The majority of those costs would be borne by the local governments. New Yorkers have consistently reelected a governor whom they know will veto any death penalty legislation which comes across his desk. Now it appears that New York may be reaping the benefit of that choice.

Significantly, no city in New York State, without the death penalty, is among the nation's top twenty-five cities in homicide rates according to statistics recently released by the FBI.[39] In particular, New York City bucked the national trend and experienced a decline in every major category of crime last year.[40] In the first four months of 1992, crime is again down across the board in New York, compared to the same period two years ago, with murders decreasing by over eleven percent.[41]

While direct causes for a decrease in crime are difficult to pinpoint, many experts have attributed New York's success to an increasingly popular concept known as community policing. Two years ago, New York had 750 foot officers on the street. Today that number is 3,000.[42] Community policing is a strategy for utilizing police officers not just as people who react to crime, but also as people who solve problems by becoming an integral part of the neighborhoods they serve.

Such programs do not come cheaply, but they do seem to be effective. In Prince George's County, Maryland, police Captain Terry Evans said their community policing program is "the only thing I've seen in twenty three years of law enforcement that's had an impact, actually turned it around."[43] Fully implemented, Prince George's community policing program will cost the county ten million per year.

The programs apparently work best where governments can afford to add officers, rather than taking from existing numbers, leaving other work unattended. This is borne out in cities like Boston where murders dropped twenty three percent in 1991, partly because of a program that put more police officers on the beat.[44] The need for more police officers is supported by a survey of Chiefs of Police from around the country, seventy percent of whom said they could no longer provide the type of crime prevention activities they did ten years ago because of too few police officers.[45]

Boston, like New York, is in a state without the death penalty, though Governor William Weld (R-Mass.) has been attempting to re-instate it. That proposal has met with opposition from the state's district attorneys. Judd Carhart, past president of the district attorneys' association, said a majority of the state's district attorneys oppose capital punishment partially on the grounds that it is a waste of money better spent on other areas of law enforcement and incarcerations.[46] Attorney General Scott Harshbarger agreed: "We need major criminal justice and court reform now to address the crisis in our criminal justice system. The death penalty, however, has no place in this reform effort. It is a simplistic, arbitrary, misguided, ineffective and costly response, cloaked in the guise of a remedy to the brutalizing violence that angers and frustrates us all."[47]

Compared to community policing and other successful programs, the death penalty, for all its cost, appears to have no effect on crime. A *New York Times* editorial noted recently that the number of executions in this country "constituted less than .001 percent of all murderers . . . and were only .000004 percent of all violent criminals. Even if U.S. executions were multiplied by a factor of ten they would still constitute an infinitesimal element of criminal justice." The public seems to agree: only 13 %of those who support capital punishment believe it deters crime.[48]

New York and Massachusetts can be contrasted with Texas which is the nation's leader in the use of the death penalty. Texas has the largest death row and has executed almost twice as many people as the next leading state. Houston alone accounts for 10% of all people executed in the United States since 1976.[49] Yet, the murder rates in three of Texas' major cities rank among the nation's top twenty five cities. In all three, Houston, Dallas and Fort Worth, the number of murders increased significantly last year.[50]

Wherever the death penalty is in place, it siphons off resources which could be going to the front line in the war against crime: to police, to correctional systems, and to neighborhood programs which have proven effective. Instead, these essential services are repeatedly cut while the death penalty continues to expand. Politicians could address this crisis, but, for the most part, they either endorse executions or remain silent.

Political Manipulation of the Death Penalty

What drives this high spending on such an ineffective program? The answer lies partly in the promotion by politicians who hope to benefit by advocating the death penalty. Even though it fails to meet the cost-benefit test applied to other government programs, many politicians use capital punishment to distinguish themselves from their opponents. Politicians have generally not posed the death penalty as one alternative among a limited number of crime fighting initiatives which the people must ultimately pay for. Rather, the death penalty is used to play on the public's fear of crime and to create an atmosphere in which the extreme view wins. The rhetoric then becomes policy and the people pay.

The Death Penalty in National Politics

Flush with his party's convincing victory in the 1988 Presidential elections, Republican National Chairman Lee Atwater urged his fellow Republicans to capitalize on the issue of crime because "almost every Democrat out there running is opposed to the death penalty."[51] Apparently, the Democrats were listening as well since politicians of all stripes rushed to proclaim their support of capital punishment.

From Florida to California, the political races in 1990 were marked by excessive attempts by politicians to appear tougher on crime by their willingness to execute people. Ironically, those who were most demonstrative about the death penalty were defeated, though seldom by opponents of capital punishment.

In this election year, the national political debate on the death penalty is more conspicuous for its silence. The utility of the death penalty as a defaming issue was lost when most of the Democratic

Presidential candidates supported the death penalty. George Bush, Bill Clinton and Ross Perot are all in favor of the death penalty, though none has made it a major campaign issue.

George Bush: From Willie Horton to the Crime Bill

In the previous campaign, George Bush was able to link a furlough for convicted murderer Willie Horton with Michael Dukakis' position against the death penalty, thus portraying Dukakis as soft on crime. This time, President Bush has sought to convey a tough image by his support for a greatly expanded federal death penalty. When recent unemployment figures indicated that the economy was going to be a negative for the Bush campaign, his advisers called for a greater emphasis on crime to bolster the President's popularity.[52]

In 1990, President Bush sought to identify the Republican Party as tough on crime. He introduced a crime bill whose centerpiece was an expansion of the federal death penalty to over forty new crimes. Not to be outdone, the Democrats endorsed a bill allowing the death penalty in over fifty new crimes. Despite two years of debate and attempts to expand the death penalty even further, the bill remains in Political gridlock. While the bill's death penalty provisions and restrictions on federal habeas corpus appeals have received the most notice, proposals for law enforcement, prison construction, boot camps and other crime fighting provisions have received little attention.

Just prior to the last presidential election in 1988, the death penalty was also promoted as a way of appearing tough on drug crime. Legislation was passed imposing the death penalty in drug-related murders but that law has resulted in only seven prosecutions and one death sentence in almost four years. Bush's bill is designed to have a much broader application. However, some parts of the current bill are also window dressing, having little to do with the public's concern about crime.

The crime bill would impose death sentences for such offenses as treason, espionage, murder in the act of destroying a maritime platform, murder of federal egg product inspectors, horse inspectors and poultry inspectors. These proposals will have no real impact on crime in the streets, which is the rationale for proposing such legislation. As one legal commentator put it: "What they mean when they say they're 'getting tough' is simply that they are talking tough."[53]

An expanded federal death penalty could also prove to be enormously expensive. One amendment approved by the Senate would impose the death penalty for murders involving weapons used in interstate commerce. The Congressional Budget Office estimated that this proposal would cost as much as $600 million over four years.[54]

Senator Thomas Daschle (D-SD) described much of the talk about the death penalty on Capitol Hill as political posturing: "We debate in codes, like the death penalty as a code for toughness on crime. The whole game is a rush to acquire the code: he who gets the code first wins — it denigrates the national debate."[55]

Bill Clinton: Insulating Himself from Attack

Although Clinton's pro-death, penalty stance has partially neutralized Bush's use of this tactic in the current campaign, on the death penalty one can never be tough enough. For example, Vice President Dan Quayle recently attacked Clinton for being soft on capital punishment (despite having presided over four executions as Arkansas Governor) because Clinton had suggested that Governor Mario Cuomo (D-NY) might make a good Supreme Court Justice.[56]

Bill Clinton has criticized Bush's manipulation of the death penalty issue: "President Bush has used an expansion of the death penalty as a cover for actually weakening the partnership of the federal government in the fight against crime."[57] However, Clinton bowed to the popular wisdom when he made a prominent demonstration of his support for the death penalty by leaving the primary campaign in January to preside over the execution of a brain damaged defendant in Arkansas.

Ever since he lost the Governor's race in Arkansas after serving only one term, Clinton has made clear his support for the death penalty. Clinton returned to office as Governor in 1983 and has granted no commutations to anyone on death row and has presided over all four of the state's executions in the modern era. However, as Arkansas was returning to executions, its murder rate was increasing: murders in Little Rock, alone, jumped forty percent in the past year.[58]

The Death Penalty in State Politics

The death penalty is almost the exclusive function of the states rather than the federal government. It is not surprising, then, that some of the most blatant attempts at political manipulation of the death penalty have occurred on the level of state politics.

Florida and Texas are two states with the largest death rows and most active execution chambers. They were also the scene of recent gubernatorial races featuring candidates boasting of their ability to secure more executions than their opponent. In 1990, Florida's Governor Bob Martinez campaigned with background shots of smirking serial killer Ted Bundy, while reminding the voters how many death warrants he had signed. Martinez was defeated by Democrat Lawton Chiles who also favors the death penalty.

The Texas Campaign: "Who Can Kill the Most Texans?"

The governor's race in Texas presented a variety of candidates vying to demonstrate their greater support of the death penalty. As populist Democrat Jim Hightower put it, the race boiled down to one issue: "Who can kill the most Texans?"[59]

Former Governor Mark White portrayed his toughness by walking through a display of large photos of the people executed during his term. Attorney General Jim Mattox insisted that he was the one who should be given credit for the thirty two executions carried out under his watch. Meanwhile, the Republican candidate, Clayton Williams showed pictures of a simulated kidnapping of young children from a school yard and then touted his backing of a separate law to impose the death penalty for killing children. His ad ended with the slogan: "That's the way to make Texas great again."[60]

In the end, the campaigns succeeded only in gaining embarrassing notoriety for Texas as Democrat Ann Richards became the eventual winner. Richards has continued Texas' leadership in carrying out the most executions of any state. However, while Texas is spending hundreds of millions of dollars on the death penalty, it is having to release other prisoners early to avoid overcrowding. Inmates serve only an average of one-fifth of their sentences. In Harris County (Houston), arguably the death penalty capital of the country, sixty seven percent of those arrested are recidivists and crime is the people's number one concern.[61]

California Politics: A Cue of Neglect

California's 1990 gubernatorial race also involved jockeying for the position of "death penalty candidate." Dianne Feinstein was the most outspoken, describing herself in commercials as "the only Democratic candidate for governor in favor of the death penalty."[62] This ploy caused her Democratic rival, John Van de Kamp, to respond with ads assuring the voters that he wouldn't let his conscience get in the way of carrying out executions. Although personally opposed to the death penalty, his ads proclaimed his record as attorney general of putting or keeping almost 300 people on California's death row and featured pictures of the condemned inmates in the background.

Van de Kamp lost to Feinstein and Feinstein then lost to Republican Pete Wilson, another strident pro-death penalty candidate. This year Feinstein is running for the Senate and all 11 of the major candidates for California's two Senate seats support the death penalty.[63]

California is in the throes of an extreme financial crisis. The state paid its workers with IOUs for two months and most social services are facing major cuts. Los Angeles County alone is considering laying off 500 sheriff's deputies to cope with the loss of state funds. Such cuts are likely to have a direct effect on public safety. As one official remarked, "The public doesn't seem to have a heightened sense of urgency about this yet, and I don't think they ever will — until they become victims themselves."[64] Nevertheless, the state has been paying an estimated ninety million per year over normal costs to carry out the death penalty.[65] With over 300 people condemned to death, California has the second largest death row in the country.

The Los Angeles riots were a stark reminder of the anger which simmers as a result of social neglect. Reforms like community policing were contemplated in L.A. but were viewed skeptically by former Police Chief Daryl Gates because no funds were available: "The first problem," Gates said in his new book, "is the need for more officers. But again, how much more can taxpayers be asked to pay?"[66] As a result, L.A.'s police force was described by one expert as "the antithesis of community policing. The department was cool, aloof, disconnected from the community."[67] The city burned.

New York Politics: Grandstanding on the Death Penalty

New York illustrates that voters are not monolithic when it comes to the death penalty. Although more executions have been carried out in New York since 1900 than in any other state, it does not have the death penalty now and has not executed anyone since 1963. For ten straight years, the state legislature has passed death penalty legislation and for ten years Governor Cuomo has vetoed the bills, continuing the tradition of Governor Hugh Carey before him. Although the majority of New Yorkers appears to support capital punishment, Cuomo has been re-elected repeatedly. Cuomo's 1990 Republican opponent, Pierre

Rinfret, built a campaign around the death penalty but failed to win voter support. Even fellow Republican and death penalty supporter Jack Kemp rejected such blatant manipulation:

> He's running on the death penalty for drug pushers. I mean, goodness gracious, if . . . that's what politics has descended into in the 1990's, who can get to the far right on the death penalty — it is a sad day. . . . I don't want to be in the Republican Party of New York if that's all they can talk about, the death penalty. I am for the death penalty, but that pales in significance to the need for a healthy economic and opportunity-oriented state, whether it is New York or the state of the economy nationally.[68]

The New York legislature has often come close to overriding Cuomo's veto. Lately, however, that movement has been losing steam. The controversy demonstrates that switching one's allegiance on the death penalty issue to join the mainstream is not always a ticket to electoral success. In the 1990 elections, three Assemblymen who once opposed the death penalty, but who had lately switched their votes, were all defeated.[69] As a result, the vote to override Cuomo's veto lost by a larger margin in the next session.

The *New York Daily News*, long a supporter of the death penalty with such subtle headlines as "FRY HIM!", has apparently become frustrated with the political game-playing surrounding the issue and now rejects the death penalty. In an editorial earlier this year, the *News* took particular aim at those pro-death penalty politicians who vote against the alternative sentence of life-without-parole because it would make their own death penalty bill harder to pass: "Why won't the Legislature adopt the obvious alternative — life without parole? Because politicians would rather grandstand on the death penalty. It is cheap political expedience, not wise public policy."[70]

The death penalty's chief proponent in the New York Assembly, Vincent Graber from Buffalo, acknowledged the kind of manipulation the *News* criticized. Graber admitted that the life-without-parole bill was rejected because it interfered with the quest for capital punishment: "This being an election year," Graber said in 1990, "I don't think the Senate is in the mood to go with mandatory life, no parole. The death penalty would become less of a campaign issue and I don't think they want to do that."[71]

Politics In Other Places

Politicians are quick to capitalize on an opportunity to promote the death penalty. Massachusetts does not have the death penalty, but when Carol Stuart, a young white, pregnant woman, was brutally murdered in 1989, the city of Boston reacted in angry shock. The media and the public were misled to believe that a young black man was the attacker and the Republican Party called a press conference within hours of Stuart's death demanding a return to capital punishment.[72] After the embarrassing truth came out that Stuart was probably murdered by her own husband, the campaign fizzled.

In Arizona, state Representative Leslie Johnson (R-Mesa) called for the death penalty for child molesters after a particularly horrendous crime in Yuma. On the floor of the House, Johnson proposed the quick fix: "If we do away with these people, if we do have the death penalty and if you are a sex offender, you're just out of here — dead, gone. And if we get a few innocent people, fine and dandy with me. I'll take the percentage, folks, because I don't want to put my children at risk anymore.[73]

And in the District of Columbia, Senator Richard Shelby (D-Ala.) proposed that the death penalty be enacted for the city by Congress after one of his aides was killed on Capitol Hill. Congress responded by cutting out the Mayor's twenty five million youth and anti-crime initiative while imposing a referendum on the death penalty. The hidden but inevitable costs resulting from having capital punishment were not addressed in the appropriations bill. But if the experience of other states is any indication, it will be years before any execution is carried out, after an expenditure of as much as $ 100 million, either from federal or DC funds.

Finally, the death penalty is manipulated by those politicians who are closest to it: the elected state attorneys and prosecutors who make the decisions on which cases to pursue the ultimate punishment. A campaign advertisement for district attorney Bob Roberts of North Carolina, for example, lists all the defendants for whom he won a death sentence. His slogan: "If one of your loved ones is murdered, who do you want to try the accused? Bob Roberts with his splendid record and experience or his inexperienced opponent."[74]

As a public defender, Attorney General Grant Woods of Arizona had argued before a judge that it would be murder if the judge sentenced his innocent client to death. Now, as chief prosecutor and staunch defender of the death penalty, Woods turned on his client, Murray Hooper, saying he is guilty and deserves the death penalty. Since Hooper is still on death row, such a representation has raised questions of legal ethics and client loyalty. Woods claims he is just doing his job.[75]

A district attorney in Georgia, Joseph Briley, was also charged with numerous breaches of legal ethics in a Supreme Court amicus brief signed by twelve legal ethics professors from around the country. When the conviction of Tony Amadeo was overturned, Briley first announced that he would again seek the death penalty. However, he later allowed the defendant to plead guilty in exchange for a life sentence after the defense proffered three expert witnesses to testify that his ethical violations should disqualify him from retrying the case. Briley's frustration at having to take the plea was summed up in his comment to one of the defense attorneys, "You've probably made me un-electable."[76]

In Kentucky, Commonwealth Attorney Ernest Jasmin made a name for himself by obtaining a death sentence against the killer of two teenagers from Trinity High School. He then campaigned as the Trinity Prosecutor, taking ads in the high school newspaper and campaigning with one of the victims' parents frequently at his side.[77]

In Nebraska, attorney general Don Stenberg took the unusual step of attaching a personal letter to his Supreme Court brief urging the execution of Harold Otey, whom he described as a "vicious killer" who "still smirks at the family of the victim. . . ."[78] While pushing publicly for Otey's death, Stenberg also sat as one of three decision makers at Otey's clemency hearing and two of his staff presented gruesome details of the murder.

In sum, there has been a steady stream of politicians attempting to capitalize on the death penalty issue in recent years. Real solutions to crime get overshadowed in the tough talk of capital punishment. When some of these politicians are successful, the death penalty gets implemented or expanded and the people begin to pay the high costs. Somewhere down the road there may be an execution, but the crime rate continues to increase. Politicians do the people a disservice by avoiding the hard economic choices that have to be made between the death penalty and more credible methods of reducing violence.

Conclusion

The death penalty is parading through the streets of America as if it were clothed in the finest robes of criminal justice. Most politicians applaud its finery; others stare in silence, too timid to proclaim that the emperor has no clothes. Instead of confronting the twin crises of the economy and violence, politicians offer the death penalty as if it were a meaningful solution to crime. At the same time, more effective and vital services to the community are being sacrificed. Voters should be told the truth about the death penalty. They should understand that there are programs that do work in reducing crime, but the resources to pay for such programs are being diverted into show executions. Being sensible about crime is not being soft on crime. Too much is at stake to allow political manipulation to silence the truth about the death penalty in America.

Epilogue — Fall 1994

"Every dollar we spend on a capital case is a dollar we can't spend anywhere else. . . . We have to let the public know what it costs" to pursue a capital case.
> John M. Bailey, Chief State's Attorney, Connecticut

Since the publication of *Millions Misspent* in the fall of 1992, more judges, prosecutors and other state officials have joined those questioning the death penalty in light of its exorbitant costs. At a time when crime is the nation's primary concern, new data confirms the Report's earlier conclusion that the death penalty is draining state treasuries of funds which could be spent on effective crime prevention measures.

The financial burden is particularly acute in counties where administrators are being forced to choose between raising taxes and bankruptcy in order to prosecute death penalty cases. While many politicians continue to ignore these costs in using the death penalty to sound tough, some prosecutors are now deciding not to seek executions because the cases are simply too expensive.

The Duke University Study

In May, 1993, a federally funded study brought a new perspective to the cost debate.[79] This model study was prompted by an American Bar Association proposal and was conducted at Duke University's Terry Sanford Institute of Public Policy. It is one of the most comprehensive and thorough analyses on this topic.

Authors Philip Cook and Donna Slawson spent two years comparing the costs of adjudicating capital and noncapital cases in North Carolina and concluded that capital cases *cost at least an extra $2.16 million per execution*, compared to what taxpayers would have spent if defendants were tried without the death penalty and sentenced to life in prison.[80] Moreover, the bulk of those costs occur at the trial level.

Applying their figures on a national level implies that $82 million was spent just for U.S. executions in 1993, and that the national bill for the death penalty has been over $500 million since the death penalty was reinstated.[81] Yet, the national concern about crime indicates that few feel safer for all this expense.

Time Is Money

Death penalty cases are so expensive because they take longer at every stage and require vast resources for both the prosecution and the defense. The authors of the North Carolina study identified 24 principal areas in which a death penalty case would likely be more expensive than if the case were tried non-capitally.[82] These areas included:

- More investigative work by both law enforcement officials and the defense team
- More pre-trial motions
- More questioning concerning individual jurors' views on capital punishment and more peremptory challenges to jurors at jury selection
- The appointment of two defense attorneys
- A longer and more complex trial
- A separate penalty phase conducted in front of a jury
- A more thorough review of the case on direct appeal
- More post-trial motions

- • Greater likelihood that counsel will be appointed for a federal habeas corpus petition
- • Greater likelihood that there will be full briefing and argument on federal review
- • More preparation for, and a longer clemency proceeding.

A little rural county in Kentucky just can't deal with (death penalty) bills like that.

Michael Mager,
Executive Director of the Kentucky
County Judge-Executives Association

The North Carolina study estimated that a death penalty trial takes about four times longer than a non-capital murder trial. And, of course, not every death penalty trial results in a death sentence. Based on the experience in North Carolina, the authors found that less than a third of capital trials resulted in a death sentence.[83] Nevertheless, each of the these trials had the extra expense associated with death penalty proceedings. The trial costs alone were about $200,000 *more for each death penalty imposed* than if no death penalty was involved.[84]

The authors computed the costs of appealing a death penalty case and subtracted the savings which accrue to the state when an execution finally occurs. The "savings," which are due to the inmate no longer being kept at state expense, only occur when an execution is actually carried out. As with the trial level, there is a "failure" rate resulting from the fact that many inmates who are sentenced to death will never be executed. Many cases will be overturned on appeal, some inmates will commit suicide, others will die of natural causes. Again, based on the experience in North Carolina, the authors estimated that only one inmate would likely be executed for every ten who are sentenced to death.[85] This is actually higher than the national rate where only about one in every eleven cases which have been resolved has resulted in an execution.[86]

Bulk of Costs at Trial Level

The importance of accounting for this failure rate is critical for two reasons. First, it represents a truer picture of what it is actually costing the state to achieve an execution. It is not just the cost of a single person's trial and appeals. That would be comparable to saying that the cost of landing a man on the moon was the cost of fuel for the one rocket which brought him there. The state has to pay more for all the trials and appeals which start out as death penalty cases but for which there will never be the "saving" associated with an execution.

Second, the per execution costs reveal that the bulk of death penalty costs occur at the *trial* level. Often those who acknowledge the high costs of the death penalty believe that the expense is due to "endless appeals." By taking into account the capital cases which will never result in an execution, the North Carolina study makes clear that the *trials* produce the largest share of death penalty costs[87] and these costs will not be substantially lessened by tinkering with the opportunities that death row inmates have to appeal. A significant financial corollary of this finding is that taxpayers must pay death penalty expenses up front, whereas the costs of a life sentence are meted out gradually over many years, making that alternative even less expensive.

Evidence from Other States

> It's going to be a fairly substantial (tax) increase. I hope the taxpayers understand.
>
> John Sims, Jasper County (Miss.) Board
> President, on death penalty prosecution costs

There have been numerous indications from other areas of the country that the death penalty is straining the budgets of state and local governments and that the financial drain is getting worse. Some counties have been brought to the brink of bankruptcy because of death penalty cases. More county commissioners have risked going to jail for balking at paying for capital prosecutions,[88] while others reluctantly raise taxes to pay the costs of even one capital case.

- In San Diego, California, the prosecution costs alone (not counting defense costs or appeals) for three capital cases averaged over half a million dollars each.[89] One estimate puts the total California death penalty expense bill at $1 billion since 1977.[90] California has executed two people during that time, one of whom refused to appeal his case.

- In Jasper County, Mississippi, the Circuit Judge and the District Attorney had to address the county supervisors to get more money for death penalty prosecutions. The only solution was to raise county taxes. "It's going to be a fairly substantial increase," said the board president, John Sims. "I hope the taxpayers understand. . . ."[91]

Life without parole could save millions of dollars. In other words, it's cheaper to lock 'em up and throw away the key. . . . As violent crime continues to escalate, it's something to consider.
Jim Mattox, former Texas Attorney General

- In Connecticut, a state with only a handful of death row inmates, *The Connecticut Law Tribune* was unable to calculate the total costs of capital punishment but concluded that the "costs are staggering."[92] State's attorney Mark Solak said he spent between 1,000 and 1,500 hours preparing one capital prosecution.[93] The defense attorney in the case noted that if his client had been given an offer of life in prison without parole he would have accepted it "in a heartbeat." "The case," he said, "would have been over in 15 minutes. . . . No one would have spent a penny."[94]

- Other items from *The Connecticut Law Tribune*'s report:
  * Jury selection in death cases can take eight weeks.[95]
  * One state's attorney in one case spent about 7 months distilling a 10,000 page trial transcript, and three other attorneys assisted him, putting in a total of 15 months' work.[96]
  * The state's public defender office spends about $138 defending an average criminal case. Death penalty cases, however, have cost over $200,000 *each* to defend.[97]

- In South Carolina, *The Sun News* reported that the bills for death penalty cases are "skyrocketing" because of a state supreme court ruling that attorneys in death penalty cases deserve reasonable fees. Before the decision, attorneys received no more than $2,500 for each death penalty case.[98]

When the law changed so defendants can be sentenced to 40 years flat time, and when you start taking into account what the taxpayers are getting for their money, it seems like some defendants should be tried . . . without the death penalty.

Judge Doug Shaver, Harris County (TX)

• It took six years to extradite Charles Ng from Canada to California mainly because Canada resisted the prospect of sending someone to a possible death sentence. Since coming to California, the case has cost Calaveras County $3.2 million, an amount which would have bankrupt the county except for the fact that the state agreed to reimburse the county until 1995. Now it looks as though the bailout will have to last until the year 2000, with millions more in expenses yet to come.[99]

• In Harris County, Texas, there are 135 pending death penalty cases. State Judge Miron Love estimated that if the death penalty is assessed in just 20 percent of these cases, it will cost the taxpayers a minimum of $60 million. Judge Love, who oversees the county's courts, remarked: "We're running the county out of money."[100]

We're running the county out of money.

Judge Miron Love, Harris County (TX),
reflecting on a projected $60 million
expense for pending death
penalty cases in that county alone.

Reactions to the High Costs

There have been many similar reactions from state and local officials who wonder about the wisdom of spending such exorbitant sums on such unpredictable and isolated cases. In Tennessee, the number of people sentenced to death has dropped because prosecutors say death penalty cases cost too much.[101]

In Texas, Judge Doug Shaver from Houston was also concerned about the high costs of so many capital cases: "I can't figure out why our county is prosecuting so many more (death) cases than comparably large counties around Texas. When the law changed so defendants can be sentenced to 40 years flat time (as an alternative to death), and when you start taking into account what the taxpayers are getting for their money, it seems like some defendants should be tried . . . without the death penalty."[102]

Former Texas Attorney General Jim Mattox agrees: "Life without parole could save millions of dollars." "In other words," he wrote, "it's cheaper to lock 'em up and throw away the key. . . . As violent crime continues to escalate, it's something to consider."[103]

California has been hit particularly hard by natural disasters and the economic recession. Many social programs have had to be cut. Yet the state continues to spend hundreds of millions of dollars on the death penalty which has resulted in two executions in seventeen years. Even supporters of the death penalty recognize that it is a financial loser. In financially strapped Orange County, Vanda Bresnan, who manages the criminal courts, remarked: "Even though I do believe in the death penalty, I wonder how long the state or county can afford it,"[104] she said. Defense attorney, Gary Proctor, who practices in the same county, believes that the solution will be found by cutting other services: "What I see happening is that other services provided to the taxpayer — such as libraries and parks — will be cut back. Certain people are not aware of the tradeoffs." He added: "Strong beliefs are easy enough to hold if you don't think they're coming out of your pocket."[105]

> *Even though I do believe in the death penalty, I wonder how long the state or county can afford it.*
>
> Vanda Bresnan,
> Manager of the Criminal Courts,
> Orange County (CA)

In rural Kentucky, tax bases are small and budgets are already stretched. When an expensive capital case is about to be heard in court, the state and county often argue for weeks about who will pay. As Michael Mager, executive director of the Kentucky County Judge-Executives Association, points out, "A little rural county in Kentucky just can't deal with bills like that."[106]

And in Connecticut, the Chief State's Attorney, John M. Bailey, echoed similar concerns: "Every dollar we spend on a capital case is a dollar we can't spend anywhere else. . . . We have to let the public know what it costs to pursue a capital case."[107]

Political Manipulation of the Death Penalty

Despite the overwhelming weight of evidence pointing to the unmanageable and growing costs of imposing capital punishment, politicians continue to ignore these costs in using the death penalty to appear tough on crime. This hypocrisy reached new heights with the passage of the federal crime bill. Every time this legislation was considered, the number of new death penalty crimes grew. While debate immediately before the bill's passage centered on whether the proposed crime prevention measures were too expensive, little was said about the costs that these new death penalties would bring or whether they were likely to do any good.

> *I know of no law-enforcement professional who believes that all the death penalty provisions and new Federal crimes would affect public safety in the slightest.*
> Robert Morgenthau, Manhattan (NY) District Attorney

Ultimately, funding for crime prevention programs was cut back but the 60 new federal death penalty crimes were left intact. Unfortunately, the legacy of the death penalty will probably outlast all the other provisions of the legislation. Federal funding for new police, prisons and programs like midnight basketball will be phased out in a few years but the costs of expanding the death penalty will last for decades. Federal prosecutions in death penalty cases are likely to be even more expensive than in the states. Thousands of offenses will now be eligible for the federal death penalty. Even if only a small fraction of these cases are pursued, the costs of additional federal prosecutors, additional federal public defenders and judges will be draining. The federal government will be joining the states in spending millions of dollars for an occasional execution, with no effect on the real problem of crime.

Some Representatives and Senators voted in conscience against the crime bill because of its death penalty provisions. But, for the most part, politics prevailed. Philip Heymann, the former U.S. Deputy Attorney General who recently resigned from the Justice Department, commented that the entire crime debate was "so mired in politics and ideology that no one in the Government dared speak the truth about the subject." The truth, as he saw it, was that the crime bill was a deeply flawed quick fix that sounded great "for the first 15 seconds," the perfect length for a campaign ad sound bite.[108]

Robert Morgenthau, the District Attorney for Manhattan, similarly castigated the politics behind expansion of the federal death penalty: "I know of no law-enforcement professional who believes that all the death penalty provisions and new Federal crimes would affect public safety in the slightest." The bill, he noted, "would provide no new Federal judges, prosecutors or courtrooms. That isn't surprising: the new crimes and death sentences are window dressing."[109]

Conclusion

> *Like a black hole, the death penalty absorbs vast quantities of resources but emanates no light.*

Recent studies of death penalty costs reinforce the existing evidence that the death penalty is becoming unmanageably expensive. Like a black hole, it absorbs vast quantities of resources but emanates no light. Nevertheless, politicians and much of the public are drawn to it in the hope of finding a quick fix to the crime problem. But as the actual costs of capital punishment become clearer, the public should be in a better position to judge the death penalty as they would other programs. If a program is highly cost intensive, given to years of litigious expense, focused on only a few individuals, and produces no measurable results, then it should be replaced by better alternatives.

Amanda Smith assisted in the preparation of this Epilogue.

* **Note:** This article originally was published February 23, 1994, as a Special Edition to the Temple LEAP Ledger, a publication of Temple LEAP, an office of the Temple University School of Law providing educational training and resources to school districts throughout the Commonwealth of Pennsylvania.

Chapter 19

The Death Penalty and Justice Blackmun*

David J.W. Vanderhoof

"From this day forward, I no longer shall tinker with the machinery of death.."

Justice Harry A. Blackmun, after a 20-year struggle with the issue of capital punishment, concluded that "the death penalty experiment has failed" and that it was time for the Court to abandon the "delusion" that capital punishment was consistent with the Constitution. His views were expressed in an unusual opinion released by the Supreme Court yesterday. Justice Blackmun's tone seemed urgent, as if in the twilight of his career he sought to reopen a dialogue on the death penalty which has all but disappeared with the retirement of Justices William J. Brennan Jr. and Thurgood Marshall, who both believed that the death penalty was inherently unconstitutional.

Justice Blackmun's discussion of his struggle was aimed toward a future in which he expressed the hope that the Court would realize that the effort to administer the death penalty fairly and consistently was "doomed to failure."

"I may not live to see that day," he said, "but I have faith that eventually it will arrive." His emotions in death penalty cases have been close to the surface before. In a 1972 dissent he said that death penalty cases are an "excruciating agony of the spirit." Last year [1993], in another dissent, he said that the impending execution of another Texas inmate, Leonel Herrera, who had asserted his innocence but could not get a Federal court hearing, came "perilously close to simple murder."

There were further developments in the Callins case:

FORT WORTH, Feb. 22 (AP) — Mr. Callins's execution was halted just a few hours before his scheduled execution by Judge Terry R. Means of Federal District Court after defense lawyers challenged the conviction on murder and robbery charges.

What has been the Supreme Court's Guidance in Administering The Death Penalty — Constitutionally?

Starting with the 1972 Furman decision, the Supreme Court has insisted that the death penalty be administered in ways that would weed out arbitrariness and prejudice on the part of juries. The common theme of the new state death penalty laws that the Court upheld in the years after the Furman decision was a set of rules intended to channel the jury's discretion by limiting the factors that the jurors could consider in choosing a death sentence over other punishments for convicted murderers.

At the time, the 200 page Furman v. Georgia opinion was the longest decision in Supreme Court history.

In a series of rulings beginning in the late 1970's, the Supreme Court also insisted that the jury be free to consider any evidence that the defendant might put forward in their own behalf. As many death penalty scholars have pointed out (as both Justices Blackmun and Scalia asserted) these two competing commands — limited discretion to weed out arbitrariness and unlimited discretion to guarantee full consideration to individual circumstances — are mutually contradictory.

Last January [1993] the Supreme Court said clemency was the "fail-safe" mechanism for prisoners asserting innocence after they have exhausted their federal habeas claims and are barred by new trial deadlines from presenting evidence of that innocence. With Chief Justice William Rehnquist writing for the majority, the court voted 6 to 3 in January that Texas prisoner Leonel Herrera couldn't bring an innocence claim in federal court because he hadn't alleged a constitutional error. Herrera was executed in May, 1993.

> *In Herrera v. Collins (1993) the Supreme Court held that, in the absence of constitutional grounds, new evidence of innocence is no reason to order a new trial. According to the majority opinion: "Where a defendant has been afforded a fair trial and convicted of the offense for which he has been charged, the constitutional presumption of innocence disappears. . . . Thus, claims of actual innocence based on newly discovered [are not] grounds for . . . relief absent an independent constitutional violation occurring in the course of the underlying state criminal proceedings."*

And Justice Blackmun is not the only member of the Supreme Court to have death penalty second thoughts. Justice Lewis F. Powell, Jr., who worked diligently to preserve the penalty's constitutionality in state cases now believes his votes were wrong and would change his votes in all cases in which he upheld the death penalty. Shortly after his retirement, Justice Powell said he would vote against capital punishment if he faced the question as a legislator. But in a new biography, his former law clerk says Justice Powell "now thinks he was wrong on the whole issue," capital punishment should be abolished, that it "serves no useful purpose." After 15 years of capital cases the justice came to believe that "the system as a whole would always be plagued by doubt and that doubting itself, [the system] would inspire resentment and contempt." If given the chance he would change his key 1987 swing vote in *McCleskey v. Kemp*, 481 U.S. 279, which rejected a race-based statistical challenge to the punishment and his insistence that capital punishment was not prohibited by the Constitution in the landmark *Furman v. Georgia*, 408 U.S. 238 (1972), which struck down state death penalties as arbitrary and capricious. [From "Justice Lewis F. Powell Jr. and the Era of Judicial Balance."]

This June [1996] the Supreme Court, unanimously and with blazing speed, upheld a law signed by President Clinton on April 24, 1996, limiting appeals by death-row inmates.

Excerpts from Justice Blackmun's Dissent in Callins v. Collins:

From this day forward, I no longer shall tinker with the machinery of death.

[Both] fairness and rationality cannot be achieved in the administration of the death penalty. . . .

For more than 20 years I have endeavored — indeed, I have struggled — . . . to develop procedural and substantive rules that would lend more than the mere appearance of fairness to the death penalty endeavor. Rather than continue to coddle the Court's delusion that the desired level of fairness has been achieved and the need for regulation eviscerated, I feel morally and intellectually obligated simply to concede that the death penalty experiment has failed.

[T]he Court has stripped "state prisoners of virtually any meaningful federal review of the constitutionality of their incarceration."

There is little doubt now that Furman's essential holding was correct. Although most of the public seems to desire, and the Constitution appears to permit, the penalty of death, it surely is beyond dispute that if the death penalty cannot be administered consistently and rationally, it may not be administered at all.

There is a heightened need for fairness in the administration of death. This unique level of fairness is born of the appreciation that death truly is different from all other punishments a society inflicts upon its citizens. "Death, in its finality, differs more from life imprisonment than a 100-year prison term differs from one of only a year or two."

While the risk of mistake in the determination of the appropriate penalty may be tolerated in other areas of the criminal law, "in capital cases the fundamental respect for humanity underlying the Eighth Amendment . . . requires consideration of the character and record of the individual offender and the circumstances of the particular offense as a constitutionally indispensable part of the process of inflicting the penalty of death."

In recent years, I have grown increasingly skeptical that "the death penalty really can be imposed fairly and in accordance with the requirements of the Eighth Amendment," given the now limited ability of the federal courts to remedy constitutional errors.

The Court's refusal last term to afford Leonel Torres Herrera an evidentiary hearing, despite his colorable showing of actual innocence, demonstrates just how far afield the Court has strayed from its statutorily and constitutionally imposed obligations.

Because I no longer can state with any confidence that this Court is able to reconcile the Eighth Amendment's competing constitutional commands, or that the federal judiciary will provide meaningful oversight to the state courts as they exercise their authority to inflict the penalty of death, I believe that the death penalty, as currently administered, is unconstitutional.

Perhaps one day this Court will develop procedural rules or verbal formulas that actually will provide consistency, fairness, and reliability in a capital-sentencing scheme. I am not optimistic that such a day will come. I am more optimistic, though, that this Court eventually will conclude that the effort to eliminate arbitrariness while preserving fairness 'in the infliction of [death] is so plainly doomed to failure that it — and the death penalty — must be abandoned altogether.' I may not live to see that day, but I have faith that eventually it will arrive. The path the Court has chosen lessens us all. I dissent.

The full text of the Court's opinion follows:

BRUCE EDWIN CALLINS, PETITIONER
v.
JAMES A. COLLINS, DIRECTOR, TEXAS
DEPARTMENT OF CRIMINAL JUSTICE,
INSTITUTIONAL DIVISION
CALLINS v. COLLINS
No. 93-7054
SUPREME COURT OF THE UNITED STATES
114 Sct. Ct. 1127 (1994)
February 22, 1994

PRIOR HISTORY: ON WRIT OF CERTIORARI TO THE UNITED
STATES COURT OF APPEALS FOR THE FIFTH CIRCUIT.
OPINION: The petition for a writ of certiorari is denied.

CONCUR: Justice Scalia, concurring.

Justice Blackmun dissents from the denial of certiorari in this
case with a statement explaining why the death penalty "as currently
administered," post, at 22, is contrary to the Constitution of the United
States.   That explanation often refers to "intellectual, moral and
personal" perceptions, but never to the text and tradition of the
Constitution. It is the latter rather than the former that ought to control.
The Fifth Amendment provides that "no person shall be held to answer
for a capital . . . crime, unless on a presentment or indictment of a
Grand Jury, . . . nor be deprived of life . . . without due process of
law." This clearly permits the death penalty to be imposed, and
establishes beyond doubt that the death penalty is not one of the "cruel
and unusual punishments" prohibited by the Eighth Amendment.

As Justice Blackmun describes, however, over the years since 1972
this Court has attached to the imposition of the death penalty two quite
incompatible sets of commands: the sentencer's discretion to impose
death must be closely confined, see Furman v. Georgia, 408 U.S. 238
(1972) (per curiam), but the sentencer's discretion not to impose death
(to extend mercy) must be unlimited, see Eddings v. Oklahoma, 455
U.S. 104 (1982); Lockett v. Ohio, 438 U.S. 586 (1978) (plurality
opinion). These commands were invented without benefit of any textual
or historical support; they are the product of just such "intellectual,
moral, and personal" perceptions as Justice Blackmun expresses today,
some of which (viz., those that have been "perceived" simultaneously

by five members of the Court) have been made part of what is called
"the Court's Eighth Amendment jurisprudence," post, at 7.

Though Justice Blackmun joins those of us who have acknowledged
the incompatibility of the Court's Furman and Lockett-Eddings lines
of jurisprudence, see Graham v. Collins, 113 S. Ct. 892, 910-911
(1993) (THOMAS, J., concurring); Walton v. Arizona, 497 U.S. 639,
656-673 (1990) (SCALIA, J., concurring in part and concurring in the
judgment), he unfortunately draws the wrong conclusion from the
acknowledgment. He says:

> "The proper course when faced with irreconcilable constitutional
> commands is not to ignore one or the other, nor to pretend that the
> dilemma does not exist, but to admit the futility of the effort to
> harmonize them. This means accepting the fact that the death penalty
> cannot be administered in accord with our Constitution." Post, at
> 19. Surely a different conclusion commends itself — to wit, that at
> least one of these judicially announced irreconcilable commands which
> cause the Constitution to prohibit what its text explicitly permits
> must be wrong.

Convictions in opposition to the death penalty are often passionate
and deeply held. That would be no excuse for reading them into a
Constitution that does not contain them, even if they represented the
convictions of a majority of Americans. Much less is there any excuse
for using that course to thrust a minority's views upon the people.
Justice Blackmun begins his statement by describing with poignancy
the death of a convicted murderer by lethal injection. He chooses, as
the case in which to make that statement, one of the less brutal of the
murders that regularly come before us — the murder of a man ripped
by a bullet suddenly and unexpectedly, with no opportunity to prepare
himself and his affairs, and left to bleed to death on the floor of a
tavern. The death-by-injection which Justice Blackmun describes looks
pretty desirable next to that. It looks even better next to some of the
other cases currently before us which Justice Blackmun did not select
as the vehicle for his announcement that the death penalty is always
unconstitutional — for example, the case of the 11-year-old girl raped
by four men and then killed by stuffing her panties down her throat.
See McCollum v. North Carolina, No. 93-7200, cert. now pending
before the Court. How enviable a quiet death by lethal injection
compared with that! If the people conclude that such more brutal deaths
may be deterred by capital punishment; indeed, if they merely conclude

that justice requires such brutal deaths to be avenged by capital punishment; the creation of false, untextual and unhistorical contradictions within "the Court's Eighth Amendment jurisprudence" should not prevent them.

DISSENT: Justice Blackmun, dissenting.

On February 23, 1994, at approximately 1:00 a.m., Bruce Edwin Callins will be executed by the State of Texas. Intravenous tubes attached to his arms will carry the instrument of death, a toxic fluid designed specifically for the purpose of killing human beings. The witnesses, standing a few feet away, will behold Callins, no longer a defendant, an appellant, or a petitioner, but a man, strapped to a gurney, and seconds away from extinction.

Within days, or perhaps hours, the memory of Callins will begin to fade. The wheels of justice will churn again, and somewhere, another jury or another judge will have the unenviable task of determining whether some human being is to live or die. We hope, of course, that the defendant whose life is at risk will be represented by competent counsel — someone who is inspired by the awareness that a less-than-vigorous defense truly could have fatal consequences for the defendant. We hope that the attorney will investigate all aspects of the case, follow all evidentiary and procedural rules, and appear before a judge who is still committed to the protection of defendants' rights — even now, as the prospect of meaningful judicial oversight has diminished. In the same vein, we hope that the prosecution, in urging the penalty of death, will have exercised its discretion wisely, free from bias, prejudice, or political motive, and will be humbled, rather than emboldened, by the awesome authority conferred by the State.

But even if we can feel confident that these actors will fulfill their roles to the best of their human ability, our collective conscience will remain uneasy. Twenty years have passed since this Court declared that the death penalty must be imposed fairly, and with reasonable consistency, or not at all, see Furman v. Georgia, 408 U.S. 238 (1972), and, despite the effort of the States and courts to devise legal formulas and procedural rules to meet this daunting challenge, the death penalty remains fraught with arbitrariness, discrimination, caprice, and mistake. This is not to say that the problems with the death penalty today are identical to those that were present 20 years ago. Rather, the problems that were pursued down one hole with procedural rules and verbal formulas have come to the surface somewhere else, just as virulent and pernicious as they were in their original form. Experience has taught us that the constitutional goal of eliminating arbitrariness and discrimination from the administration of death, see Furman v. Georgia, supra, can never be achieved without compromising an equally essential component of fundamental fairness — individualized sentencing. See Lockett v. Ohio, 438 U.S. 586 (1978).

It is tempting, when faced with conflicting constitutional commands, to sacrifice one for the other or to assume that an acceptable balance between them already has been struck. In the context of the death penalty, however, such jurisprudential maneuvers are wholly inappropriate. The death penalty must be imposed "fairly, and with reasonable consistency, or not at all." Eddings v. Oklahoma, 455 U.S. 104, 112 (1982).

To be fair, a capital sentencing scheme must treat each person convicted of a capital offense with that "degree of respect due the uniqueness of the individual." Lockett v. Ohio, 438 U.S., at 605 (plurality opinion). That means affording the sentencer the power and discretion to grant mercy in a particular case, and providing avenues for the consideration of any and all relevant mitigating evidence that would justify a sentence less than death. Reasonable consistency, on the other hand, requires that the death penalty be inflicted even handedly, in accordance with reason and objective standards, rather than by whim, caprice, or prejudice. Finally, because human error is inevitable, and because our criminal justice system is less than perfect, searching appellate review of death sentences and their underlying convictions is a prerequisite to a constitutional death penalty scheme.

On their face, these goals of individual fairness, reasonable consistency, and absence of error appear to be attainable: Courts are in the very business of erecting procedural devices from which fair, equitable, and reliable outcomes are presumed to flow. Yet, in the death penalty area, this Court, in my view, has engaged in a futile effort to balance these constitutional demands, and now is retreating not only from the Furman promise of consistency and rationality, but from the requirement of individualized sentencing as well. Having virtually conceded that both fairness and rationality cannot be achieved in the administration of the death penalty, see McCleskey v. Kemp, 481 U.S. 279, 313, n. 37 (1987), the Court has chosen to deregulate the entire enterprise, replacing, it would seem, substantive constitutional requirements with mere aesthetics, and abdicating its statutorily and constitutionally imposed duty to provide meaningful judicial oversight to the administration of death by the States.

From this day forward, I no longer shall tinker with the machinery of death. For more than 20 years I have endeavored — indeed, I have struggled — along with a majority of this Court, to develop procedural and substantive rules that would lend more than the mere appearance of fairness to the death penalty endeavor.[1]   Rather than continue to coddle the Court's delusion that the desired level of fairness has been achieved and the need for regulation eviscerated, I feel morally and intellectually obligated simply to concede that the death penalty experiment has failed.   It is virtually self-evident to me now that no combination of procedural rules or substantive regulations ever can save the death penalty from its inherent constitutional deficiencies. The basic question — does the system accurately and consistently determine which defendants "deserve" to die? — cannot be answered in the affirmative.   It is not simply that this Court has allowed vague aggravating circumstances to be employed, see, e.g., Arave v. Creech, U.S. (1993), relevant mitigating evidence to be disregarded, see, e.g., Johnson v. Texas, U.S. (1993), and vital judicial review to be blocked, see e.g., Coleman v. Thompson, 501 U.S. (1991).   The problem is that the inevitability of factual, legal, and moral error gives us a system that we know must wrongly kill some defendants, a system that fails to deliver the fair, consistent, and reliable sentences of death required by the Constitution.[2]

I

In 1971, in an opinion which has proved partly prophetic, the second Justice Harlan, writing for the Court, observed:

> "Those who have come to grips with the hard task of actually attempting to draft means of channeling capital sentencing discretion have confirmed the lesson taught by the history recounted above. To identify before the fact those characteristics of criminal homicides and their perpetrators which call for the death penalty, and to express these characteristics in language which can be fairly understood and applied by the sentencing authority, appear to be tasks which are beyond present human ability. . . . For a court to attempt to catalog the appropriate factors in this elusive area could inhibit rather than expand the scope of consideration, for no list of circumstances would ever be really complete." McGautha v. California, 402 U.S. 183,

204, 208 (1971). In McGautha, the petitioner argued that a statute which left the penalty of death entirely in the jury's discretion, without any standards to govern its imposition, violated the Fourteenth Amendment. Although the Court did not deny that serious risks were associated with a sentencer's unbounded discretion, the Court found no remedy in the Constitution for the inevitable failings of human judgment.

A year later, the Court reversed its course completely in Furman v. Georgia, 408 U.S. 238 (1972) (per curiam, with each of the nine Justices writing separately). The concurring Justices argued that the glaring inequities in the administration of death, the standardless discretion wielded by judges and juries, and the pervasive racial and economic discrimination, rendered the death penalty, at least as administered, "cruel and unusual" within the meaning of the Eighth Amendment. Justice White explained that, out of the hundreds of people convicted of murder every year, only a handful were sent to their deaths, and that there was "no meaningful basis for distinguishing the few cases in which [the death penalty] is imposed from the many cases in which it is not." 408 U.S., at 313. If any discernible basis could be identified for the selection of those few who were chosen to die, it was "the constitutionally impermissible basis of race." Id., at 310 (Stewart, J., concurring).

I dissented in Furman. Despite my intellectual, moral, and personal objections to the death penalty, I refrained from joining the majority because I found objectionable the Court's abrupt change of position in the single year that had passed since McGautha. While I agreed that the Eighth Amendment's prohibition against cruel and unusual punishments "'may acquire meaning as public opinion becomes enlightened by a humane justice,'" 408 U.S., at 409, quoting *Weems v. United States*, 217 U.S. 349, 378 (1910), I objected to the "suddenness of the Court's perception of progress in the human attitude since decisions of only a short while ago." 408 U.S., at 410. Four years after Furman was decided, I concurred in the judgment in *Gregg v. Georgia*, 428 U.S. 153 (1976), and its companion cases which upheld death sentences rendered under statutes passed after Furman was decided. See *Proffitt v. Florida*, 428 U.S. 242, 261 (1976), and *Jurek v. Texas*, 428 U.S. 262, 279 (1976). Cf. *Woodson v. North Carolina*, 428 U.S. 280, 307 (1976), and *Roberts v. Louisiana*, 428 U.S. 325, 363 (1976).

A

There is little doubt now that Furman's essential holding was correct. Although most of the public seems to desire, and the Constitution appears to permit, the penalty of death, it surely is beyond dispute that if the death penalty cannot be administered consistently and rationally, it may not be administered at all. *Eddings v. Oklahoma*, 455 U.S., at 112. I never have quarreled with this principle; in my mind, the real meaning of Furman's diverse concurring opinions did not emerge until some years after Furman was decided. See *Gregg v. Georgia*, 428 U.S., at 189 (opinion of Stewart, Powell, and STEVENS, JJ.) ("Furman mandates that where discretion is afforded a sentencing body on a matter so grave as the determination of whether a human life should be taken or spared, that discretion must be suitably directed and limited so as to minimize the risk of wholly arbitrary and capricious action"). Since Gregg, I faithfully have adhered to the Furman holding and have come to believe that it is indispensable to the Court's Eighth Amendment jurisprudence.

Delivering on the Furman promise, however, has proved to be another matter. Furman aspired to eliminate the vestiges of racism and the effects of poverty in capital sentencing; it deplored the "wanton" and "random" infliction of death by a government with constitutionally limited power. Furman demanded that the sentencer's discretion be directed and limited by procedural rules and objective standards in order to minimize the risk of arbitrary and capricious sentences of death.

In the years following Furman, serious efforts were made to comply with its mandate. State legislatures and appellate courts struggled to provide judges and juries with sensible and objective guidelines for determining who should live and who should die. Some States attempted to define who is "deserving" of the death penalty through the use of carefully chosen adjectives, reserving the death penalty for those who commit crimes that are "especially heinous, atrocious, or cruel," see Fla. Stat." 921.141(5)(h) (Supp. 1976), or "wantonly vile, horrible or inhuman," see Ga. Code Ann." 27-2534.1(b)(7) (1978). Other States enacted mandatory death penalty statutes, reading Furman as an invitation to eliminate sentencer discretion altogether. See, e.g., N.C. Gen. Stat." 14-17 (Cum. Supp. 1975). But see *Woodson v. North Carolina*, 428 U.S. 280 (1976) (invalidating mandatory death penalty statutes). Still other States specified aggravating and mitigating factors that were to be considered by the sentencer and weighed against one another in a calculated and rational manner. See, e.g., Ga. Code. Ann." 17-10-30(c) (1982); cf. Tex. Code Crim. Proc. Ann., Art. 37.071(c)-(e) (Vernon 1981 and Supp. 1989) (identifying "special issues" to be considered by the sentencer when determining the appropriate sentence).

Unfortunately, all this experimentation and ingenuity yielded little of what Furman demanded. It soon became apparent that discretion could not be eliminated from capital sentencing without threatening the fundamental fairness due a defendant when life is at stake. Just as contemporary society was no longer tolerant of the random or discriminatory infliction of the penalty of death, see Furman, supra, evolving standards of decency required due consideration of the uniqueness of each individual defendant when imposing society's ultimate penalty. See Woodson, 428 U.S., at 301 (opinion of Stewart, Powell, and STEVENS, JJ.) referring to *Trop v. Dulles*, 356 U.S. 86, 101 (1958) (plurality opinion).

This development in the American conscience would have presented no constitutional dilemma if fairness to the individual could be achieved without sacrificing the consistency and rationality promised in Furman. But over the past two decades, efforts to balance these competing constitutional commands have been to no avail. Experience has shown that the consistency and rationality promised in Furman are inversely related to the fairness owed the individual when considering a sentence of death. A step toward consistency is a step away from fairness.

B

There is a heightened need for fairness in the administration of death. This unique level of fairness is born of the appreciation that death truly is different from all other punishments a society inflicts upon its citizens. "Death, in its finality, differs more from life imprisonment than a 100-year prison term differs from one of only a year or two." Woodson, 428 U.S., at 305 (opinion of Stewart, Powell, and STEVENS, JJ.). Because of the qualitative difference of the death penalty, "there is a corresponding difference in the need for reliability in the determination that death is the appropriate punishment in a specific case." Ibid. In Woodson, a decision striking down mandatory death penalty statutes as unconstitutional, a plurality of the Court explained: "A process that accords no significance to relevant facets of the character and record of the individual offender or the circumstances of the particular offense excludes from consideration in fixing the ultimate punishment of death the possibility of compassionate or mitigating factors stemming from the diverse frailties of humankind." Id., at 304.

While the risk of mistake in the determination of the appropriate penalty may be tolerated in other areas of the criminal law, "in capital cases the fundamental respect for humanity underlying the Eighth Amendment . . . requires consideration of the character and record of the individual offender and the circumstances of the particular offense as a constitutionally indispensable part of the process of inflicting the penalty of death." Ibid. Thus, although individualized sentencing in capital cases was not considered essential at the time the Constitution was adopted, Woodson recognized that American standards of decency could no longer tolerate a capital sentencing process that failed to afford a defendant individualized consideration in the determination whether he or she should live or die. Id., at 301.

The Court elaborated on the principle of individualized sentencing in *Lockett v. Ohio*, 438 U.S. 586 (1978). In that case, a plurality acknowledged that strict restraints on sentencer discretion are necessary to achieve the consistency and rationality promised in Furman, but held that, in the end, the sentencer must retain unbridled discretion to afford mercy. Any process or procedure that prevents the sentencer from considering "as a mitigating factor, any aspect of a defendant's character or record and any circumstances of the offense that the defendant proffers as a basis for a sentence less than death," creates the constitutionally intolerable risk that "the death penalty will be imposed in spite of factors which may call for a less severe penalty." Id., at 604-605 (emphasis in original). See also *Sumner v. Shuman*, 483 U.S. 66 (1987) (invalidating a mandatory death penalty statute reserving the death penalty for life-term inmates convicted of murder). The Court's duty under the Constitution therefore is to "develop a system of capital punishment at once consistent and principled but also humane and sensible to the uniqueness of the individual." *Eddings v. Oklahoma*, 455 U.S., at 110.

C

I believe the Woodson-Lockett line of cases to be fundamentally sound and rooted in American standards of decency that have evolved over time. The notion of prohibiting a sentencer from exercising its discretion "to dispense mercy on the basis of factors too intangible to write into a statute," Gregg, 428 U.S., at 222 (White, J., concurring), is offensive to our sense of fundamental fairness and respect for the uniqueness of the individual. In *California v. Brown*, 479 U.S. 538 (1987), I said in dissent:

> The sentencer's ability to respond with mercy towards a defendant has always struck me as a particularly valuable aspect of the capital sentencing procedure. . . . We adhere so strongly to our belief that a sentencer should have the opportunity to spare a capital defendant's life on account of compassion for the individual because, recognizing that the capital sentencing decision must be made in the context of 'contemporary values,' *Gregg v. Georgia*, 428 U.S., at 181 (opinion of Stewart, POWELL, and STEVENS, JJ.), we see in the sentencer's expression of mercy a distinctive feature of our society that we deeply value. (Id., at 562-563.)

Yet, as several Members of the Court have recognized, there is real "tension" between the need for fairness to the individual and the consistency promised in Furman. See *Franklin v. Lynaugh*, 487 U.S. 164, 182 (1988) (plurality opinion); *California v. Brown*, 479 U.S., at 544 (O'CONNOR, J., concurring); *McCleskey v. Kemp*, 481 U.S., at 363 (BLACKMUN, J., dissenting); *Graham v. Collins*, U.S., (1993) (THOMAS, J., concurring). On the one hand, discretion in capital sentencing must be "'controlled by clear and objective standards so as to produce non-discriminatory [and reasoned] application.'" Gregg, 428 U.S., at 198 (opinion of Stewart, Powell, and STEVENS, JJ.), quoting *Coley v. State*, 231 Ga. 829, 834, 204 S.E.2d 612, 615 (1974). On the other hand, the Constitution also requires that the sentencer be able to consider "any relevant mitigating evidence regarding the defendant's character or background, and the circumstances of the particular offense." *California v. Brown*, 479 U.S. 538, 544 (1987) (O'CONNOR, J., concurring). The power to consider mitigating evidence that would warrant a sentence less than death is meaningless unless the sentencer has the discretion and authority to dispense mercy based on that evidence. Thus, the Constitution, by requiring a heightened degree of fairness to the individual, and also a greater degree of equality and rationality in the administration of death, demands sentencer discretion that is at once generously expanded and severely restricted.

This dilemma was laid bare in *Penry v. Lynaugh*, 492 U.S. 302 (1989). The defendant in Penry challenged the Texas death penalty statute, arguing that it failed to allow the sentencing jury to give full mitigating effect to his evidence of mental retardation and history of child abuse. The Texas statute required the jury, during the penalty phase, to answer three "special issues"; if the jury unanimously answered "yes" to each issue, the trial court was obligated to sentence the defendant to death. Tex. Code Crim. Proc. Ann., Art. 37.071(c)-(e) (Vernon 1981 and Supp. 1989). Only one of the three issues — whether the defendant posed a "continuing threat to society" — was related to the evidence Penry offered in mitigation. But Penry's evidence of mental retardation and child abuse was a two-edged sword as it related to that special issue: "it diminished his blameworthiness for his crime even as it indicated that there [was] a probability that he [would] be dangerous in the future." 492 U.S., at 324. The Court therefore reversed Penry's death sentence, explaining that a reasonable juror could have believed that the statute prohibited a sentence less than death based upon his mitigating evidence. Id., at 326.

After Penry, the paradox underlying the Court's post-Furman jurisprudence was undeniable. Texas had complied with Furman by severely limiting the sentencer's discretion, but those very limitations rendered Penry's death sentence unconstitutional.

D

The theory underlying Penry and Lockett is that an appropriate balance can be struck between the Furman promise of consistency and the Lockett requirement of individualized sentencing if the death penalty is conceptualized as consisting of two distinct stages.[3] In the first stage of capital sentencing, the demands of Furman are met by "narrowing" the class of death-eligible offenders according to objective, fact-bound characteristics of the defendant or the circumstances of the offense. Once the pool of death-eligible defendants has been reduced, the sentencer retains the discretion to consider whatever relevant mitigating evidence the defendant chooses to offer. See *Graham v. Collins*, U.S., at (STEVENS, J., dissenting) (slip op. 3) (arguing that providing full discretion to the sentencer is not inconsistent with Furman and may actually help to protect against arbitrary and capricious 26] sentencing).

Over time, I have come to conclude that even this approach is unacceptable: It simply reduces, rather than eliminates, the number of people subject to arbitrary sentencing.[4] It is the decision to sentence a defendant to death — not merely the decision to make a defendant eligible for death — that may not be arbitrary. While one might hope that providing the sentencer with as much relevant mitigating evidence as possible will lead to more rational and consistent sentences, experience has taught otherwise. It seems that the decision whether a human being should live or die is so inherently subjective — rife with all of life's understandings, experiences, prejudices, and passions — that it inevitably defies the rationality and consistency required by the Constitution.

E

The arbitrariness inherent in the sentencer's discretion to afford mercy is exacerbated by the problem of race. Even under the most sophisticated death penalty statutes, race continues to play a major role in determining who shall live and who shall die. Perhaps it should not be surprising that the biases and prejudices that infect society generally would influence the determination of who is sentenced to death, even within the narrower pool of death-eligible defendants selected according to objective standards. No matter how narrowly the pool of death-eligible defendants is drawn according to objective standards, Furman's promise still will go unfulfilled so long as the sentencer is free to exercise unbridled discretion within the smaller group and thereby to discriminate. "'The power to be lenient [also] is the power to discriminate.'" *McCleskey v. Kemp*, 481 U.S., at 312, quoting K. Davis, Discretionary Justice 170 (1973).

A renowned example of racism infecting a capital-sentencing scheme is documented in *McCleskey v. Kemp*, 481 U.S. 279 (1987). Warren McCleskey, an African-American, argued that the Georgia 28] capital-sentencing scheme was administered in a racially discriminatory manner, in violation of the Eighth and Fourteenth Amendments. In support of his claim, he proffered a highly reliable statistical study (the Baldus study) which indicated that, "after taking into account some 230 nonracial factors that might legitimately influence a sentencer, the jury more likely than not would have spared McCleskey's life had his victim been black." 481 U.S., at 325 (emphasis in original) (Brennan, J., dissenting). The Baldus study further demonstrated that blacks who kill whites are sentenced to death "at nearly 22 times the rate of blacks who kill blacks, and more than 7 times the rate of whites who kill blacks." Id., at 327 (emphasis in original).

Despite this staggering evidence of racial prejudice infecting Georgia's capital-sentencing scheme, the majority turned its back on McCleskey's claims, apparently troubled by the fact that Georgia had instituted more procedural and substantive safeguards than most other States since Furman, but was still unable to stamp out the virus of racism. Faced with the apparent failure 29] of traditional legal devices to cure the evils identified in Furman, the majority wondered aloud whether the consistency and rationality demanded by the dissent could ever be achieved without sacrificing the discretion which is essential to fair treatment of individual defendants:

> It is difficult to imagine guidelines that would produce the predictability sought by the dissent without sacrificing the discretion essential to a humane and fair system of criminal justice. . . . The dissent repeatedly emphasizes the need for 'a uniquely high degree of rationality in imposing the death penalty'. . . . Again, no suggestion is made as to how greater 'rationality' could be achieved under any type of statute that authorizes capital punishment. . . . Given these safeguards already inherent in the imposition and review of capital sentences, the dissent's call for greater rationality is no less than a claim that a capital punishment system cannot be administered in accord with the Constitution. (Id., at 314-315, n. 37.)

I joined most of Justice Brennan's significant dissent which expounded McCleskey's Eighth Amendment claim, and I wrote separately, 30] id., at 345, to explain that McCleskey also had a solid equal protection argument under the Fourteenth Amendment. I still adhere to the views set forth in both dissents, and, as far as I know, there has been no serious effort to impeach the Baldus study. Nor, for that matter, have proponents of capital punishment provided any reason to believe that the findings of that study are unique to Georgia.

The fact that we may not be capable of devising procedural or substantive rules to prevent the more subtle and often unconscious forms of racism from creeping into the system does not justify the wholesale abandonment of the Furman promise. To the contrary, where a morally irrelevant — indeed, a repugnant — consideration plays a major role in the determination of who shall live and who shall die, it suggests that the continued enforcement of the death penalty in light of its clear and admitted defects is deserving of a "sober second thought." Justice Brennan explained:

Those whom we would banish from society or from the human community itself often speak in too faint a voice to be heard above society's demand for punishment. It is the particular role 31] of courts to hear these voices, for the Constitution declares that the majoritarian chorus may not alone dictate the conditions of social life. The Court thus fulfills, rather than disrupts, the scheme of separation of powers by closely scrutinizing the imposition of the death penalty, for no decision of a society is more deserving of the 'sober second thought.' Stone, The Common Law in the United States, 50 Harv. L. Rev. 4, 25 (1936). (Id., at 343.)

F

In the years since *McCleskey*, I have come to wonder whether there was truth in the majority's suggestion that discrimination and arbitrariness could not be purged from the administration of capital punishment without sacrificing the equally essential component of fairness — individualized sentencing. Viewed in this way, the consistency promised in *Furman* and the fairness to the individual demanded in *Lockett* are not only inversely related, but irreconcilable in the context of capital punishment. Any statute or procedure that could effectively eliminate arbitrariness from the administration of death would also restrict the sentencer's discretion to such an extent that the sentencer would be 32] unable to give full consideration to the unique characteristics of each defendant and the circumstances of the offense. By the same token, any statute or procedure that would provide the sentencer with sufficient discretion to consider fully and act upon the unique circumstances of each defendant would "throw open the back door to arbitrary and irrational sentencing." *Graham v. Collins*, U.S., at (THOMAS, J., concurring) (slip op. 17). All efforts to strike an appropriate balance between these conflicting constitutional commands are futile because there is a heightened need for both in the administration of death.

But even if the constitutional requirements of consistency and fairness are theoretically reconcilable in the context of capital punishment, it is clear that this Court is not prepared to meet the challenge. In apparent frustration over its inability to strike an appropriate balance between the Furman promise of consistency and the Lockett requirement of individualized sentencing, the Court has retreated from the field,[5] allowing relevant mitigating evidence to be discarded,[6] vague aggravating circumstances to be employed,[7] and providing 33] no indication that the problem of race in the administration of death will ever be addressed. In fact some members of the Court openly have acknowledged a willingness simply to pick one of the competing constitutional commands and sacrifice the other. See Graham, U.S., at (THOMAS, J., concurring) (calling for the reversal of Penry); *Walton v. Arizona*, 497 U.S. 639, 673 (1990) (SCALIA, J., concurring in part and concurring in the judgment) (announcing that he will no longer enforce the requirement of individualized sentencing, and reasoning that either Furman or Lockett is wrong and a choice must be made between the two). These developments are troubling, as they ensure that death will continue to be meted out in this country arbitrarily and discriminatorily, and without that "degree of respect due the uniqueness of the individual." Lockett, 438 U.S., at 605. In my view, the proper course when faced with irreconcilable constitutional commands is not to ignore one or the other, nor to pretend that the dilemma does not exist, but to admit the futility of the effort to harmonize them. This 34] means accepting the fact that the death penalty cannot be administered in accord with our Constitution.

The Court has also refused to hold the death penalty unconstitutional per se for juveniles, see *Stanford v. Kentucky*, 492 U.S. 361 (1989), and the mentally retarded, see *Penry v. Lynaugh*, 492 U.S. 302 (1989).

II

My belief that this Court would not enforce the death penalty (even if it could) in accordance with the Constitution is buttressed by the Court's "obvious eagerness to do away with any restriction on the States' power to execute whomever and however they please." Herrera, U.S., at (BLACKMUN, J., dissenting) (slip op. 18). I have explained at length on numerous occasions that my willingness to enforce the capital punishment statutes enacted by the States and the Federal Government, "notwithstanding my own deep moral reservations . . . has always rested on an understanding that certain procedural safeguards, 36] chief among them the federal judiciary's power to reach and correct claims of constitutional error on federal habeas review, would ensure that death sentences are fairly imposed." Sawyer v. Whitley, U.S., (1992) (BLACKMUN, J., concurring in the judgment) (slip op. 8-9). See also *Herrera v. Collins*, U.S., at (BLACKMUN, J., dissenting). In recent years, I have grown increasingly skeptical that "the death penalty really can be imposed fairly and in accordance with the requirements of the Eighth Amendment," given the now limited ability of the federal courts to remedy constitutional errors. Sawyer, U.S., at (BLACKMUN, J., concurring in the judgment) (slip op.1).

Federal courts are required by statute to entertain petitions from state prisoners who allege that they are held "in violation of the Constitution or the treaties of the United States." 28 U.S.C. " 2254(a). Serious review of these claims helps to ensure that government does not secure the penalty of death by depriving a defendant of his or her constitutional rights. At the time I voted with the majority to uphold the 37] constitutionality of the death penalty in *Gregg v. Georgia*, 428 U.S. 153, 227 (1976), federal courts possessed much broader authority than they do today to address claims of constitutional error on habeas review. In 1976, there were few procedural barriers to the federal judiciary's review of a State's capital sentencing scheme, or the fairness and reliability of a State's decision to impose death in a particular case. Since then, however, the Court has "erected unprecedented and unwarranted barriers" to the federal judiciary's review of the constitutional claims of capital defendants. Sawyer, U.S., at (BLACKMUN, J., concurring in the judgment) (slip op. 2). See, e.g., *Herrera v. Collins*, supra; *Coleman v. Thompson*, 501 U.S. (1991); *McCleskey v. Zant*, 499 U.S. (1991); *Keeney v. Tamayo-Reyes*, U.S. (1992) (overruling *Townsend v. Sain*, 372 U.S. 293 (1963), in part); *Teague v. Lane*, 489 U.S. 288 (1989); *Butler v. McKellar*, 494 U.S. 407 (1990).

The Court's refusal last term to afford Leonel Torres Herrera an evidentiary hearing, despite his colorable showing of actual innocence, demonstrates just how far afield the Court has strayed from its statutorily and constitutionally imposed obligations. See *Herrera v. Collins*, supra. In Herrera, only a bare majority of this Court could bring itself to state forthrightly that the execution of an actually innocent person violates the Eighth Amendment. This concession was made only in the course of erecting nearly insurmountable barriers to a defendant's ability to get a hearing on a claim of actual innocence. Ibid. Certainly there will be individuals who are actually innocent who will be unable to make a better showing than what was made by Herrera without the benefit of an evidentiary hearing.[8] The Court is unmoved by this dilemma, however; it prefers "finality" in death sentences to reliable determinations of a capital defendant's guilt. Because I no longer can state with any confidence that this Court is able to reconcile the Eighth

Amendment's competing constitutional commands, or that the federal judiciary will provide meaningful oversight to the state courts as they 39] exercise their authority to inflict the penalty of death, I believe that the death penalty, as currently administered, is unconstitutional.

III

Perhaps one day this Court will develop procedural rules or verbal formulas that actually will provide consistency, fairness, and reliability in a capital-sentencing scheme. I am not optimistic that such a day will come. I am more optimistic, though, that this Court eventually will conclude that the effort to eliminate arbitrariness while preserving fairness "in the infliction of [death] is so plainly doomed to failure that it — and the death penalty — must 40] be abandoned altogether." *Godfrey v. Georgia*, 446 U.S. 420, 442 (1980) (Marshall, J., concurring in the judgment). I may not live to see that day, but I have faith that eventually it will arrive. The path the Court has chosen lessens us all. I dissent.

Chapter 20

Hanging, Twisting in the Wind: Justice Thurgood Marshall, Lynching and the Death Penalty

David J.W. Vanderhoof

Justice Thurgood Marshall was born in the year of our Lord, 1908[1]. That year eighty-nine African-Americans were lynched in the United States.[2]

"Lynched For Theft of A Cow"
"10,000 View Body of Lynched Colored Man on Sunday"
"Sunday School Children are Among Sunday Throngs that Gaze at Half-Naked Body of Victim Brutally Murdered by White Mob in Maryland"

His parents read these headlines in their hometown newspaper, the *Baltimore Sun*,[3] year. For thirty years lynch mobs struck roughly once every three days.[4] Between 1889 and 1932, 2954 African-Americans were executed by lynch mobs,[5] a period which coincided with a newfound power and status for African Americans.[6] Four thousand, seven hundred, forty three Americans have been lynched in forty of these United States.[7]

Roots

by Emily Whittle

At the end of the Civil War
my great-grandfather walked
four hundred miles back home
to Georgia and gave his gun up.
Said he'd seen enough dead
men and beasts to cure a man
of hunting, forever.

Not long after that he stumbled in the night
upon four men in sheets
about to lynch a Negro.
In those days one knew
all one's neighbors.
He yelled, "What you plannin'
to do with that man?"
They yelled, "Kill him!"
He said, "You do, and I'll
turn your names into the
authorities, every last one of you!"
They said, "You do, and we'll shoot you, too."
They did.
The next day, he did.
And that night,
as he sat with his family
at supper,
they did.

A poetic account of a friend's oral family history

Justice Marshall was born in an era when lynchings were twice as common as legal executions.[8] At that time, unlike today, executions were public and often festive events. Ostensibly, the lynch mob intervened to purge the community of an evil in their midst. Lynching was a response to the public's demand for swift and terrible justice. I ask you to reflect on this comment by a faceless member of a lynch mob of 500 recorded by a reporter who covered the event, for it describes a sense of community service: "When we left home tonight, our wives, daughters, and sisters kissed us good bye and told us to do our duty, and we're trying to do it as citizens."[9] The members of the town watch were often dressed in white robes or other uniforms. Lynch mobs served a civic purpose.

What this town needs is a good old fashioned lynching. The real thing. With all the trimmings. It would be like going to church. Puts things in their proper perspective. Reminding everybody of who they are, where they stand. Divides the world simple and pure. Good or bad. Oppressors and oppressed. Black or white.

> John Edgar Wideman, The Lynchers 60 (1973).

Mississippi Governor James K. Vardaman once remarked that he had no conscientious objection to lynching. In fact he said that he lacked respect for any white man who would shun lynchers.[10] Lynch mobs operated with implicit state sanction, and members of the mob were seldom punished. Lynchings were often an outlet for displaced hostility of the white populace.

A lynching could be provoked by the mere allegation of a crime, or suggestion of a taboo violated. Scott Burton and William Donegan were lynched in 1908, the year Justice Marshall was born. This is their story:

> A white man was stabbed to death after he discovered a black intruder in his daughter's bedroom. The killing shook the town and after a young white woman accused a black man of attempted rape a mob of thousands descended upon the black section of town. The men pillaged black neighborhoods and decided to make an example of Burton and Donegan. Scott Burton, an elderly black barber, was chosen after he tried to defend his home and family. Dragged through the streets, he was lynched and mutilated. William Donegan, an 84 year old shoe maker was chosen because his wife of thirty years was white. The mob lynched Donegan, slashed his throat and hacked his body apart. Although 117 indictments were handed down against the mob members, only one was found guilty of any crime.[11]

This happened within shouting distance of the Liberty Bell. Well, about thirty two miles southwest. A few years later, in 1911, a mob in Coatesville, Pennsylvania lynched Zachariah Walker before a crowd estimated at 2000-5000. Walker, a mill worker, earlier in the day shot a policeman in self defense. The mob quickly tracked him down. Walker put a pistol to his head and pulled the trigger. Only wounded, he was taken to a hospital. A chant demanding a lynching rose from the crowd which formed outside. Later the mob dragged him from his hospital bed. Reporters recorded his plea, "For God's Sake, give a man a chance. I killed [the policeman] in self defense. Don't give me a crooked death because I'm not white." He was clubbed and forced onto a makeshift funeral pyre where he was burned alive. His singed fingers were later collected as relics.[12]

The future Justice Marshall was a child, young man and inquiring student during the lynching era and I expect it formed part of his impression that "justice" and "due process" were illusionary concepts for Americans of color. It was also a time when many states were reconsidering the death penalty. Public and legislative debate was vocal, confusing and results contradictory. Ten states abolished capital punishment between 1897-1917: Colorado (1897), Kansas (1907), Minnesota (1911), Washington (1913), Oregon (1914), South Dakota (1915), North Dakota (1915), Tennessee (1915), Arizona (1916) and Missouri (1917). Eight of these states reinstated the death penalty between 1901-1939: Colorado (1901), Arizona (1918), Tennessee (1919), Missouri (1919), Washington (1919), Oregon (1920), Kansas (1935) and South Dakota (1939).[13] Hugo A. Bedau, who many consider to be the dean of capital punishment researchers, has questioned the reasons for reintroducing the death penalty in states only a few years after it had been abolished but apparently was never able to determine why. He concluded his analysis with the following comment, "Surprising though it may be . . . the full story has never been told."[14] It is clear, however, that the death penalty has traditionally been administered in a racist fashion,[15] and states with the highest concentrations of non-white citizens use the death penalty most frequently.[16]

Whatever may be recorded in the transcripts of legislative debate, or the unique triggering events in the history of the death penalty of any particular state, most of the states which abolished the death penalty had very small non-white populations. Only two of these states had more than 5% minority populations. In general, states with homogeneous populations and a small minority population are more receptive to lenient or less severe criminal penalties.[17] There are exceptions.

Montana's last hanging was in 1943. It hung a black man who had confessed to killing a white woman. In 1989, a federal court halted Montana's next planned execution and questioned the plea bargain with a white co-defendant while the state refused even to negotiate with his black accomplice who the state sought to hang.[18]

The hangman's noose is not fitted solely to blacks. Between 1910 and 1916, Arizona executed only Hispanics.[19]

Lynching almost disappeared from the American landscape in the 1940's but, I suggest, its lesson has not been forgotten. In plays, novels, and poems, black writers describe this "peculiarly American ritual"[20] which tend to translate historical accounts. Lynching is an integral part of the black experience and has particular resonance to a growing death row prison population comprised mostly of minorities, the majority of whom are black. Consider its impact on a young lawyer in the formative years of his profession.

In 1946, while in Columbia, Tennessee, on NAACP business, Thurgood Marshall was rescued from a lynch mob. He was stopped on a lonely road by sheriff's officers and highway patrolman while clansmen waited nearby at the Duck River. The future Justice of the U.S. Supreme Court was rescued by an armed escort of local blacks who grabbed him from police custody. The next day they returned to the scene and found a lynch rope and noose still hanging from a tree by the river. They cut it down and gave it to Marshall for a souvenir.[21] An investigation was requested, but no officers were ever prosecuted and, even more strangely, no charges were ever brought against Marshall's black rescuers, who were well known to local police.

Senator Sam Ervin, Jr., questioning Thurgood Marshall during hearings to confirm Marshall's nomination to the Supreme Court, lamented that the *Miranda* would exclude voluntary confessions, something defense lawyer Marshall had first-hand experience of, as he had represented many clients whose "voluntary" confessions had been offered at trial. The former defense lawyer responded, "I tried a case in Oklahoma where the man 'voluntarily' confessed after he was beaten up for six days."[22]

When Thurgood Marshall joined the Supreme Court in 1967, the Constitution had not been read to limit the use of the death penalty.[23] He approached capital cases employing a skill he honed as a civil rights lawyer in the 1940's and 1950's when he learned — as good trial lawyers do who try a case with an eye on the appeal — the benefit of "building a record." And when he built that record in death penalty cases, it revealed the distance between the law's lofty guarantees and the painful reality of discrimination. In his final fifteen years on the Court, Justice Marshall examined how states administered the death penalty and he recorded the extent to which the death penalty was inevitably linked to race and class.[24]

Justice Marshall's perspective in approaching death penalty cases was that of a criminal defense lawyer; the gut-wrenching experience of having the life or liberty of a fellow human being riding on some tactical/legal choice he may have missed in Court on any given day. Justice O'Connor reflected on how Justice Marshall's stories "would, by and by, perhaps change the way I see the world."[25] He told, she recounted, of a case he lost as trial counsel for a black man accused of raping a white woman. The prosecutor offered a life sentence in exchange for a guilty plea. When told of the offer, Marshall's client exclaimed: "Plead guilty to what? Raping that woman? You gotta be kidding. I won't do it." As Justice Marshall told the story, "That's when I knew I had an innocent man. . . . The guy was found guilty and sentenced to death. But he never raped that woman." He added: "Oh well, he was just a Negro."[26] The application of 'the law' and the interpretation of constitutional rights takes place in a field and death."[27]

Perhaps the greatest gift Justice Marshall presented to the Supreme Court was his intuitive understanding that the Constitution is not an abstraction. Reading his opinions reminds us that the constitutionality of the death penalty should be measured by what states actually do, and not by some general musing about what a state could or should do. He did not rely exclusively or even primarily on his moral commitments; it was the trial lawyer's practical considerations that leap out at me when I reflect on his discussion. And I, as a white man, a generation his junior, understand his lawyerly presentation. To me it is compelling reading. As I studied to become a lawyer, as I appeared in court, I learned part of my craft from that trial lawyer on the Supreme Court. And one day, as I stood beside a small young black man waiting for the jury to take or spare his life, I understood better the lawyer's moral and ethical standard he established for me to follow.

Starting with the 1972 *Furman* decision, the Supreme Court has insisted that the death penalty be administered in a manner that would weed out arbitrariness and prejudice. A common theme of the new state death penalty statutes the Court upheld in the years after the *Furman* case was a set of rules intended to channel the jury's discretion by limiting the factors that jurors may consider in choosing a death sentence over other punishments for convicted murderers. The Court also insisted that juries be free to consider evidence the defendant might put forward in their own behalf known to most of us as mitigating factors.

Most of Justice Marshall's death penalty work, particularly his dissents from denial of certiorari in capital cases, challenged the Court's

decisions on their own terms.[28]   He attempted to demonstrate that the
death penalty, even if acceptable as a punishment in the abstract, was
not in fact being administered in a fair and nondiscriminatory manner.[29]
From 1976, when the Court first upheld the death penalty, until 1991
when Thurgood Marshall left the Court, death penalty cases invariably
included dissents by Justices Brennan, Marshall or both. In more than
2,100 cases they reiterated their opinion that the death penalty is cruel
and unusual punishment and in violation of the Eight Amendment.[30]
Their repeated dissents raise the question of morality of the law. The
death penalty is, of course, emotionally charged with moral overtones.
The position of Justices Brennan and Marshall was a legal statement.
But whose morality? To Brennan the constitution encompassed a moral
standard of "cruel and unusual punishment" which respects human
dignity which a state fails to respect when it imposes the death penalty.
The envolving stands of decency provide the substance of the Eighth
Amendment. Justice Marshall sought to influence the values of an
informed citizenry and to ask that they question the constitutionality
of the death penalty. He believed that if people just knew and understood
they would conclude that the death penalty was "shocking, unjust,
and unacceptable."[31]

On March 8, 1995, New York reinstated the death penalty and
became the 38th state with capital punishment.[32] But why? Fear of
crime has increased when our cities are becoming safer, much safer.
Yes, even New York City was safer that summer than it has been for
years. In July 1995, New York City's murder, robbery and burglary
rates plummeted to their lowest levels in a quarter century. The decline
in the murder rate — a 31.8% drop compared with last year — is
amazing. In 1995 the citizens of Baltimore, Cleveland, Houston,
Jacksonville, Los Angeles, Memphis, Milwaukee, Nashville,
Philadelphia, Pittsburgh, San Antonio, San Diego and San Francisco
all saw their murder rates drop by better than 10%. The 32% drop in
Houston's murder rate for the first six months of 1995 was slightly
better than New York's 31% slide; Phoenix and Chicago were not too
far behind. But New York's drop in virtually every crime category
was more sustained and steeper than the experience of any other major
U.S. city.[33] No city can match New York's record of a sustained and
accelerating decrease in the crime rate during the last five years. An
election promise to reinstate New York's death penalty was fulfilled
and went into effect September 1, 1995.[34]

On June 7, 1995, in its first major decision, South Africa's new
Supreme Court, in a unanimous opinion, abolished the death penalty,

underscoring the importance of the issue in a country where, for decades, executions were used not just as a weapon against common crime, but as a means of terror to enforce a system of racial separation known as apartheid. "Retribution cannot be accorded the same weight under our Constitution as the right to life and dignity. . . . It has not been shown that the death sentence would be materially more effective to deter or prevent murder than the alternative sentence of life imprisonment would be,"[35] explained one justice. "It's making us a civilized society. It shows we actually do mean business when we say we have reverence for life," said Archbishop Desmond Tutu, the Anglican primate of Southern Africa.[36]

Despite progress, racism continues to pervade the administration of the death penalty in America. A close look will identify that "disgraceful, distorting effects of racial discrimination and poverty continue to be painfully visible in the imposition of death sentences."[37] The race of the defendant may be the most important variable in applying the death penalty. If the victim is white the death penalty is four times more likely than if the victim is of another race.[38] In the United States about half of the people murdered each year are black. Yet since 1977, when a firing squad in Utah initiated our modern era of capital punishment, the overwhelming majority of people who have been executed — 85% — had killed a white person. Only 11% had killed a black person.[39]

Numerous studies have examined these apparent racial disparities and arrive at some basic conclusions:

- Disparities in death sentencing are most often related to the race of the victim.
- Bias does not necessarily occur at the most visible point of the judicial process — when juries decide whether to recommend death. Often, disparities arise from earlier decisions by prosecutors, like whether to allow the defendant to plead guilty to a lesser charge or whether to ask for the death penalty at all.
- Racial disparities are concentrated among certain kinds of murder cases which account for perhaps one-fifth to one-fourth of the total. In a majority of murders — crimes of passion, killings in barroom brawls — the death penalty is rarely imposed. In a small number of particularly grisly crimes like multiple murders, death sentences are frequent

without regard to race. But for murders that fall into a middle ground — the killing of a shopkeeper in a robbery, say, or a murder by a person with a serious felony record — prosecutors and juries are more likely to agonize over the propriety of a death sentence, and hidden biases are more likely to creep in, the studies suggest.[40]

The General Accounting Office reviewed studies which considered the impact of race and concluded that, "In 82 percent of the studies, the race of victim was found to influence the likelihood of being charged with capital murder or receiving the death penalty."[41]

Responding to the public call to get tough on crime, Congress in 1988 enacted a federal death penalty for murders committed by drug dealers. Of those targeted under this law between 1988 and 1993, 73% were black and 13% were Latino.[42] As of March 1994 all 10 federal death penalty prosecutions authorized by the Clinton administration were against black defendants.[43] Today, the United States has the world's highest known rate of incarceration.[44] The length of our prison terms has also increased as has the number of individuals on death row. The federal prison population has more than tripled since 1980. Nearly half (48%) of that population is black, although African-Americans constitute only 12% of the total U.S. population.[45] Black men in the United States are incarcerated at a rate four times that of black men during apartheid in South Africa. One out of every four young black men in this country is either imprisoned, on probation, or on parole at any given moment. Alarmingly, there are more young black men in prison and in jail than in college.[46]

Justice Marshall passed away in 1992. That year these united (but mainly our southern) states, executed 31 Americans, 40% were African Americans.[47] Was it solely because of the color of their skin or was it because of their poverty, lack of education, or race?[48]

Reflecting on 15 years of death penalty cases during his tenure on the Supreme Court, Justice Lewis F. Powell Jr., if given the opportunity, would change his vote in all capital cases in which he upheld the death penalty, including his key swing vote[49] in 1987 which rejected a race-based statistical challenge to capital punishment and his insistence in 1972 that the death penalty was not prohibited by the Constitution.[50] For he now thinks he was wrong on the whole issue, and that capital punishment should be abolished for it "serves no useful purpose."[51]

As long as Justice Marshall sat on the Supreme Court, we had persistent reminders of the failed promise of "Liberty and Justice for All."

> I remain hopeful that even if the Court is unwilling to accept the view that the death penalty is so barbaric that it is in all circumstances cruel and unusual punishment forbidden by the Eighth and Fourteenth Amendments, it may eventually conclude that the effort to eliminate arbitrariness in the infliction of that ultimate sanction is so plainly doomed to failure that it — and the death penalty — must be abandoned altogether.[52]

With the departure of Justices Marshall, Brennan and Blackmun, the human and moral tenor from the Supreme Court has been altered because its denials of review in capital cases no longer bear any special indication that a person's life is at stake. From the streets of Philadelphia, where I walk in the fading shadows of our founding fathers, I ask, what is the meaning today of "We The People" and are all equal?

Chapter 21

Capital Punishment and Offenders with Mental Retardation

Emily A. Reed

Introduction

O ffenders with mental retardation should never be sentenced to death nor executed. In order to understand why this is so, one must first understand what mental retardation is, and what its implications are or capital sentencing.

This article presents a definition of mental retardation and an explanation of the characteristics of persons with mental retardation as they relate to capital crimes. It then summarizes the reasons why offenders with mental retardation should never be put to death.

Definition of Mental Retardation

Individuals with mental retardation are special, uncomplicated people. According to the American Association on Mental Retardation, mental retardation means "significantly sub-average general intellectual functioning existing concurrently with deficits in adaptive behavior and manifested during the developmental period."[1] This definition can be divided into three parts to clarify its meaning.

The first part, "significantly sub-average general intellectual functioning," means that the retarded person has an Intelligence Quotient (IQ) score of 70 or less.[2] IQs below 70 are at least "two standard deviations below" the average person's or "mean score" for the whole population. The average American has an IQ of 100.[3] Ninety-seven to ninety-eight percent of the population has IQs of 70 or more.[4] Thus the mentally retarded fall into the bottom two to three percent of the U.S. population in intellectual functioning.

Adults with mental retardation never have a mental age greater than twelve years old. Alfred Binet, the creator of the IQ test, also developed the concept of "mental age." Mental age means that "an adult with certain types of mental deficiencies cannot function in terms of reasoning and understanding beyond the level of an average child" of a given age.[5] Adults with mental ages of children always have "a substantial mental disability."[6] By definition, they perpetually have "significant limitation in . . . effectiveness in meeting the standards of maturation, learning, personal independence, and/or social responsibility that are expected for [their] age level and cultural group."[7] Their handicap pervades "in every dimension" of their "functioning, including . . . language, memory, attention, ability to control impulsiveness, moral development, self-concept, self-perception, suggestibility, knowledge of basic information, and general motivation."[8]

The second part, "deficits in adaptive behavior," means that the retarded have behavioral problems and deficient life skills that derive from their intellectual inadequacies.[9] By definition, the mentally retarded have lower than average "ability to cope with and function in the everyday world."[10] These deficits prevent the retarded from surviving in the world without the help of an extensive familial and/or social service support system.[11]

The third part, manifestation of the handicap "during the developmental period" means that onset of the low IQ and lack of adaptive skills began prior to age twenty-two.[12]

The importance of this definition is that the prohibition of capital punishment for all mentally retarded persons *per se* hinges on the content of these elements.

Mental Retardation Attributes

In more detail, the inherent cognitive disability of persons with mental retardation is made up of multiple handicapping attributes.

First, persons with mental retardation are characterized by cognitive impairment which includes limited understanding, basic knowledge, memory, and communicative skills.[13] They have few concepts of basic facts and life. Their lack of elemental formal knowledge is often aggravated by improper childhood habilitation and schooling. Their sparse mental aptitude contributes to their inability to speak logically.[14] They are simple people.

Second, although some mentally retarded people can distinguish right from wrong, all the mentally retarded have limits in moral development and reasoning.[15]

> . . . moral reasoning ability develops in stages, incrementally over time, and is dependent on an individual's intellectual ability and developmental level. . . . Mental retardation limits the ability of individuals to reach full moral reasoning ability.[16]

Thus all individuals with mental retardation have "immature concepts of moral blameworthiness."[17]

Third, this cognitive deficit is evidenced by an inability to grasp the basic relationship between cause and effect, a lack of foresight, and an inability to foresee the consequences of actions.

Fourth, people with mental retardation lack intellectual flexibility, a deficit which prevents them from learning from their past mistakes. They have "a pattern of persisting in behaviors even after they [such behaviors] have proven counterproductive or unsuccessful."[18]

Fifth, the mentally retarded have short attention spans and lack full impulse control.[19] These problems lead to deficits in "attention focus and selectivity in the attention process." [20] Lack of ability to attend leads to impulsiveness. They act on "strong emotion without the intervention of judgment."[21]

Conversely, they lack the *mens rea* needed to formulate fully the specific intent to commit a criminal act. Under the concept of diminished capacity, their limited understanding of their own culpability circumscribes their liability and blameworthiness so that their degree of guilt is never total or complete.[22]

Thus although there are variations in the degree of mental retardation, and the severe and profoundly retarded[23] have greater disabilities than the mild and moderately retarded,[24] ALL mentally retarded people are below the threshold of normal intellectual and adaptive functioning. Even those with IQs in the 60-70 range have low intellectual capacity.

It is important to say in passing that the word "mild" is an unfortunate and misleading choice of words for persons with IQs in the 55-70 range. Whereas mild is meant to indicate the degree of disability relevant to the other categories of mental retardation, it inadvertently connotes a meaning of not being qualitatively different from normal intelligence. In fact, however, persons in the mild range of mental retardation have real deficits in intellectual and adaptive behavior which grievously limit their life abilities.[25] As a prominent member of the Association for Retarded Citizens said, "Why don't we talk about amputation and say that a person is mildly amputated if they lost one leg?"[26]

Even in the upper range of mild retardation (65-70 IQ), the mentally retarded lack the capacity to make adequate and sufficient distinctions between right and wrong. Persons with mild retardation are capable of completing at the most about the sixth grade,[27] and when they reach chronological maturity, they require "guidance and assistance when under unusual social or economic stress."[28] A Georgia district court's opinion illustrates these points. The court gave a straightforward explanation of the limitations of accused murderer, William A. Smith, IQ 65, that is, in the high mild category. It clarified that the defendant "had poor reading and verbal skills and that his memory, reasoning ability, and other skills . . . were severely impaired."[29] Similarly, persons with moderate retardation can complete about the second grade. As adults they require "supervision and guidance when subjected to even mild social or economic stress."[30]

Based on these characteristics and the definition of mental retardation iterated above, thirteen arguments can be made as to why capital punishment should be banned for all offenders with mental retardation. The following sections delineate these arguments.

Culpability and the **Per Se** *Definition*

That individuals with mental retardation do not commit crimes in any greater numbers than the general population and that there is no direct causal link between mental retardation and criminality is now widely accepted among the criminal justice community and experts in mental disabilities.[31] When the mentally retarded do commit crimes, their lack of understanding of causality and consequences, their impairments in general comprehension and cognition, their impulsiveness, deficits in ethical and moral reasoning ability, and diminished degree of deliberateness in acting, *per se* prevent persons with mental retardation from being fully culpable for their criminal actions. Without full culpability, offenders with mental retardation can never merit the full punishment of death.

Disproportionality

Execution is the utmost of punishments. The Constitution requires that an offender and the characteristics of the offense be equal to the highest degree of culpability for death to be a proportionate sanction. Because full culpability is extremely difficult to assess with certainty, and the penalty is bitter and final, only about one percent of murderers are sentenced to death. Only a small portion of these are actually executed.

By definition, all persons with mental retardation are in the bottom two percent of the population in intellectual functioning. Because of their limited capabilities, they can never be in the top one percent of defendants who are most culpable and therefore deserving of execution. The most severe punishment is disproportionate to the least functioning citizens. The cleavage between the two is so wide that no individual can simultaneously be in both categories.

Deterrence

Punishment serves the purpose of deterring folks from criminal activity for fear of it. Special deterrence refers to deterrence of specific individuals. Capital punishment of the murderer is the epitome of deterrence because the offender is gone from life and can no longer commit crimes.

However, life imprisonment deters individuals equally as well by incapacitation and separation from society. It honors humanity and the American constitutional emphasis on civil rights and liberties. It is more benevolent than execution.

On a second level, punishing criminals is said to deter the general public from committing crimes. The death penalty aims to divert both the body politic and people with mental retardation in general from future murders.

Deterrence assumes that human beings act rationally. They see what happens to the murderer and avoid killing to avoid being killed. The general public undoubtedly understands this deterrence relationship, but potential murderers do not universally act on it. Murders are frequently committed in the heat of passion without reasoning about consequences. If murderers think about it at all, they believe that they will get away with it or, if caught, at most serve a few years in prison. As death sentence appeals take longer and longer and the certainty of punishment diminishes, the general deterrence value of capital punishment deteriorates. Assuming deterrence works at all for the general public, taking the murderer who is mentally retarded out of the small pool of those executed would have little effect on it.

Where a potential murderer with mental retardation exists, capital punishment has marginal deterrence value. Persons with mental retardation lack the intellectual capacity to understand the deterrence relationship. They have no conception of whether murderers are or are not executed in their state. Even if deterrence could be fully understood by individuals who have mental retardation, their diminished impulse control prevents them from tailoring their actions to their understanding.

Execution of offenders with mental retardation does not work to deter the general public or the retarded. It does deter the murderer with mental retardation who is executed, but life imprisonment better serves other goals of society.

Retribution

Retribution, the theory of "just desserts," calls for a life for a life. However, modern religions and spirituality teach kindness and forgiveness, mercy and a gentler philosophy. Exacting death from the mentally handicapped is barbaric vengeance unworthy of a civilized and humanitarian nation.

Just desserts requires only that the scales of crime and punishment be equal. The most serious crime should receive the most severe penalty that society authorizes. Nothing in the desserts theory requires that execution be that punishment. At the top of the scale, justice is served equally as well by life imprisonment as by the death penalty. Life in prison is no longer (if it formerly was) a crueler punishment than execution, because prison systems are recognizing and accommodating the needs of inmates who have mental retardation.

When vengeance and retribution are applied to the handicapped, they are barbaric acts unworthy of an advanced, civilized society. They serve no other purpose than the needless infliction of pain on the bewildered.

Societal Consensus

The Supreme Court used the methodology of relying on lack of state legislature activity and inconclusive public opinion to refuse to ban the death penalty for persons with mental retardation in the landmark case of *Penry v. Lynaugh* decided in 1989.[32]

This method makes the court little more than a mirror of societal and political consensus, while its constitutional and historical role is far greater, that of the Final Arbitrator of legal principles and the Constitution itself. By relying on societal consensus or lack thereof, it abrogates its substantive constitutional role.

Assuming *arguendo* that the methodology has validity, the Court erred in its assessment of societal consensus. A plethora of objective and convincing evidence exists that the American people do not want offenders with mental retardation to be executed. Sources for this evidence include public opinion polls, the development of habilitative programs for persons with mental retardation, sentencing practices, case law, and federal statutes.

Authority

All authorities and experts in the field of mental retardation and the law hold that people with mental retardation should never be executed. These distinguished professional authorities include the American Association on Mental Retardation, nine other mental disability support and advocacy groups who joined in filing an *amicus* brief in the *Penry* case, and the American Bar Association. The Supreme

Court, a generalist policy-making body with only limited knowledge of mental retardation, ignored the expertise of the proven authorities in the field when it authorized the *Penry* penalty. In doing so, it made a critical policy error.

Statistics

Individuals who are mentally retarded comprise approximately two percent of the general population in the United States, yet they are far greater proportions of correctional populations, including those given death sentences and those executed. The killer who has mental retardation, most frequently Black and poor, is typically defended by inadequate counsel untutored in the debilitating characteristics of mental retardation and unskilled in the defense of capital cases. In a nation based on the protection of minority rights from tyrannical majorities, it is unworthy for a virtually unprotected minority, people with mental retardation, to receive the most severe punishment of a majoritarian society in greater proportion than other criminals.

Mitigation

Most states' capital sentencing statutes and the Supreme Court have held that the mitigating effects of mental retardation must be elucidated at trial because these effects are relevant and essential to the determination of an equitable and proportionate punishment. Each factor of mitigation associated with the nature of mental retardation must be weighed independently, and the accumulated weight of all such factors creates a preponderance of evidence substantial enough to establish a presumption of life for the offenders with mental retardation.

However, aggravating factors can also be introduced to counterbalance mitigation. When such factors as the brutality of a crime or the offender's future dangerousness are vividly portrayed to the court and jury, these factors may outweigh the mitigation of mental retardation. This is especially true if mental retardation is presented and viewed as increasing the defendant's threat to society, that is, as an aggravating rather than mitigating factor. Such an equivocal consideration of the nature of mental retardation, that is, viewing it as aggravating because of future dangerousness, or mitigating because of diminished culpability, is arbitrary and capricious. The Supreme Court's requirements for revision of death penalty statutes in the 1970s were targeted precisely at removing such wanton discretion from sentencing authorities. Under the *Penry* decision, that arbitrary discretion has been restored.

Thus case-specific remedies are never sufficient to guarantee the protection of the rights of defendants with mental retardation because they permit arbitrary discretion in the determination of the mitigating or aggravating quality of mental retardation. When the death penalty is applied in this way, it denies fundamental due process to the defendant and is cruel and unusual punishment prohibited by the Eighth Amendment.

Child Execution

Children are the little people aged twelve or under. They aren't teenagers yet. Alas, the wonder, naiveté and innocence of childhood end when teenage begins.

Childhood characteristics include less experience, less education, less perception, less responsibility for actions, less aptitude to evaluate actions' consequences, more susceptibility to peer pressure and emotional influences than adults.[33] Children have a lesser ability to constrain their conduct and to plan for the long term.[34] Even though children by tradition are held to know right from wrong by the age of seven,[35] they are incapable of acting with the same degree of culpability as adults or even teenagers. American society's indisputable refusal to execute young children[36] is predicated on these characteristics and the fact that children's "irresponsible conduct is not as morally reprehensible as that of" adults.[37] Thus, it is totally improper to impose the adult penalty of capital punishment on children.

As an advanced and humanitarian civilization grounded in law and constitution, the United States absolutely prohibits[38] strapping a child of twelve or under into the electric chair and sending mega-volts through him until he jerks uncontrollably and dies. Although the death penalty may be applied to teenagers as young as sixteen at the time of the murder,[39] it is never imposed on children twelve or younger. Minors younger than teens are not executed in this country because it defies common decency and social mores to put children to death, however reprehensible the crime. Society does not want to execute the first grader who drowns his baby sisters in the bathtub, carves them into turkey soup with a kitchen knife, and fiendishly says they deserved it for tormenting him.

Similarly, adults with mental retardation are functionally children in fully grown bodies. Mentally retarded persons are childlike "in every morally relevant way."[40] Early case law recognized this factor even in the nineteenth century, long before the concept of "mental age" was developed to describe the phenomenon.[41]

The concept of mental age is used to delineate the level of intellectual development in terms of chronological age. Persons with mental retardation never have a mental age greater than twelve.[42] Their functional childhood is defined precisely like chronological childhood — twelve years old or younger. Like children, the mentally retarded have immature intellects, diminished understanding, and childish behavior patterns. Like children, they have underdeveloped powers to "form criminal intent."[43] Like children, they always lack full intentional abilities.

Because children are ultimately never held criminally responsible nor executed, neither should people with mental retardation be, whatever their chronological age. Whether their developmental age is lesser or greater within the childhood range, that is, whether they are mentally seven or ten or twelve, persons with mental retardation should not be held criminally liable like adults in the capital sentencing process, just as children of these ages are not so held. Mentally retarded functional childhood stands in its own right as a reason not to execute persons with mental retardation. To execute a mentally retarded functional child who commits a brutal murder is just as socially intolerable and cruel and unusual punishment as executing the seven or ten or twelve year old.

On May 24, 1990, Senator Joseph Biden, sponsor of the Omnibus Crime Bill of 1990, eloquently summarized this logic as he pled before the U.S. Senate for passage of the prohibition of the death penalty clause in the federal anti-crime bill. In an impassioned plea he stated:

> For God's sake, if we acknowledge you should not put children to death, acknowledge that we should not as a nation put to death the mentally retarded. . . .
>
> The Supreme Court says it is all right to put mentally retarded people to death. Just because the Supreme Court said we can, that does not mean we should. . . . My God, what have we come to?[44]

Right from Wrong

Whether people with mental retardation know right from wrong and can be executed on the basis of this knowledge has been legally debated for at least two centuries. The first legal guideline for judging this issue, the M'naghten rule, held that those who cannot distinguish right from wrong cannot be held criminally responsible. Gradually M'naghten was limited to the criminally insane, and persons with mental retardation were excluded.

In 1954, dissatisfaction with this formula led to the adoption of the Durham test. Durham stated that mental illness, a curable condition, must be distinguished from mental defect, which includes the lifelong condition of mental retardation. Crimes resulting from mental defect have diminished culpability.

However, in 1962 in *McDonald v. United States*,[45] the Durham test was again narrowed, and juries and judges were left to determine the content of mental defect based on expert testimony. Establishing the fact of mental retardation would not automatically validate reduced criminal responsibility.

Disillusioned with judicial interpretation of the right-from-wrong issue, the American Law Institute subsequently adopted a diminished culpability standard as a part of the Model Penal Code. It stated that a person with mental retardation is not criminally culpable if he or she lacks the substantial capacity to appreciate an action's criminality because of mental defect. People with mental retardation cannot entertain general criminal intent.

The American Bar Association's Mental Health Standards carry this interpretation even further. They explicitly state that mental defect refers to mental retardation, and an offender with mental retardation is not criminally responsible if he or she cannot appreciate the wrongfulness of his or her actions. Under the ABA rule, a person with mental retardation is treated precisely the same as a mentally ill person. Neither can be executed because of their diminished capacities and culpability. Thus it seems clear that a person who cannot distinguish right from wrong at all cannot be executed.

The issue then becomes whether those offenders with mental retardation who are believed to understand the lawlessness of their actions can be executed. Mental retardation experts hold that persons with mental retardation never have full understanding of the difference between right and wrong. Even those who do have some elemental comprehension of this moral standard should never be given the death penalty because their understanding is incomplete. The killer with mental retardation can be held responsible for his actions equally as well by life imprisonment, a more humane solution to this dilemma.

Most recently, the U.S. Senate made a clear-cut and decisive determination of the issue in the passage of the Crime Control Act of 1990. Key senators stated the universal premise that children are never executed even though they traditionally can distinguish right from wrong by age seven. Despite the Supreme Court's allowance of the execution of teenagers as young as fifteen, the Senate would not tolerate such cruelty. It supported banning these executions and all those of even younger children in the 1990 Crime Control Act.

Similarly, persons with mental retardation who never have a mental age beyond twelve should never be executed. They are still children in mind and spirit even if they primitively understand the difference between right and wrong.

Multiple Claims

Critics contend that banning the mentally retarded death penalty will allow killers who are in fact criminally responsible to avoid the death penalty. They say that multiple claims of mental retardation will be made by indigent defendants. This will create an enormous taxpayer burden because public payment of mental retardation evaluations will be required. There are several answers to these multiple claims arguments.

First, although multiple claims may be made, the prosecution will argue against this, and the jury will determine whether the defendant fits the definition of mental retardation, as in all contentions made by the defense in the American system of adjudication.

Further, no one can feign mental retardation. It is a so apparent and distinguishable lifelong condition that the U.S. Senate, in drafting the 1990 Crime Control Act, determined that mental retardation does not even need to be defined.

Practically, even though expensive evaluations will be required when a mental retardation claim is made, these will be limited to capital cases. Funding for evaluations and defense of indigent defendants is increasingly available from *pro bono* sources.

Finally, the contention that the cost to the public is too much to bear is philosophically specious. Where life or death is at issue, the cost of protecting the rights of the accused is never too much to pay. Society is willing to sustain the cost of years of appeals to insure that the rights of the condemned are protected when the death penalty is applied. It should be no less willing to pay a relatively small amount up-front to avoid such greater costs later.

Mainstreaming, Individualism and the "Right to Execution"

Some people who deal with people with mental retardation say they do not want to see them treated differently from anyone else. If we allow execution of the non-mentally retarded, then we should also allow it for individuals with mental retardation.

Inclusion in the American Dream for people with mental retardation does not include the "right to execution." Mainstreaming into American life of individuals with mental retardation is to allow them to enjoy all the benefits and privileges of society that non-handicapped citizens enjoy. It does not include the right to negative benefits or costs, deprivations or punishments, especially the worst punishment society can hand out, execution.

There is no right to be executed for offenders with mental retardation because execution is not a benefit, privilege or right. It is the deprivation of a right, the right to live.

Treating persons with mental retardation like everyone else in terms of execution is continuation of the discrimination and deprivation of the rights of the mentally handicapped that has historically existed. People with mental retardation have long been given the worst of treatment. Mainstreaming and treating them like everyone else is to stop this. It is to treat people with mental retardation like everyone else on the positive side of rights, not on the deprivation of rights.

Such a movement to promote individual treatment, although well-meaning, is a dangerous thing. There are unintended negative consequences associated with it. It carries the threat of destroying the hard-won statutory and constitutional protections that identification of minorities as legal classes has come to mean. Without such protections, the floodgates would open for denial of the civil rights of defendants with mental retardation and renewed massive discrimination against them.

Georgia

A final argument made against banning the death penalty holds that the lead of an unsophisticated Deep South state like Georgia, the first to ban the death penalty for persons with mental retardation, should not be followed by more progressive states outside the South.

This is a superficial argument based on prejudice. The issue should be decided on the merits, not on where the concept was first implemented. The death penalty applied to people with mental retardation falls unequally on minorities, and Georgia has deliberately taken steps to remedy this.

The argument is in another sense moot since the federal government and several other states have also banned the mentally retarded death penalty.

Georgia became the trail blazer because its citizens were appalled at the execution of Jerome Bowden in 1986. Other states can avoid the same mistake of having the injustice of an execution of a person with mental retardation poignantly brought home to it. Other states can avoid Georgia's error by emulating its legislative and judicial remedies before, rather than after, they face the chilling reality of a mentally retarded execution.

Endnotes

Chapter 1

1. John Laurence, *A History of Capital Punishment*, (N.Y.: The Citadel Press, 1960), 1-3
2. Michael Kronenwetter, *Capital Punishment: A Reference Handbook*, (Santa Barbara, CA: ABC-CLIO, Inc., 1993), 71
3. *Capital Punishment:...,* p. 72
4. *Capital Punishment:...,* p. 72; *A History of Capital ...,* 4-9
5. *A History of Capital...,* 9-14
6. *Capital Punishment:...,* 72-73
7. Hugo Adam Bedau, *The Death Penalty in America*, (N.Y.: Oxford University Press, 1982)
8. *The Death Penalty in America*, 7
9. Phillip English Mackey, *Voices Against Death: American Opposition to Capital Punishment*, 1787-1975, (N.Y.: Burt Franklin & Co., Inc., 1976), xi-xii
10. *The Death Penalty in America*, 7
11. *Voices Against Death*, 7-8
12. Cesare Beccaria, *On Crimes and Punishment*, trans. Henry Paolucci, (Indianapolis: Bobbs-Merrill, 1963).
13. *Voices Against Death*, xvi-xvii
14. *Voices Against Death*, xix-xxv
15. *Voices Against Death*, xvii-xviii
16. *Voices Against Death*, xxx-xxxi
17. *The Death Penalty in America*, 15
18. *Voices Against Death*, xxxii-xxxiv, xli
19. *Voices Against Death*, xlvii-xlix
20. *The Death Penalty in America*, 17
21. FBI Uniform Crime Report 1992; The Sentencing Project.

Chapter 2

1. See Ex Parte Grayson, Ala. Supr., 479 So.2d 76,78-80 (1985).
2. See *Goodwin v. Balkcom*, 11th Cir., 684 F.2d 794, 805-10 (1982).
3. *McCleskey v. Kemp*, 481 U.S. at 325 (Brennan, J., dissenting).
4. See *McCollum v. North Carolina*, No. 93-7200, cert now pending before this court.
5. *McCollum v. North Carolina*, No. 93-7200 (Blackmun, J., dissenting from the denial of certiorari).

Chapter 8
Racist Beliefs

Arguments

*   **For David Dawson** (Counsel of Record, Bernard J. O'Donnel, Assistant
    Public Defender, Office of the Public Defender, 820 North French Street,
    Wilmington, DE 19801; telephone (302)577-3220):

    Dawson's sentence of death is invalid because the state of Delaware
    asserted his constitutionally protected beliefs as an aggravating
    circumstance supporting the sentence.

*   **For the State of Delaware** (Counsel of Record, Gary A. Myers, Deputy
    Attorney General, Delaware Department of Justice, 1 South Race Street,
    PO Box 508, Georgetown, DE 19947; telephone (302)856-5353):

    Neither the First Amendment nor the due process clause prevents a
    sentencing jury from considering all evidence reflecting on the capital
    offender's character, including evidence that he had embraced a racist
    prison gang.

Amicus Briefs
In Support of David Dawson

A joint brief by the American Civil Liberties Union, the ACLU of
Delaware, and the National Association of Criminal Defense Lawyers
(Counsel of Record, Michael A. Bamberger; Sonnenschein Nath &
Rosenthal, 900 Third Avenue, New York, NY 10022; telephone (212)891-
2000)

In Support of the State of Delaware

The United States of America (Counsel of Record, Kenneth W. Starr,
Department of Justice, Washington DC 20530; telephone (202) 514-2217.

Chapter 8 Notes

1. *Penry v. Lynaugh* 492 U.S. 302 (1989); *Skipper v. South Carolina*, 476
    U.S. 1 (1986); *Eddings v. Oklahoma*, 455 U.S. 104 (1982).
2. *McCleskey v. Kemp*, 481 U.S. 279 (1987); *Pulley v. Harris*, 465 U.S.
    37 (1984); *Gregg v. Georgia*, 428 U.S. 153 (1976) (plurality opinion).
3. *Frisby v. Shultz*, 487 U.S. 474 (19988)
4. *Texas v. Johnson*, 491 U.S. 397 (1989)
5. *NAACP v. Button*, 371 U.S. 415 (1963).
6. 462 U.S. 862 (1983).
7. 581 A.2d 1078 (Del. 1990).

8. *Brandenburg v. Ohio*, 395 U.S. 444 (1969)
9. *NAACP v. Button*, 371 U.S. 415 (1963
10. *Texas v. Johnson*, 491 U.S. 397 (1989).
11. *Texas v. Johnson; United States v. Eichman*, 110 S.Ct. 2404 (1990).
12. *Eddings v. Ohio*, 438 U.S. 586 (1978) (plurality opinion).
13. 462 U.S. 862 (emphasis added).

Chapter 9

1. EX, 21; 23-24
2. Mt. 5:39

Chapter 10

Arguments

• **For Derrick Morgan** (Counsel of Record, Allen H. Andrews, III, Assistant Defender, Office of the State Appellate Defender, Supreme Court Unit, PO Box 5720, 400 South Ninth Street, STE 101, Springfield, IL 62705; telephone (217)782-1989):

The trial court's refusal to ask whether potential jurors would automatically impose a death sentence if the convicted petitioner of murder violated due process and the Sixth Amendment guarantee of an impartial jury.

• **For the State of Illinois** (Counsel of Record, Renee G. Goldfarb, Assistant State's Attorney, Cook County State's Attorney Office, 309 Richard J. Daley Center, Chicago, IL 60602; telephone (312)443-5496):

1.   The Sixth and Fourteenth Amendments should not include a specific requirement that state court judges question jurors on whether they would always return a death penalty verdict upon finding the a defendant guilty of murder.
2.   Voir dire, not easily the subject of appellate review, should be left to the discretion of the trial judges.
3.   Morgan's suggestion that he is entitled to life qualify prospective jurors by asking the inverse of the Witherspoon question is erroneous in light of this Court's holdings and in light of modern death penalty legislation's.

Amicus Briefs
In Support of Derrick Morgan
The American Civil Liberties Union and the American Civil Liberties Union of Illinois (Counsel of Record, Robert L. Graham; Jenner & Block, One IBM Plaza, Chicago, IL 60611; telephone (312)222-9350

Chapter 10 Notes

1. *Wardius v. Oregon*, 412 U.S. 470 (1973); *Turney v. Ohio*, 273 U.S. 522 (1927)
2. *Ristaino v. Ross*, 424 U.S. 589 (1976); *Fay v. New York*, 332 U.S. 288 (1947)
3. *Turner v. Murray*, 476 U.S. 28 (1986) (plurality opinion); *Irvin v. Dowd*, 366 U.S. 717 (1961)
4. *People v. Morgan*, 568 N.E.2d 755 (Ill. 1991)
5. *Skipper v. State*, 363 S.E.2d 835 (Ga. 1988); *Stanford v. Commonwealth*, S.W.2d 781 (Ky. 1987) ("We do not disagree with defendant that he had a right to life qualify the jury."); *State v. Norton*, 675 P.2d 577 (Utah 1983) ("The court should inquire, when so requested by the defendant, whether there are any jurors whose convictions would make them feel compelled to vote for capital punishment for all persons convicted of murder."); *Patterson v. Commonwealth*, 283 S.E. 2d 212 (Va. 1981) (fairness requires that the defendant in a capital case be allowed to "life qualify" prospective jurors); *Poole v. State*, 194 So.2d 903 (Fla. 1967); *State v. Henry*, 198 So. 910 (La. 1940)
6. *Mu'min v. Virginia*, 111 S.Ct. 1899 (1991)

Chapter 13

1. See *Sentencing for Life: Americans Embrace Alternatives to the Death Penalty 6*, Death Penalty Information Center (April 1993).
2. Hearings on innocence and the death penalty were also held before the Senate Judiciary Committee on April 1, 1993.
3. The principal sources for this information are news articles, M. Radelet, H. Bedau, & C. Putnam, *In Spite of Innocence* (1992), H. Bedau & M. Radelet, *Miscarriages of Justice in Potentially Capital Cases*, 40 Stanford L. Rev. 21 (1987), and the files of the National Coalition to Abolish the Death Penalty.
4. M. Radelet, H. Bedau, & C. Putnam, *In Spite of Innocence* 121 (1992).
5. *Id.* at 124-125. The juries at both trials were all white.
6. *Id.* at 134.
7. See also Davies, *White Lies: Rape, Murder, and Justice Texas Style* (1991).
8. See P. Applebome, "Black Man Freed After Years on Death Row in Alabama," *The New York Times*, March 3, 1993 at A1.
9. See "Five Years on Death Row," *The Washington Post*, March 6, 1993, at A20.
10. See P. Applebome, note 11 above, at B11.
11. *Martinez-Macias v. Collins*, 979 F.2d 1067 (5th Cir. 1992).
12. For a list of death row inmates who were reprieved within 72 hours of their scheduled executions, See Bedau & Radelet, at 72.

13. M. Lacey & S. Hubler, "L.A. Awards Two Freed Inmates $7 Million," *Los Angeles Times*, Jan 27, 1993, at B1.
14. C. Carmody, "The Brady Rule: Is it Working?," *The National Law Journal*, May 17, 1993 at 1.
15. See, e.g., S. Skowron, "New DNA Testing Provides Hope for Some Inmates," *The Los Angeles Times*, July 4, 1993, at A26 (Maryland's time limit for admitting new evidence is one year after the judgment becomes final).
16. See R. Marcus, "Execution Stalled on 11th Hour Claim of Innocence," *The Washington Post*, Feb 25, 1992, at A3: "Lawyers for the state of Texas and a death row prisoner engaged in a last-minute sprint through the federal court system over the execution, which had been scheduled to take place before sunrise." The execution did not take place that night because a Texas state court decided to issue a stay. Herrera's case was argued before the Supreme Court on Oct. 7, 1992. The Court decided Herrera was not entitled to a hearing on his innocence claims, and he was executed in May, 1993.
17. M. Allen, "Coleman is Electrocuted," *Richmond Times-Dispatch*, May 21, 1992 at A11.
18. *Coleman v. Thompson*, 111 S. Ct. 2546 (1991).
19. See e.g., J. Smolowe, "Must This Man Die?" *Time Magazine*, May 18, 1992 at 41.
20. See Bedau, et al., supra, at 68.
21. *Id.* at 56-57.
22. *Id.* at 128.
23. See G. Small, "Nine Year Prison Nightmare Comes to an End as Accused Killer is Exonerated," *The Baltimore Sun*, June 29, 1993, at 1A.
24. See also P. Valentine, "Jailed for Murder, Freed by DNA," *The Washington Post*, June 29, 1993, at A1.
25. See *A Study of Representation in Capital Cases in Texas*, The Spangenberg Group 1993. at vi ("the rate of compensation provided to court-appointed attorneys in capital cases is absurdly low and does not cover the cost of providing representation").
26. See, e.g., S. Bright, "In Defense of Life, Enforcing the Bill of Rights on Behalf of Poor, Minority, And Disadvantaged Persons Facing the Death Penalty," 57 *Missouri L. Rev* 849, (1992).
27. See Subcommittee hearings May 22, June 27, and July 17, 1991.
28. See, e.g. *Brecht v. Abrahamson*, 123 L.Ed.2d 353 (1992) (relaxing the standard in federal habeas for finding error to be harmless).
29. See *Herrera v. Collins*, slip op. No. 91-7328 (Jan 25, 1993), at 19, n.8.
30. *Id.* at 19-20, n. 9-11.
31. See D. Savage, "Court Urged to OK Execution Despite Evidence," *Los Angeles Times*, Oct. 8, 1992, at A1: "'Let's say you have a videotape which conclusively shows the suspect is innocent,' said Justice Anthony M. Kennedy, addressing the state's attorney. 'Is it a federal constitutional violation to execute the person?'

'No. It would not be violative of the Constitution,' replied Texas Assistant Attorney Gen. Margaret P. Griffey."

32. See *Murray v. Giarratano*, 492 U.S. 1 (1989) (states not required to provide counsel to indigent death row prisoners after direct appeal). Once a case moves into federal habeas litigation, federal law allows for the appointment of counsel but crucial issues may have been waived before then.

33. See R. Smothers, "A Shortage of Lawyers to Help the Condemned," *The New York Times*, June 4, 1993, at A21; see also H. Chiang, "Judge Sees 'Time Bomb' on Death Row," *San Francisco Chronicle*, Aug. 18, 1993 (105 of the 370 Calif. death row inmates have no attorneys).

34. See *Herrera*, supra, at 20.

35. *Graham v. Collins*, 122 L.Ed.2d 260 (1993).

36. *Coleman v. Thompson*, 111 S. Ct. 2546 (1991).

37. See *McCleskey v. Zant*, 111 S. Ct. 1454 (1991).

38. See *Herrera*, supra, at 23, n. 14.

39. See "Clemency: Fail-safe System of Political Football?" *The Oakland Tribune*, June 27, 1993 (41 additional clemencies have been granted for judicial expediency, to save time and expense after court rulings requiring a new sentencing).

40. See, e.g., J. Berry, "Governors Shy Away From Death Row Pardons," *The Dallas Morning News*, Aug. 15, 1993, at 1J.

41. See "New Turns in Case of a Texan Scheduled to Die," *The New York Times*, Aug. 13, 1993 (stay was ordered pending appeal of judge's order).

42. B. Reeves, "Execution Stay Upheld," *The Lincoln* (Nebraska) *Star*, Aug. 6, 1992, at 1.

43. *Herrera v. Collins*, slip op. No. 91-7328-Dissent (Jan. 25, 1993) (emphasis in original), at 11.

Chapter 17

APPENDIX

Methodology Used In Poll

The latest poll results cited in this Report are based on a nationwide telephone survey of 1,000 registered voters conducted between February 28 and March 1, 1993 by Greenberg/Lake and the Tarrance Group. The sample was distributed based upon voter turnout in the last three presidential elections. A sample of this type is likely to yield a margin of error of +/-3. 1 %.

Chapter 17 Notes

1. H. Zeisel & A. Gallup, "Death Penalty Sentiment in the United States," 5 *Journal of Quantitative Criminology* 285, 287 (1989).

2. See, e.g., *Death Penalty Sentencing: Research Indicates Pattern of Racial Disparities*, U.S. General Accounting Office, at 5 (1990).

3. A. Gallup & F. Newport, *Death Penalty Support Remains Strong, But Most Feel Unfairly Applied*, The Gallup Poll News Service, June 26, 1991, at 4.

4. See, e.g., *Millions Misspent: What Politicians Don't Say About the High Costs of the Death Penalty*, The Death Penalty Information Center (1992).

5. J. Horgan, Scientific American, July 1990, at 17 ("More than a century of research in the United States and other countries . . . has produced no evidence that capital punishment reduces the rate of murder or other violent crime.").

6. See, e.g., Tabak & Lane, "The Execution of Injustice: A Cost and Lack-of-Benefit Analysis of the Death Penalty," 23 *Loyola of Los Angeles Law Review* 59 (1989).

7. Radelet, Bedau, & Putnam, *In Spite of Innocence: Erroneous Convictions in Capital Cases* (1992).

8. *Id.* at 271.

9. *Herrera v. Collins*, No. 91-7328, slip opinion, at 26 (Jan. 25, 1993).

10. See Pierce & Radelet, "The Role and Consequences of the Death Penalty in American Politics," 18 *N.Y.U. Review of Law & Social Change* 711, 718 (1990-1991).

11. See P. Applebome, "Black Man Freed After Years on Death Row in Alabama," *The New York Times*, March 3, 1993, at A1.

12. CBS-TV News show "60 Minutes," broadcast Nov. 22, 1992, showed the case unraveling with one of the chief witnesses saying he lied at the trial.

13. For other examples of prosecutorial misconduct in death penalty trials, see *Killing Justice: Government Misconduct and the Death Penalty*, Death Penalty Information Center (1992).

14. Information regarding the various polls is on file with the Death Penalty Information Center

15. W. Bowers & M. Vandiver, *New Yorkers Want an Alternative to the Death Penalty*, Executive Summary, appendix summarizing other state polls (1991).

16. Zeisel & Gallup, note 7, at 290.

17. M. Leary, *Counter-Trend to Death Penalty Emerging in California*, Pacific News Service, April 20-24, 1992, at 6 (reporting on California and national polls); see also Gallup & Newport, note 9.

18. See Bowers & Vandiver, note 21, at 3,13.

19. Bowers & Vandiver, *Nebraskans Want an Alternative to the Death Penalty*, Executive Summary, at 7-8 (1991).

20. See Bowers & Vandiver, note 21, at 2,6.

21. Cambridge Survey Research, *Attitudes in the State of Florida on the Death Penalty*, Executive Summary, at 5 (1986).

22. Grasmick & Bursik, *Attitudes of Oklahomans Toward the Death Penalty*, Univ. of Oklahoma, at 21, 25 (1988).

23. See, e.g., J. DeParle, "Abstract Death Penalty Meets Real Execution," *The New York Times*, June 30, 1991 (only 36% of those in a Justice

Department survey voted for the death penalty in simulated cases typical of those punishable by death).

24. See Lane, note 2, at 333.
25. Marquart & Sorenson, "A National Study of the Furman-Commuted Inmates: Assessing the Threat to Society from Capital Offenders," 23 *Loyola of Los Angeles Law Review* 5, 23 (1989).
26. See J. Wright, "Life-Without-Parole: An Alternative to Death or Not Much of a Life At All?" 43 *Vanderbilt Law Review* 529 (1990) for state statutes regarding life without parole sentences, especially at notes 70-129 and accompany text. Some statutes have a specific sentence of life without parole; in other states the restriction is in the parole regulations. In addition to the states designated by Wright, Colorado, Oregon, Utah and the District of Columbia now have sentences of life without parole for some offenses.
27. See *Funding the Justice System: A Call to Action*, the American Bar Association, at 54 (1992).
28. B. Denson, "The Pros, Cons of Throwing Away Key," *The Houston Post*, July 14, 1991, at A-1.
29. See note 5.
30. A. Malcolm, "Capital Punishment Is Popular, But So Are Its Alternatives," *The New York Times*, Sept. 10, 1989, at 4E.
31. See Denson, note 34, at A-1.
32. J. Kerkhove, "Lifer?" *The Messenger*, July-Sept., 1992, at 19.
33. Letter from Robert Gold to the Death Penalty Information Center, Jan. 26, 1993.
34. See Michigan Department of Corrections Memoranda, Feb. 10, 1993 (Terry Murphy), and April 11, 1991.
35. For example, all 36 States that authorize capital Punishment have provisions for clemency. *Herrera v. Collins*, No. 917328, slip opinion, at 23, n. 14 (Jan. 25, 1993).
36. M. Radelet, *Clemency in Post-Furman Cases*, manuscript (Nov. 29, 1991).
37. See notes 5, 38 & 40 above.
38. *Herrera*, No. 91-7328, slip opinion, at 20 (footnotes omitted).
39. M. Leary, *Counter-Trend to Death Penalty Emerging in California*, Pacific News Service, April 20-24, 1992, at 6.
40. E. Kolbert, "As Vote on Death Penalty Nears, Cuomo Advocates Life Sentences," *The New York Times*, June 19, 1989.
41. "The View From the Jury Box," *The National Law Journal*, Feb. 22, 1993, at S2.
42. See note 1.
43. See Paduano & Smith, "Deathly Errors: Juror Misperceptions Concerning Parole in the Imposition of the Death Penalty," 18 *Columbia Human Rights Law Review* 211, 216 (1987).

44. See Lane, note 2, at 390 (emphasis added). Ten of the twelve jurors expressed similar concerns.
45. *Id.* at 383.
46. *Id.* at 334.
47. *Id.* at 334, n.42.
48. See W. Hood, "Note: The Meaning of "Life" for Virginia Jurors and Its Effect on Reliability in Capital Sentencing," 75 *Virginia Law Review* 1605, 1624-25 (1989).
49. See, e.g., Dayan, Mahler, & Widenhouse, "Searching for an Impartial Sentencer Through Jury Selection in Capital Trials," 23 *Loyola of Los Angeles Law Review* 151, 164-176 (1989).
50. *King v. Lynaugh*, 828 F.2d 257, 260 (5th Cir. 1987) (emphasis added).
51. Cypress Research and Development Corporation, letter and report to the Loyola Death Penalty Resource Center, Aug. 31, 1990.
52. *The Sunday Times* (London), Mar. 18, 1990 (quoted in G. Pierce & M. Radelet, "The Role and Consequences of the Death Penalty in American Politics," 18 *N.Y.U. Review of Law & Social Change* 711, 725 (1990-91)).
53. *Californians' Attitudes About the Death Penalty: Results of a Statewide Survey*, public opinion poll implemented by the Field Research Corporation in Dec., 1989.
54. See Bowers & Vandiver, note 21, at 3 & 9.
55. "Death Verdicts Slip as No-Parole Grows," *The Daily Oklahoman*, Nov. 10, 1992.
56. Bureau of Justice Statistics, *Capital Punishment 1991*, at 8 (October 1992).
57. See Bureau of Justice Statistics, *Report to the Nation on Crime and Justice*, Second Edition, at 41-42 (March, 1988).
58. B. Denson, see note 34.
59. See Marquart & Sorenson, note 31. In 1972, all the existing death sentences were overturned by the Supreme Court's decision in *Furman v. Georgia*. In 1989, Marquart and Sorenson looked at the cases of the 558 inmates whose death sentences were commuted to life imprisonment by *Furman*. Of these, 243 of the inmates were released to the community. Only one of those released committed a new homicide. *Id.* at 22-24.
60. See note 63 (ages of those arrested for violent crime); see also *Capital Punishment* 1991, note 62, at 10 (ages of those admitted to death row).
61. Katz, "In Mich., Life Without Parole," *Newsday*, June 20, 1989, at 5. Thomas Coughlin, (former) Commissioner of the New York State Department of Correctional Services made similar statements about "true lifers" in New York. See Tabak & Lane, note 12, at 124-25.
62. See Wright, note 32, at 549.
63. S. Eisele, "Lifers Help Youths Stay Out of Jail," *Philadelphia Inquirer*, Mar. 20, 1991, at 1-B.

64. See M. Mauer, *Americans Behind Bars: A Comparison of International Rates of Incarceration*, The Sentencing Project, at Table 1 (Jan., 1991).

65. W. Bowers & M. Vandiver, "People Want an Alternative to the Death Penalty: A New Look at Public Opinion," (draft, to be published in *Law & Society Review*), Jan. 15, 1993.

66. See, e.g., B. Galaway, "Restitution As Innovation or Unfilled Promise?" 52 *Federal Probation* 3 (1988). Arlington, VA (1993).

67. See *Restitution: Eligibility Types of Restitution Allowed* (Draft), National Victim Center, Arlington, VA (1993).

68. See, e.g., *Millions Misspent*, note 10.

69. Letter from Marietta Jaeger to the Death Penalty Information Center, Feb. 17, 1993.

70. Memorandum to Senator Joseph Biden, Chairman, Senate Judiciary Committee, from James S. Liebman, Professor of Law, Columbia University School of Law: *Rate of Reversible Constitutional Error in State Capital Convictions and Sentences that Underwent Federal Habeas Corpus Review Between 1976-1991 (Revised)*, July 15, 1991, at 4; see also Editorial: "Virginia Murder, Federal Review," *The Washington Post*, Dec. 6, 1991. Forty percent of the cases that survive review in state court are reversed in federal courts.

71. Payton, "How Parents of Slain Children Cope," *Oakland Tribune*, Mar. 6, 1987, at C7.

72. T. Mathis, 1 The Voice 2, publication of Murder Victims Families for Reconciliation (March 1992) (quoting her mother).

73. Letter from William Pelke to the Death Penalty Information Center, Feb. 7, 1993.

74. M. Cuomo, "New York State Shouldn't Kill People," *The New York Times*, June 17, 1989.

75. M. Humbert, "Annual Death Penalty Battle Resumes in NYS," *The Cortland Standard*, Feb. 5, 1990, at 11.

76. "Instead of Death Penalty, Life Without Parole," Editorial, *The New York Daily News*, May 20, 1992, at 34.

77. "Jolt to Death Penalty: Voters Reject 2 of Its Backers," *N.Y. Daily News*, Sept. 13, 1990, at 11.

78. Coley, *Senate Eliminates Life Without Parole Sentence*, UPI, March 19, 1986.

79. S. Friedman, "No-parole Irks Prosecutors," *Houston Post*, May 6, 1991, at A1.

Chapter 18

1. S. Magagnini, "Closing Death Row Would Save State $90 Million a Year," *The Sacramento Bee*, March 28, 1988, at 1.

2. Kansas Legislative Research Department study, cited in D. Von Drehle, "Bottom Line: Life in Prison One-sixth as Expensive," *The Miami Herald*, July 10, 1988, at 12A.

3. C. Hoppe, "Executions Cost Texas Millions," *The Dallas Morning News*, March 8, 1992, at IA.
4. D. Von Drehle, "Bottom Line: Life in Prison One-sixth as Expensive," *The Miami Herald*, July 10, 1988, at 12A.
5. Magagnini, see note 1.
6. The New York Department of Correctional Services study cited in Moran & Ellis, "Death Penalty: Luxury Item," *New York Newsday*, June 14, 1989, at 60; see also the Massachusetts Bar Association Section News, *The Dollar and Human Costs of the Death Penalty*, April 1992, at 5.
7. *Funding the Justice System: A Call to Action*, A report by the American Bar Association, August, 1992, at ii, 3 (emphasis in original) (hereinafter, ABA Study).
8. *Id.* at 16.
9. M. Garey, "The Cost of Taking A Life: Dollars and Sense of the Death Penalty," 18 *University of California Davis Law Review* 1221, 1261 (1985).
10. ABA Study, see note 7, at 2 1.
11. Von Drehle, see note 4.
12. *Id.*
13. Moran & Ellis, see note 6, at 62
14. ABA Study, see note 7, Table: Indicators of a National Problem: 1991, at ii-iii.
15. *Id.*, Attachment, at 54.
16. L. Bienen, "No Savings in Lives or Money with Death Penalty," *The New York Times*, August 7, 1988; see also D. Grothaus, "Death, Dollars and Scales of Justice," *The Houston Post*, December 7, 1986 at 3B (Harris County, with almost half of the state's capital cases, spent $86.3 million since 1980).
17. ABA Study, see note 7, at 18.
18. *Id.*, Attachment, at 18.
19. Testimony of Carole Carpenter on behalf of the National Association of Counties before the U.S. Senate Subcommittee on Juvenile Justice, April 29, 1992, at 7.
20. Harshbarger, Statement on Reinstating the Death Penalty in the Commonwealth, Massachusetts Bar Association, see note 6, at 3.
21. Tabak & Lane, "Judicial Activism and Legislative "Reform" of Federal Habeas Corpus: A Critical Analysis of Recent Developments and Current Proposals," 55 *Albany Law Review* 1, 31(1991).
22. Magagnini, see note 1.
23. Magagnini, "Sierra County Robs Police to Pay Lawyers," *The Sacramento Bee*, March 28, 1988.
24. Phone conversation, September 15, 1992.
25. See Magagnini, note 2; see also *Corenevsky v. Superior Court of Imperial County*, 682 P.2d 360 (Calif. 1984).
26. "Commissioners Jailed Over Fees," *American Bar Association Journal*, February, 1992.

27. "Lincoln Commissioners Pick Jail Over Legal Fees," *The Atlanta Constitution*, Oct. 24, 199 1.
28. K. Wood, "Can State Afford Fourth Prosecution of Spraggins?" *Fulton County Daily Report*, March 3, 1988, at 1.
29. "Marwell Murder Trial May Up Kemper Taxes," *The Meridian Star* (Mississippi), July 21, 1992; phone conversation with Michael Luke, September 11, 1992.
30. "Public Defender System Needed," *The Yazoo Herald*, July 6, 1991.
31. Hoppe, *The Dallas Morning News*, see note 3.
32. *Id*.
33. J. Painter, "Death Penalty Seen as Too Costly for Oregon's Pocketbook," *The Oregonian* (Portland), July 27, 1987.
34. Kansas, for example, estimated that the annual cost for implementing the death penalty would be $11.4 million, of which $9.2 million would be for trial costs. Kansas Legislative Research Dept. Memorandum, Feb. 11, 1987. New York estimated a cost of $1.8 million per case, through the first level of appeals, of which $1.5 million would be trial costs. *Capital Losses: The Price of The Death Penalty for New York State*, NY State Defenders Association, Albany, 1982.
35. Magagnini, see note 1.
36. M. Hansen, "Politics and the Death Penalty," *The Palm Beach Review's Florida Supreme Court Report*, Feb. 25, 1991, at I OB, 26B.
37. D. Kaplan, "Death Mill, USA," *The National Law Journal*, May 9, 1989, at 40.
38. See Capital Losses, note 34.
39. U.S. Dept. of Justice, Uniform Crime Report, preliminary annual release, April 26, 1992; see also *Richmond-Times Dispatch*, April 27, 1992 for chart of 25 cities based on the Uniform Crime Report.
40. G. James, "In Every Category, Crime Reports Fell Last Year in New York City," *The New York Times*, March 26, 1992, at Al.
41. *The New York Times*, Aug. 4, 1992, chart at B2.
42. C. Wolff, "Brown Legacy: Community Policing," *The New York Times*, Aug. 4, 1992, at B2.
43. E. Meyer, "Policing With People in Mind," *The Washington Post*, June 15, 1992, at Al, 8.
44. T. Squitieri, "Murder Rate is Up in Usually Slow First Quarter," *USA Today*, April 3, 1992, at 8A.
45. National Association of Chiefs of Police, 4th National Poll, 1991.
46. K. Cullen, "Death Penalty Criticized by County Prosecutors," *The Boston Globe*, Jan. 26, 1992.
47. S. Harshbarger, see note 20.
48. "Death, Life and the Presidency," *The New York Times*, January 25, 1992.
49. J. Kennedy, "Why Houston Leads in Death Row Cases," *The Los Angeles Times*, July 2, 1992 (Washington edition).

50. See note 39.
51. "Republican Leaders Praise Atwater After Memo Flap," *The Courier-Journal* (Louisville, KY), June 17, 1989.
52. M. Wines, "Bad Economic News Forces Bush to Refocus Re-election Strategy," *The New York Times*, July 4, 1992, at AI.
53. D. Von Drehle, "A Broader Federal Death Penalty: Prelude to Bloodbath or Paper Tiger?" *The Washington Post*, November 29, 199 1, at A29, quoting Franklin Zang, director of the Earl Warren Legal Institute.
54. Letter from Robert D. Reischauer, Director of the Congressional Budget Office to Charles E. Schumer, Chairman of the House Subcommittee on Crime and Criminal Justice, September 20, 1991.
55. H. Dewar, "On Capitol Hill, Symbols Triumph," *The Washington Post*, November 26, 1991 at Al.
56. K. Sack, "Arkansan Portrayed As Soft," *The New York Times*, August 25, 1992, at A18.
57. E. Dionne, "Clinton Charges Bush With Inaction on Crime," *The Washington Post*, February 22, 1992.
58. See note 39.
59. S. Grady, "Savagery of Bush-Dukakis Race Lingers," *The Albuquerque Journal*, March 14, 1990.
60. S. Attlesey, "GOP Launches New Ad Attack Against Richards," *The Dallas Morning News*, September 29, 1990.
61. C. Pesce, "Houston Fears It's Being 'Eaten Up By Crime'," *USA Today*, October 21, 1991.
62. M. Oreskes, "The Political Stampede on Execution," *The New York Times*, April 4, 1990, at Al 6.
63. L. Mecoy & H. Sample, "Candidates Waffle on Execution," *The San Francisco Daily Journal*, April 21, 1992, at 7.
64. J. Miller, "Counties Brace for Cuts in Police and Other Services," *The Los Angeles Times*, September 1, 1992 (Wash. edit.), quoting Grover Trask, Riverside County District Attorney.
65. See Magagnini, note 2.
66. D. Gates, Chief. "My Life in the LAPD," (1992) quoted in *Newsweek*, May 11, 1992, at 39.
67. "Blacks and Cops: Up Against the Wall," *Newsweek*, May 11, 1992, at 52-3, quoting Wesley Skogan of Northwestern University.
68. G. Ifill, "Kemp Attacks GOP Challenger to Cuomo," *The Washington Post*, June 7, 1990.
69. "A Welcome Defeat for Death," *The New York Times*, November 14, 1990 (editorial) at A28.
70. "Instead of Death Penalty, Life Without Parole," *The New York Daily News*, May 20, 1992, at 34.
71. M. Humbert, "Annual Death Penalty Battle Resumes in AIYS," *The Cortland Standard*, February 5, 1990, at I 1.
72. "Black Leaders Demand that Flynn Apologize," *The Boston Globe*, January 5, 1990.

73. B. Medlyn, "Arizona Child Crime Laws Among Toughest, Officials Say," *The Phoenix Gazette*, July 9, 1988, at B 12.
74. *The Salisbury Post*, May 5, 1990 (advertisement).
75. P. Manson, "Woods Fought Death Penalty as a Lawyer, Now Backs It," *The Arizona Republic*, March 17, 1992.
76. K. Wood, "Plea Deal Lets DA Avert Abashment," *Fulton County Daily Report*, October 22, 1990.
77. See C. Willis, "Lawyers Accuse Jasmin of Prosecuting Case for 'Political Gain'," *The Courier-Journal* (Louisville, KY), Feb. 25, 1992, at B I.
78. Letter from Stenberg to the Chief Deputy Clerk of the U.S. Supreme Court, August 4, 1992.
79. P. Cook and D. Slawson, *The Costs of Processing Murder Cases in North Carolina* (May, 1993).
80. *Id.* at 98.
81. There were 38 executions in the U.S. in 1993 and there have been 252 executions since 1976 as of Sept. 20, 1994. See NAACP Legal Defense & Educational Fund, Inc., *Death Row, U.S.A.* 5 (Summer 1994) (7 additional executions occurred since that publication).
82. P. Cook, note 79, at 22-23.
83. *Id.* at 68.
84. *Id.* at 70.
85. *Id.* at 98.
86. Bureau of Justice Statistics, *Capital Punishment 1992*, at 10, Appendix table 1 (1993) (of 4,704 people sentenced to death, 2,129 were removed from death row, including 188 executions).
87. See P. Cook, note 79, at 97 Table 9.1.
88. See J. Gerth, "Counties Balk at Paying Experts to Testify for Indigents," *Louisville Courier-Journal*, April 4, 1994, at 1.
89. See B. Callahan, "Lawyers No Longer Get Millions in Capital Cases," *San Diego Tribune*, June 26, 1994, at A-1, A-18 (prosecutions of David Lucas, Ronaldo Ayala, and Billy Ray Waldon).
90. C. Linder, "Capital Cases Are Crippling State Courts," *The Sacramento Bee*, Sept. 5, 1993, at Forum 1.
91. M. Hatcher, "Judge and D.A. Warn Supervisors About High Cost of Capital Murder Trials," *Jasper County News*, Mar. 9, 1994.
92. E. Simon, "Death Be Not Cheap," *Connecticut Law Tribune*, November 29, 1993, at 1, 12.
93. *Id.* at 13.
94. *Id.*
95. *Id.*
96. *Id.*
97. *Id.* at 12.
98. B. Kudelka, "The High Cost of Pursuing the Death Penalty," *The Sun News* (Myrtle Beach, SC), May 1, 1994, at 1A.

99. T. Philip, "Only Funds Going Fast in Ng Case," *The Sacramento Bee*, July 19, 1994, at A1.
100. J. Makeig, "Capital Justice Takes a Lot of County Capital," *The Houston Chronicle*, Aug. 15, 1994.
101. "Death Sentences Fall in Tenn.; Costs Cited," *The Commercial Appeal* (Memphis), Sept. 6, 1994 (Associated Press).
102. J. Makeig, note 100.
103. J. Mattox, "Texas' Death Penalty Dilemma," *The Dallas Morning News*, Aug. 25, 1993.
104. A. Tugend, "Death Penalty's High Cost," *The Orange County Register*, Aug. 9, 1993, at 1.
105. *Id.* at 2.
106. J. Gerth, "Counties Balk at Paying Experts to Testify for Indigents," *Louisville Courier-Journal*, April 4, 1994, at 1.
107. J. Gerth, "Counties Balk at Paying Experts to Testify for Indigents," *Louisville Courier-Journal*, April 4, 1994, at 1.
108. D. Johnston, "Ex-O Special Attacks Crime Bill Backed by Clinton," *New York Times*, February 16, 1994, at A1.
109. R. Morgenthau, "47 New Death Penalties. Big Deal," *New York Times*, November 10, 1993, at A27.

Chapter 19

1. As a member of the United States Court of Appeals, I voted to enforce the death penalty, even as I stated publicly that I doubted its moral, social, and constitutional legitimacy. See *Feguer v. United States*, 302 F.2d 214 (CA8), cert. denied, 371 U.S. 872 (1962); *Pope v. United States*, 372 F.2d 710 (CA8 1967) (en banc), vacated and remanded, 392 U.S. 651 (1968); *Maxwell v. Bishop*, 398 F.2d 138, 153-154 (CA8 1968), vacated and remanded, 398 U.S. 262 (1970). See *Furman v. Georgia*, 408 U.S. 238, 405 (1972).
2. Because I conclude that no sentence of death may be constitutionally imposed under our death penalty scheme, I do not address Callins' individual claims of error. I note, though, that the Court has stripped "state prisoners of virtually any meaningful federal review of the constitutionality of their incarceration." *Butler v. McKellar*, 494 U.S. 407, 417 (1990) (Brennan, J., dissenting) (emphasis in original). Even if Callins had a legitimate claim of constitutional error, this Court would be deaf to it on federal habeas unless "the state court's rejection of the constitutional challenge was so clearly invalid under then-prevailing legal standards that the decision could not be defended by any reasonable jurist." *Id.*, at 417-418 (emphasis in original). That a capital defendant facing imminent execution is required to meet such a standard before the Court will remedy constitutional violations is indefensible.

3. See Sundby, "The Lockett Paradox: Reconciling Guided Discretion and Unguided Mitigation in Capital Sentencing," 38 *UCLA L. Rev.* 1147, 1162 (1991).

4. The narrowing of death-eligible defendants into a smaller subgroup coupled with the unbridled discretion to pick among them arguably emphasizes rather than ameliorates the inherent arbitrariness of the death penalty. S. Gillers, "Deciding Who Dies," 129 *U. Pa. L. Rev.* 1, 27-28 (1980) (arguing that the inherent arbitrariness of the death penalty is only magnified by post-Furman statutes that allow the jury to choose among similarly situated defendants).

5. See *Clemons v. Mississippi*, 494 U.S. 738 (1990) (concluding that appellate courts may engage in a reweighing of aggravating and mitigating circumstances in order to "cure" error in capital sentencing); *Blystone v. Pennsylvania*, 494 U.S. 310 (1990) (upholding a death penalty statute mandating death where aggravating, but no mitigating, circumstances are present, thus divesting the jury of its ability to make an individualized determination that death is the appropriate punishment in a particular case).

6. See *Johnson v. Texas*, U.S. (1993) (affirming death sentence even though the jurors were not allowed to give full mitigating effect to the defendant's youth under the Texas death penalty statute); *Graham v. Collins*, U.S. (1993). See also *Saffle v. Parks*, 494 U.S. 484 (1990) (upholding death sentence where jurors were instructed to avoid "any influence of sympathy," because the claim was raised on federal habeas and a ruling for the petitioner would constitute a "new rule" of constitutional law); *Boyde v. California*, 494 U.S. 370 (1990) (upholding death sentence where jurors reasonably may have believed that they could not consider the defendant's mitigating evidence regarding his character and background); *Walton v. Arizona*, 497 U.S. 639 (1990) (affirming placement upon the defendant of the burden to establish mitigating circumstances sufficient to call for leniency).

7. See *Arave v. Creech*, U.S. (1993) (holding that an Idaho statute, as interpreted by the Idaho Supreme Court, which authorizes the death penalty for those murderers who have displayed "utter disregard for human life," genuinely narrows the class of death-eligible defendants); *Lewis v. Jeffers*, 497 U.S. 764 (1990) (affirming lenient standard for the review of the constitutional adequacy of aggravating circumstances).

8. Even the most sophisticated death penalty schemes are unable to prevent human error from condemning the innocent. Innocent persons have been executed, see Bedau & Radelet, "Miscarriages of Justice in Potentially Capital Cases," 40 *Stan. L. Rev.* 21, 36, 173-179 (1987), perhaps recently, see *Herrera v. Collins*, supra, and will continue to be executed under our death penalty scheme.

Chapter 20

1. As a defense lawyer Justice Marshall brought a unique perspective to the Supreme Court. Justice Marshall - the lawyer/justice is explored in; Gerald F. Uelmen, *Justice Thurgood Marshall and the Death Penalty: A Former Criminal Defense Lawyer on the Supreme Court*, 26 Ariz. St. L.J. 403 (1994); Mark Tushnet, *Lawyer Thurgood Marshall*, 44 Stan. L. Rev. 1277 (1992) (discussing Justice Marshall's work as a trial lawyer by a former law clerk); Jordan Steiker, "The Long Road Up From Barbarism: Thurgood Marshall and the Death Penalty," 71 *Tex. L. Rev.* 1131, 1163 (1993)(A perspective is provided by a former law clerk); Sandra Day O'Connor, "Thurgood Marshall: The Influence of a Raconteur," 44 *Stan. L. Rev.* 1217 (1992) (recalling Marshall's tendency, as a Supreme Court Justice, to tell his colleagues stories that "made clear what legal briefs often obscure: the impact of legal rules on human lives"); Anthony M. Kennedy, "The Voice of Thurgood Marshall," 44 *Stan. L. Rev.* 1221 (1992); Tracey Maclin, "Justice Thurgood Marshall: Taking the Fourth Amendment Seriously," 77 *Cornell L. Rev.* 723 (1992); Martha Minow, "A Tribute to Justice Thurgood Marshall," 105 *Harv. L. Rev.* 66 (1991); Wendy Brown-Scott, "Justice Thurgood Marshall and the Integrative Ideal," 26 *Ariz. St. L.J.* 535 (1994).

   I also suggest the following books: John P. MacKenzie, "Thurgood Marshall," in 4 *The Justices of the United States Supreme Court*, Leon Friedman & Fred L. Israel eds.,(1980); Michael D. Davis & Hunter R. Clark, *Thurgood Marshall* (1992); and a personal bibliography by Justice Marshall's good friend Carl T. Rowan, *Dream Makers, Dream Breakers, The World of Justice Thurgood Marshall*, Little Brown & Co.(1993); and for a history of NAACP Legal Defense and Education Fund, *Crusaders in the Courts*, Jack Greenberg, HarperCollins, Basic Books (1994).

2. Foreword, 6 Harv. Black Letter J. 1, 2 (1989). In the year I was born, there were three (3) lynchings as there were in 1964 when my oldest daughter was born. Statistics maintained by the Archives at Tuskegee Institute and reported in; Robert L. Zangrando, *The NAACP Crusade Against Lynching, 1909-1950*, Temple University Press (1980).

3. Carl T. Rowan, *Dream Makers, Dream Breakers, The World of Justice Thurgood Marshall* 28 (Little, Brown & Co. 1993).

4. Sabrina L. McLaughlin, "High-tech Lynchings in an Age of Evolving Standards of Decency," 3 *San Diego Justice J.* 177, 199 (1995) citing James M. SoRelle, "The 'Waco Horror': The Lynching of Jesse Washington," in *Lynching, Racial Violence, and Law* 303, 303, Paul Finkelman, ed.(1992); Robert L. Zangrando, *The NAACP Crusade Against Lynching, 1909-1950*, Temple University Press (1980); James R. McGovern, *Anatomy of a Lynching: The Killing of Claud Neal*, Louisiana State University Press (1982).

5. Arthur F. Raper, *The Tragedy of Lynching* 480-1 (1933).
6. Sabrina L. McLaughlin, "High-tech Lynchings in an Age of Evolving Standards of Decency," 3 *San Diego Justice J.* 177-78 (1995).
7. Robert L. Zangrando, *The NAACP Crusade Against Lynching, 1909-1950*, Temple University Press, 5&6, Tables 1 & 2,(1980) [statistics collected by the archives at Tuskegee Institute]. There have been 712 documented lynchings in the five states I lived; Pennsylvania (8), New Jersey (2), Utah (8), Virginia (100), Texas (493), and North Carolina (101).
8. Paul Finkelman, *Lynching, Racial Violence, and Law* 210 (1992).
9. Sabrina L. McLaughlin, "High-tech Lynchings in an Age of Evolving Standards of Decency," 3 *San Diego Justice J.* 177, 199 (1995) citing James M. SoRelle, "The 'Waco Horror': The Lynching of Jesse Washington," in *Lynching, Racial Violence, and Law* 303, 307 (Paul Finkelman ed., 1992).
10. George C. Rable, "The South and the Politics of Antilynching Legislation, 1920-1940," in *Lynching, Racial Violence, and Law* 227, 228 (Paul Finkelman ed., 1992).
11. James L. Crouthamel, "The Springfield Race Riot of 1908," in *Lynching, Racial Violence and Law* 76, 76-93 (Paul Finkelman ed., 1992).
12. William Ziglar, "Community on Trial: The Coatesville Lynching of 1911," in *Lynching, Racial Violence and Law* 323, 323-29 (Paul Finkelman ed., 1992).
13. John F. Galliher, Gregory Ray & Brent Cook, "Abolition and Reinstatement of Capital Punishment During the Progressive Era and Early 20th Century," 83 *J. Crim. L.* 538 at 541 (1992).
14. Hugo A. Bedau, *The Death Penalty in America* at 22 (3d ed. 1982).
15. William J. Bowers et al., *Legal Homicide: Death as Punishment in America, 1864-1982* (1984).
16. U.S. Department of Justice, *Capital Punishment* (1973).
17. John F. Galliher, Gregory Ray & Brent Cook, "Abolition and Reinstatement of Capital Punishment During the Progressive Era and Early 20th Century," 83 *J. Crim. L.* 538 at 542 (1992).
18. *Coleman v. McCormick*, 874 F.2d 1280 (1989).
19. *Executions in Arizona 1910-1965*, Arizona State Historical Society.
20. Trudier Harris, *Exorcizing Blackness: Historical and Literary Lynching and Burning Rituals* (1984), supra note 12, at 1, quoting Sutton Grigg, *The Hindered Hand* (1905). Among the numerous fictional works by black American authors that address lynching are James Baldwin, *Going to Meet the Man* (1968), William Wells Brown, *Clotel* (1853), Charles Waddell Chesnutt, *The Marrow of Tradition* (1901), Paul Laurence Dunbar, "The Tragedy at Three Forks," in *The Strength of Gideon and Other Stories* (1900), Ralph Ellison, "The Birthmark," 36 *New Masses* (1940), Sutton Grigg, *The Hindered Hand* (1905), Langston Hughes, *Home, in The Ways of White Folks* (1933), James Weldon Johnson, "Brothers — American Drama," in *St. Peter Relates an Incident* (1935),

Claude McKay, "The Lynching," in *Selected Poems of Claude McKay* (1953), Jean Toomer, *Cane* (1923), Alice Walker, "The Flowers," in *In Love and In Trouble: Stories of Black Women* (1973), Margaret Walker, *Jubilee* (1967), Walter White, *The Fire in the Flint* (1924), John Edgar Wideman, *The Lynchers* (1973), Richard Wright, "Between the World and Me," 2 *The Partisan Review* 18 (1935), Richard Wright, *The Long Dream* (1958). See generally Trudier Harris, *Exorcizing Blackness: Historical and Literary Lynching and Burning Rituals* (1984).

21. Carl T. Rowan, *Dream Makers, Dream Breakers, The World of Justice Thurgood Marshall* 4, 107-12 (Little, Brown & Co. 1993).

22. The case he referred to was *Lyons v. Oklahoma* 322 U.S. 596 (1944) which he also lost in the Supreme Court. The client however was sparred the death penalty and sentenced to life. John P. MacKenzie, "Thurgood Marshall," in 4 *The Justices of the United States Supreme Court 1789-1978* 3063, 3084-87 (Leon Friedman & Fred L. Israel eds., 1980). Senator Ervin, and many southern Senators, voted against Thurgood Marshall's confirmation.

23. Jordan Steiker, Essay: "The Long Road Up from Barbarism: Thurgood Marshall and the Death Penalty," 71 *Tex. L. Rev.* 1131, 1134 (1993).

24. Jordan Steiker, Essay: "The Long Road Up from Barbarism: Thurgood Marshall and the Death Penalty," 71 *Tex. L. Rev.* 1131, 1163 (1993).

25. Sandra Day O'Connor, "Thurgood Marshall: The Influence of a Raconteur," 44 *Stan. L. Rev.* 1217, 1218 (1992).

26. Sandra Day O'Connor, "Thurgood Marshall: The Influence of a Raconteur," 44 *Stan. L. Rev.* 1217, 1220 (1992).

27. I wish I could take credit for these words but I can't they come from Robert Cover, "Violence and the Word," 95 *Yale L.J.* 1601 (1986).

28. The day after his retirement from the Court Justice Marshall told a press conference that when interviewing prospective law clerks he always asked them if they liked working on dissents, "If they said 'no' they didn't get the job," Marshall said, "I only picked those that liked to write dissenting opinions." Anthony Lewis, "Marshall Urges Bush to Pick 'The Best,'" *New York Times*, June 1991 at A8. To explore the power of a well founded dissent I suggest, Alan Barth, *Prophets with Honor, Great Dissents and Great Dissenters in the Supreme Court*, Vintage Books, (1975).

29. Jordan Steiker, Essay: "The Long Road Up from Barbarism: Thurgood Marshall and the Death Penalty," 71 *Tex. L. Rev.* 1131, 1134 (1993).

30. Michael Mello, "Adhering to Our Views: Justices Brennan and Marshall and the Relentless Dissent to Death Penalty as a Punishment," 22 *Fla. St. U.I. Rev.* 592, 593 (1995).

31. *Furman v. Georgia*, 408 U.S., 361 (1972).

32. James Dao, "Death Penalty in New York Reinstated after 18 Years; Pataki Sees Justice Served," *The New York Times*, Page A1, March 8, 1995.

33. Clifford Krauss, "Crime Lab; Mystery of New York, the Suddenly Safer City," Section 4; Page 1, *The New York Times*, July 23, 1995; Editorial, "Bringing the Murder Rate Down," *The New York Times*, Section A; Page 12, July 17; Clifford Krauss, "Murder Rate Plunges in New York City," *The New York Times*, Section 1; Page 1, July 8, 1995.

34. James Dao, "Death Penalty in New York Reinstated after 18 Years; Pataki Sees Justice Served," Section A; Page 1, *The New York Times*, March 8, 1995.

35. Howard W. French, "South Africa's Supreme Court Abolishes Death Penalty," *The New York Times*, June 7, 1995.

36. Howard W. French, "South Africa's Supreme Court Abolishes Death Penalty," *The New York Times*, June 7, 1995, quoting an interview with the Archbishop conducted by the South African Press Association.

37. *Godfrey v. Georgia*, 446 U.S. 420, 439 (1980) (Marshall, J., concurring).

38. Glenn L. Pierce and Michael L. Radeler, "The Role and Consequences of the Death Penalty in American Politics," 18 *N.Y.U. Rev. L. & Soc. Change* 711 (1990/1991).

39. Erik Eckholm, "Studies Find Death Penalty Tied to Race Of the Victims," Section B; Page 1, *The New York Times*, February 24, 1995. The concluding part of a series; "Punishable By Death: Lessons for New York."

40. Erik Eckholm, "Studies Find Death Penalty Tied to Race Of the Victims," Section B; Page 1, *The New York Times*, February 24, 1995. The concluding part of a series; "Punishable By Death: Lessons for New York."

41. General Accounting Office, Death Penalty, Sentencing Research Indicated Pattern of Racial Disparities, 1990.

42. Nkechi Taifai, "Laying Down the Law, Race by Race; Criminal Sentencing Falls Disproportionately Hard on Blacks and Latinos," Pg. S36, *Legal Times*, October 10, 1994.

43. Report: "Death Penalty Focuses On Blacks," Pg. 6, *The Legal Intelligencer*, March 17, 1994.

44. "American Imprisonment Rates Are World's Highest," *Overcrowded Times*, pg. 1, March 1991. See also comments of Kevin Reed, staff attorney, NAACP Legal Defense and Educational Fund, Inc. which appear in as part of an edited panel discussion, Kevin Reed, Richard Wilson, Joan Fitzpatrick, "Race, Criminal Justice and the Death Penalty, 15 *Whittier L. Rev.* 395 (1994). It is interesting to note that South Africa has the second highest incarceration rate.

45. NAACP Legal Defense and Educational Fund, Inc., 1992-93 Presidential Transition Paper No. 7, *Crime and the Nation's Response to it: Increasing Devastation and Expenditure of Public Funds With No Accompanying Benefit* 2 (1993).

46. Nkechi Taifai, "Laying Down the Law, Race by Race; Criminal Sentencing Falls Disproportionately Hard on Blacks and Latinos," Pg. S36, *Legal Times*, October 10, 1994.

47. See statistics in Execution Update (ACLU/Capital Punishment Project, Washington, D.C.; NAACP Legal Defense and Educational Fund, New York, N.Y.), Apr. 15, 1993; *Death Row, U.S.A.* "Snapshot," *Execution Update* (ACLU/Capital Punishment Project, Washington, D.C.; NAACP Legal Defense and Educational Fund, New York, N.Y.), Apr. 15, 1993.
48. See Helen Prejean, C.S.J., *Dead Man Walking* 47-51 (1993). William J. Bowers et al., *Legal Homicide: Death as Punishment in America, 1864-1982* (1984).
49. *McCleskey v. Kemp*, 481 U.S. 279 (1987).
50. *Furman v. Georgia*, 408 U.S. 238 (1972).
51. Marcia Coyle, "Powell Recants Death Penalty View," *The National Law Journal*, June 13, 1994. A former law clerk, Prof. John C. Jeffries Jr. of the University of Virginia School of Law has written a biography of Lewis F. Powell Jr., *Justice Lewis F. Powell Jr. and the Era of Judicial Balance*.
52. *Godfrey v. Georgia*, 446 U.S. 420 at 442 (1980) (Marshall, J., concurring).

Chapter 21

1. Herbert J. Grossman, ed., American Association on Mental Retardation (previously Deficiency), *Classification Mental Retardation* (1983), 11.
2. *See* Emily F. Reed, "Legal Rights of Mentally Retarded Offenders: Hospice and Habilitation," *Criminal Law Bulletin* 25 (September-October 1989):412.
3. John Blume and David Bruck, "Sentencing the Mentally Retarded to Death: An Eighth Amendment Analysis," *Arkansas Law Review* 41 (1988):731.
4. American Association on Mental Retardation Brief for Appellant (hereafter AAMR Brief), 5, *Penry v. Lynaugh*, 492 U.S. 302, 109 S.Ct. 2934, 106 L.Ed 2d 256 (1989).
5. Blume and Bruck, 747.
6. Testimony of James W. Ellis, President, American Association on Mental Retardation, United States Senate, Committee on the Judiciary, 27 September 1989, 4. *See also Penry v. Lynaugh*, 109 S.Ct. 2934, 2961 (Brennan and Marshall, concurring in part and dissenting in part).
7. H. Grossman, 11, 76, quoted in Penry, 109 S.Ct. 2934, 2960, (Brennan and Marshall, concurring in part and dissenting in part).
8. AAMR Brief, 6.
9. Blume and Bruck, 731.
10. *Cleburne v. Cleburne Living Center, Inc.* 473 U.S. 432, 442, 87 L.Ed 2d 313, 105 S.Ct. 3249 (1985) quoted in Penry, 109 S.Ct. 2935, 2961 (Brennan and Marshall, concurring in part and dissenting in part).
11. *See* Reed, "Legal Rights," 412. *See also*, American Bar Association, ABA House of Delegates, "Recommendation," February 1989, 2.
12. *See* Reed, "Legal Rights," 412.

13. Blume and Bruck, 732, 734.
14. *Ibid.*, 734.
15. Richard Burr, "The Death Penalty," paper presented at *A Presidential Forum - Offenders with Mental Retardation and the Criminal Justice System*, President's Commission on Mental Retardation, Washington, D.C., 16 September 1989. *See also* Testimony of Ellis, 4-5. AAMR Brief, 8.
16. AAMR Brief, 8.
17. Blume and Bruck, 733.
18. AAMR Brief, 8.
19. Blume and Bruck, 733.
20. AAMR Brief, 7.
21. Burr, 2.
22. Donald Hermann, Howard Singer, and Mary Robbers, "Sentencing of the Mentally Retarded Criminal Defendant," *Arkansas Law Review* 41 (1988):802.
23. Penury, 109 sect. 2934, 2954.
24. Burr, 3.
25. *Ibid. See also* James W. Ellis and Ruth Luckasson, "Mentally Retarded Criminal Defendants," *George Washington Law Review* 53 (1985):423. Penry, 109 S.Ct. 2934, 2960-2961 (Brennan and Marshall, concurring in part and dissenting in part).
26. *Smith v. State*, 290 S.E.2d 47 (1982).
27. *Fleming v. Zant*, 386 S.E.2d 339, 347 (Ga.1989).
28. *Ibid.*
29. *Smith v. Kemp*, 664 F.Supp. 500 (M.D. Ga. 1987) quoted in Philip L. Fetzer, "Execution of the Mentally Retarded: A Punishment without Justification," *South Carolina Law Review* 40 (Winter 1989):426.
30. John J. Gruttadaurio, "Consistency in the Application of the Death Penalty to Juveniles and the Mentally Impaired: A Suggested Legislative Approach," *Cincinnati Law Review* 58 (1989):233.
31. *See* Testimony of Ellis, 5; Ellis and Luckasson, 426.
32. *Penry v. Lynaugh*, 492 U.S. 302, 106 L.Ed 2d 256, 109 S.Ct. 2934 (1989).
33. *Thompson v. Oklahoma*, 108 S. Ct. 2687, 2692, 2699 (1988).
34. *Eddings v. Oklahoma*, 455 U.S. 104, 115, n. 11 (1982).
35. Testimony of Senator Joseph R. Biden (D-Del), Congressional Record-Senate, S6875, S6881, 24 May 1990.
36. Blume and Bruck, 759.
37. *Thompson v. Oklahoma* , 108 S.Ct. 2687, 2699 (1988).
38. *Ibid.*
39. The Supreme Court held in *Stanford v. Kentucky*; *Wilkens v. Missouri*, 492 U.S. 361; 109 S.Ct. 2969; 106 L.Ed. 2d 386 (1989), cases decided the same day as *Penry*, that teenagers aged sixteen and seventeen can be

executed. However, it had previously held in *Thompson v. Oklahoma*, 108 S. Ct. 2687 (1988), that fifteen-year-olds could not. Thus the minimum execution age is now sixteen.

40. Blume and Bruck, 759.
41. *Ibid.*, 748-749, 759.
42. *See* Testimony of Ellis, 4. *See also* Penry, 109 S.Ct. 2934, 2961-2962, 2962, fn. 2 (Brennan and Marshall, concurring in part and dissenting in part).
43. Hermann, Singer and Roberts, 766.
44. Testimony of Biden, S6875, S6881. *See also* Helen Dewar, "Senate Votes to Protect Retarded from Execution," *Washington Post*, 25 May 1990, sec. A.
45. *McDonald v. United States*, 312 F.2d 847 (D.C. Cir. 1962).

Index

Page numbers followed by *f* or *n* indicated figures or notes, respectively.

families of murder victims, 149-50
Family Court, 45
Farrell, Mike, 117
Fay v. New York, 228*n*
federal government: Crime Control
Act, 222; death penalty prosecu-
tions, 209; drug death penalty,
ix, 209; habeas corpus review,
15, 230*n*; Omnibus Crime Bill,
163-64, 177-78, 220
Federal Witness Protection Program, 90
Feguer v. United States, 239*n*
Feinstein, Dianne, 145-46, 165-66
Ferber, Neil, 100
Ferguson, Cheryl Dee, 104
fictional works that address
lynching, 242*n*
First Amendment protections, 66
first degree murder, 36, 48, 123-24;
eligibility for parole, 140, 140*f*
Flamer, William, 22, 59, 63
Florida: aggravating circumstances,
31; capital case process, 14;
capital punishment law, 26, 31-
32, 190; clemency, 114; death
penalty costs, 153, 155, 160;
death sentences, 146; eligibility
for parole, 140*f*; innocent
persons sentenced to death, 97-
103; mitigating circumstances,
32; *Poole v. State*, 228*n*; *Proffitt
v. Florida*, 32-33, 189; public
opinion, 137-38; recession, 156;
state politics, 164-65
Frank, Daniel, 3
Franklin v. Lynaugh, 193
Frisby v. Shultz, 226*n*
Furman v. Georgia, 8, 10, 25, 73,
180-81, 189-90, 233*n*, 239*n*,
243*n*, 245*n*; dissent, 95-96;
legislative response to, 28-29

Gallup polls, 137
gas chambers, 7

Gates, Daryl, 166
Georgia: aggravating circumstances,
26-27, 190-91; capital punishment law, 26-27, 190; *Coley v.
State*, 193; death penalty, 18,
144; death penalty costs, 153,
157-58; death sentences, 143-44;
death sentences for innocent
persons, 98-101, 103; death
sentences for persons with mental
retardation, 224; defense
counsel, 17; eligibility for
parole, 140*f*; *Furman v. Georgia*,
8, 10, 25, 28-29, 73, 95-96,
180-81, 189-90, 243*n*, 245*n*;
Godfrey v. Georgia, 200, 244*n*-
245*n*; *Gregg v. Georgia*, 8, 10,
26-28, 33, 38, 70, 189-90, 193,
199, 226*n*; *McCleskey v. Kemp*,
195; public opinion, 137;
recession, 156; *Skipper v. State*,
228*n*; state politics, 169
Giddens, Charles Ray, 99
Gladish, Thomas, 98, 109
Glover, Danny, 117-18
Godfrey v. Georgia, 200, 244*n*-
245*n*
Goodwin, Terry Lee, 17
Goodwin v. Balkcom, 225*n*
Graber, Vincent, 151, 167
Graham, Barbara, 8
Graham, Gary, 113-14, 117-19
Graham v. Collins, 193-94, 197,
230*n*, 240*n*
grandstanding, 166-67
Great Act, 4
Greece: Draconian Code of Athens,
1
Greenberg/Lake poll, 133, 137, 230
Greer, Richard, 98, 109
Gregg, Troy Leon, 26
Gregg v. Georgia, 8, 10, 26-28, 70,
189-90, 193, 199, 226*n*;
dissenting opinion, 33, 38
Griffey, Margaret P., 230*n*

Van de Kamp, John, 165-66
Vardaman, James K., 203
verdict, final, 129-31
Vermont: capital crimes, 5; capital
punishment in, 8; life without
parole sentences, 139*f*
victims, 55-57; families of, 149-50
Violent Crime Control and Law
Enforcement Act, ix-x
Virginia: death penalty, 3-5; death
sentences, 145; eligibility for
parole, 140*f*, 144-45; life
sentences, 145; life without
parole sentences, 139*f*; lynchings, 242*n*; *Mu'min v. Virginia*,
81, 228*n*; *Patterson v. Commonwealth*, 228*n*; public opinion,
137
voir dire, 50, 122
voluntary confessions, 205

Wagner, R. Thomas, Jr., 129-31
Walker, Zachariah, 203-4
Wallace, Robert, 101
Walton v. Arizona, 198, 240*n*
Wardius v. Oregon, 79, 228*n*
Washington: death penalty, 7, 204;
life without parole sentences,
139*f*
Waxton, Luby, 34
WBOC, 59-64
Weems v. United States, 9, 189
Weld, William, 161
Weltner, Charles, 143
Westinghouse Company, 7
West Virginia: capital punishment
in, 8; life without parole
sentences, 139*f*; public opinion,
137
White, Byron, 26, 38; *Bell* deci-
sion, 42; *Furman v. Georgia*
opinion, 29, 189; *Jurek v. Texas*
opinion, 30; *Lockett v. Ohio*
decision, 41; *Proffitt v. Florida*

decision, 32; *Woodson v. North
Carolina* dissent, 36
White, Mark, 165
Whites: executions, 74
Wideman, Edgar, 203
Wilhoit, Gregory R., 97, 103
Wilkens v. Missouri, 246*n*
Wilkerson v. Utah, 9
Williams, Clayton, 165
Williams, Darby, 100
William the Conqueror, 2
Wilson, Holly, 89-93
Wilson, Pete, 166
Wisconsin: death penalty, 6; life
without parole sentences, 139*f*;
restitution, 148
Witherspoon v. Illinois, 77
women: executions, 74; murdered,
55-57
Woods, Grant, 168-69
Woodson, James Tyrone, 34
Woodson v. North Carolina, 34-37,
189-91
Wyoming: life without parole
sentences, 139*f*

Zant v. Stephens, 66, 69

About the Authors

Senator Joseph Biden has served as Chairmen of the Committee on the Judiciary from 1987 until January 1995. He has earned international recognition as a leading policy innovator, and as an effective negotiator and spokesman, on issues ranging from crime prevention and drug control to international relations and arms control.

Michael Reggio is the Law-Related Education Coordinator for the Oklahoma Bar Association. He is an adjunct fauclty member of University of Central Oklahoma (Edmond). His recent publications include publications in *Chronicles of Oklahoma, Del Sol New Mexico,* and *Update On Law-Related Education.*

Kevin O'Connell is an attorney who specializes in defending people accused of crime. He currently represents 4 members of Delaware's "DEATH ROW", and was the attorney for Andre Deputy who was executed by the State of Delaware in 1994. Kevin is a founding member and Co-President of Delaware Citizens opposed to the Death Penalty.

Dr. Isidore Starr, widely recognized as the "Father of Law-Related Education", is a member of the Advisory Commission to the American Bar Association's Special Committee on Youth Education for Citizenship. Mr. Starr taught social sstudies in the New York Public Schools for many years before embarking on a second career as a Professor of Education at Queens College. Dr. Starr is the author of many articles and books on constitutional issues.

Judge Richard S. Gebelein was appointed to the Superior Court of Delaware in 1984. Prior to that appointment he had served as a prosecutor in the state Office of Attorney General, as Chief Assistant Public Defender, and as Attorney General of Delaware. In addition, Judge Gebelein practiced law with the law firm of Wilson and Whittington.

Steven P. Wood, Esq. has served as a Deputy Attorney General in the Criminal Division of the Department of Justice of the State of Delaware sincee 1985. He is a senior prosecutor, and currently heads the Department Felony Trial Unit. He has prosecuted many murder cases, including one in which the defendant was convicted, sentenced to death and executed. He is a graduate of Emory University School of Law, where he occasionally serves on the faculty of the school's National Institute of Trial Advocacy program.

Thomas P. Gordon had been Chief of Police of the New Castle County Police Department since March 1989. He holds a Master of Science Degree in Human Resources Management and is a graduate of the FBI National Academy, the Secret Service Protection Program and the Senior Management Institute of Police of the Police Executive Research Forum and Harvard University. Colonel Gordon served as co-commander of the Pennell serial murder investigation, who was executed.

Jim Courtney is the Dover Bureau Chief at WBOC, a CBS affiliate. He has held that position for 5½ years.

Anita Richardson is editor and senior analyst for the America Bar Association's *PREVIEW of United States Supreme Court Cases.* Her *On The Docket* column which also covers the Supreme Court appears September through May in the Journal of the American Bar Association. Dr. Richardson is a member of the adjunct faculty of the John Marshall Law School-Chicago where she teaches appellate advococacy. She also offers a seminar in death penalty jurisprudence.

Horacio D. Lewis, who does volunteer work in Delaware prisons and developed and taught a college level course on "Courts & Connections", currently consults in the areas of cultural diversity and civil rights. Dr. Lewis has been an adjunct faculty member of Wilmington College, University of Delaware, Delaware State University and Delaware Technical Community College.

Cliff Calloway is an inmate at Sussex County Correctional Institute. He was incarcerated at the same time and was personally acquainted with Andre Duputy, Kenneth DeShieldss, and Steven Penell, all of whom have been executed.

Holly Wilson is the aunt of a murdered victim and the sister of a rape victim. Because of these incidednts, she brings a unique personal perpective to these issues. Steven Pennell, convicted murderer, was the first person executed since the re-enactment of the death penalty in Delaware. She is an advocate for the death penalty.

Richard Dieter is the Executive Director of the Death Penalty Information Center in Washingotn, D.C. The Center, founded in 1990, is a non-profit organization serving the public and the media with analysis and information on issues concerning capital punishment. He has appeared on *NBC Nightly News, CBS Evening News, The Today Show, CNN Headline News, C-Span, Court-TV* and many other programs.

Ginny Carroll was named *Newsweek's* Houston Bureau Chief in April 1989. Carroll was the lead reporter for *Newsweek's* coverage of the siege at the Branch Davidan compound in Waco, Texas. She was a major contributor to *Newsweek's* three cover stories on the tragedy: "Secrets of the Cult" (3/15/93), "Death Wish" (5/3/93) and "Children of the Cult" (5/17/93).

Joseph M. Asher is an attorney with the Wilmington, Delaware office of Skadden, Arps, Slate, Meagher & Flom. His primary practice is in the area of corporate and commercial litigation.

Andrew McKinley Jefferson, Esquire, is an associate attorney with the law firm of Potter Anderson and Corroon in Wilmington, Delaware. He practices in the areas of corporate law and complex litigation.

Tom Wagner has served as the State Auditor of Delaware, and as a member of the Board of Pardons, since 1989. Mr. Wagner is the first State Auditor in Delaware's history with formal accounting experience, and will become President of the National State Auditor's Association in June of 1997. Information regarding his strides in performance auditing has been published by the organization's national newsletter entitled NASACT NEWS.

David Vanderhoof is an Assitant Professor, Department of Sociology, Social Work & Criminal Justice, at the Univeristy of North Carolina at Pembroke. He was a trial lawyer for over twenty years. As a prosecutor, he never sought the death penalty, and as defense counsel assisted in most unusual capital cases. Professor Vanderhoof is morally and ethically opposed to capital punishment.

266 *About the Authors*

Dr. Emily Reed is a Data Adminstrator for the Delaware Services for Children, Youth & Their Families. She is an adjunct fauclty member of University of Delaware. A few of her recent publications include *The Penry Penalty, "Vieiwpoint: The Death Penalty's Inequities," and State's Restrict Executions of the Mentally Retarded."*

About the Editor

B orn in Philadelphia, Pennsylvania as Laura Elizabeth Randa, Laura now resides in West Chester, Pennsylvania with her husband Don E. King, Jr. Laura is currently employed by Solvay Pharmaceutical Company working as a mental health representative in Philadelphia.

Since graduation from The Ohio State University in 1988, Laura has served as a state, regional and national coordinator of law-related education programs. As Executive Director of Delaware Teachers' Academy for Service Learning, Laura first conceived of this publication while working with students that were eager to learn about the death penalty.

As Laura's influence grew through her involvement in national law-related education, so did this publication. The work before you is a labor of love that presents many facets of this extremely complicated issue. After six years of effort on the part of many, *Societies Final Solution: A History and Discussion of the Death Penalty* is now available in bookstores throughout the United States.